Mostly Guilty

A Low-Flying Barrister's Working Life

Michael Challinger

16pt

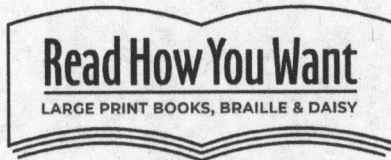
Read How You Want
LARGE PRINT BOOKS, BRAILLE & DAISY

Copyright Page from the Original Book

Published by Hybrid Publishers

Melbourne Victoria Australia

© Michael Challinger 2021

www.hybridpublishers.com.au

First published 2021

A catalogue record for this
book is available from the
National Library of Australia

NATIONAL
LIBRARY
OF AUSTRALIA

Cover design: Gittus Graphics
Typeset in Adobe Garamond Pro
Printed in Australia by McPherson's Printing Group

TABLE OF CONTENTS

Mostly Guilty

Michael Challinger grew up in Melbourne and attended Nunawading High School and Monash University, where he studied law and Russian. He is a music lover and inveterate traveller. He has worked in the law in Papua New Guinea and London and practises now at the Melbourne Bar.

Also by Michael Challinger

Port Moresby Mixed Doubles
Shawline
Historic Court Houses of Victoria
Anzacs in Arkhangel

1

Low-level Lawyer

About my clients

I'm sitting in the interview room outside Court 3. It's a bare cubicle with a table and a couple of chairs. Facing me across the table sits my client Darren. He's a likeable hoon with a boyish grin and hair as if he's been through a wind tunnel. He lounges back in his chair, professing not to know anything about the case against him. I've got a copy of the allegations in front of me and offer to read them to him.

'Go for it,' he says. 'What are they allegating this time?'

I read aloud: *'The accused forced the sliding door using a screwdriver...'*

'That's bullshit,' he says. His expression is a mix of bravado and incredulity.

'...and entered the study.'

'Is that what they say? It's bullshit!'

'*He ransacked the drawers and removed a wallet containing $400, a portable disc drive and a set of Bose headphones.*'

'Crap.'

'*He placed them in a grey backpack.*'

'Complete crap!'

'*He started to disconnect the computer from the monitor.*'

'It's all bullshit! Where's their witnesses?'

'They won't need witnesses,' I say. 'It's all on security video.'

'Fuck, is it?'

'Afraid so.'

Darren goes quiet, then shrugs cheerfully. 'Okay, maybe I done it after all.'

So begins my working day.

I'm a barrister who specialises in criminal law. I represent people charged with committing crimes and I go to court to defend them. Mainly, I appear in Magistrates' Courts, which form the bottom rung of our legal system.

My clients aren't the high achievers of the criminal world. They don't commit murders or billion-dollar company frauds; in any event stuff like that is way beyond my expertise. To run those sorts of cases you need to be a real high-flyer, a Queen's Counsel[1] – which is like a black belt in law.

A few of my snootier colleagues disdain the Magistrates' Court as some sort of sheltered workshop for barristers. I don't agree. Lowly as Magistrates' Courts may be, they're where the vast majority of Australia's criminal cases are heard. They're where most people who've had a brush with the law end up, and where even the most hardened crims generally began their careers.

My cases don't go on appeal to the High Court. They don't make headlines. To some onlookers they may seem inconsequential. Not to my clients, though, and not to me.

My court work gives me a unique opportunity to observe human behaviour. The people I deal with are people under pressure; they're either contesting their cases or answering for their failings – for their dishonesty,

[1] Also termed an SC, or Senior Counsel. The two are the same; QC is the term the monarchists prefer.

violence, carelessness and lack of self-control. Their cases are full of human interest. This book was written because I wanted to record and share what I've spent much of my working life doing.

Who are my clients then, and what are they like? The answer is that in many ways they're just ordinary people like you and me. During World War I the philosopher Bertrand Russell was sent to jail for opposing the war and spent six months locked up with common criminals. In his opinion his fellow prisoners were no worse morally than the public at large; they were just less intelligent, as proved by their having been caught.

Yet others of my clients *are* different from the rest of us. While you and I are at work, this group are still in bed. They think people who work for their living are freakish goody-goodies. They're too busy to have a job themselves; they have 'issues' instead. They have 'a lot going on' in their lives which preoccupy them to the exclusion of things like holding down a job, obeying the law or getting up in the morning.

Unlike us, clients like these have a circle of acquaintances who offer them lifts in stolen cars, lend them dodgy mobile phones and borrow their ID to sell someone else's digital camera at Cash Converters.

Curiously, they rarely know each other's names – not when speaking to the police, at any rate. The best they can offer is a nickname or two: Plugger, Wingnut, Corky or Animal (not *the* Animal, just Animal). Surnames are out of the question. So are addresses; often they don't even know their own. 'Sorry, Sergeant, can't remember the street name, I've only lived there six months. I just know how to get home.'

Events are mostly beyond their control. Things just happen to them. They're always on the receiving end, tossed like corks on the ocean of life. Their whole lives are spent being in the wrong place at the wrong time.

As they walk past car yards late at night, chain-wire fences come unravelled. Gaps appear, just wide enough for a bloke to wriggle through.

Windows turn out to be unlocked. Factory doors pop open of their own accord. The clients take a peep inside, just out of curiosity. Who wouldn't?

Some of my clients make a habit of finding number plates by the side of the road. On the spur of the moment they attach them to their own unregistered cars, then fill up with petrol and forget to pay. They come across bags of jewellery and foreign currency on nature strips and form every intention of handing them in to their nearest police station. Somehow, though, weeks or months pass and the cops pay them a visit before they've got around to it.

I appeared for a fellow once who was caught at 3a.m. by the roadside, standing next to a locked office safe weighing a quarter of a ton. He'd noticed a carload of strangers struggling to move it out of the path of traffic, and lent them a hand. Just being a Good Samaritan he was, but the others left suddenly when they noticed a blue light approaching.

Strange things like this happen all the time to some of my clients. How did the safe make its way onto the road in the first place? A mystery. Truly, their lives are full of the inexplicable. Even the bloke with drugs up his rectum said they weren't his and he didn't know how they'd got there!

Occasionally, my clients have second thoughts. They realise they're doing the wrong thing and try to distance themselves. One bloke was pinching an outboard motor from someone's ute when he had a change of heart. Yes, his conscience got the better of him and he was in the act of putting the outboard back when the police turned up. In this scenario 'conscience' means that inner voice telling him he was about to be caught.

There's one thing that does apply consistently to my clients: they're selective in what they tell me. They draw my attention to whatever favours their case but leave me to find out the adverse things myself. These days police interviews are recorded on disc and the accused is given a copy. If the fellow has lost his disc or 'forgotten' to give it to me, it's a sure bet that what's on it is unhelpful. Clients turn up protesting their innocence when they've already confessed to everything on the disc.

While they do seek my advice, many of my clients think they know better than I do. One bloke was facing a mandatory jail sentence but in his opinion he could get a good behaviour bond. 'The police say I can get a bond,' he insisted.

'Well, you can't.'

'The police say the judges can let me off. They can change the law.'

'Sorry, mate, but they can't. I'm telling you.'

'My mother's checked it all out. She should know, she works at Craigieburn Police Station.'

'In what capacity?' I ask.

'She's the cleaner.'

You may have noticed my use of the masculine pronouns 'he' and 'him' in referring to my clients. I'm not being sexist, just accurate. Like airline pilots and civil engineers, the majority of law-breakers are males. According to the statistics, women form only about 18 per cent of criminal offenders. A similar gender imbalance used to apply to judges and magistrates, but not any more. The number of male and female judicial officers is now about equal; indeed, in Victoria female magistrates currently outnumber males.

Among ourselves, we lawyers abbreviate the word 'magistrate' to something we pronounce 'madge-oh'. I use the word in this book though there's no way to write it without breaking the rules of English spelling. The best I can manage is to write it as 'mago'.

I hope what follows doesn't seem cynical. I hope, too, that it won't wholly undermine the mystique of the legal profession. Lawyers are not as arrogant, devious and money-grubbing as people believe. And lest these pages suggest otherwise, many lawyers stick up for the underdog. Many defend people's civil liberties and human rights, and strive to reform bad laws. Many give their time and skill free of charge to help the disadvantaged. I do so unintentionally when my clients fail to pay me.

Finally, I should mention that what passes between a client and his barrister is privileged, which means it's private and confidential. While everything I recount in this book is true and actually happened, to preserve that confidentiality no names in this book are true ones. I have also changed places, times, dates, sometimes descriptions and occasionally gender.

If you think you recognise yourself – or someone you know – in these pages, you are mistaken. Apart from those who have consented, the only person identifiable in this book is me.

2

Copping it Sweet

Pleas of guilty

Many people in the wider community are interested in the legal system. Those who know I'm a barrister[2] give me the benefit of their opinions. Some tell me society's ills are all the fault of the legal system. Most tell me sentences are too lenient and harangue me about the latest crime wave as reported in the *Herald Sun.*

It turns out, though, that a lot of these armchair experts have never actually been in a court. The only courtroom they've seen is the one on

---

[2] Solicitors and barristers are both lawyers, but barristers specialise in court work. Many solicitors appear regularly in court but they do other legal work as well – drawing wills and contracts, transferring land, etc. The distinction is something like that between a medical GP and a specialist.

'Judge Judy' on Channel 10. For their benefit, then, here's what a Magistrates' Court is like.

A panelled desk runs the full width of the room. The polished timber looks expensive and the trim is brushed aluminium. Sometimes there's even smoked glass in the decor. If it wasn't for the state crest on the back wall, you'd think it was the counter of some fancy wine bar. But that's no friendly barman sitting up there, nor an obliging barmaid. No, that stern-faced figure is a magistrate and he or she has the power to send you away for anything up to five years.

The courtroom's hushed, like churches used to be. A name is called and a young bloke slouches to the front row of seats. His jacket's open and the slogan on his T-shirt shows: it reads 'Born to be Pissed'. His lawyer, in dark suit and conservative tie, advances to the bar-table and announces his appearance. Let's say his name is Cox (mainly because it is).

'Thank you, Mr Cox,' says the mago. She knows Cox's name because it's been entered on the court's computer.

Besides, he's appeared before her dozens, if not a hundred times, usually saying pretty much what he's about to say today.

The mago studies her computer screen. 'Five charges,' she says, glancing at the police prosecutor. 'All proceeding?'

The prosecutor is female too. She sits on the right, the side nearest the witness box. Today she's handling sixty cases and she's dragged the briefs of evidence into court in a black-wheeled suitcase so big she'd have to pay excess baggage to get it onto a plane. She's arranged the briefs in rows and they cover her end of the table like a big, bumpy tablecloth. She runs her fingers across them and finds the right brief. She glances at the cover sheet. 'Charge 4 to be withdrawn, Your Honour,' she says.

Charge 4 is resisting police. It's coming out because charge 3, assaulting police, encompasses the resistance as well. That's how it works: overlapping charges are withdrawn or multiple charges rolled into one. Police methodology deems a crime solved once an arrest is made, so it doesn't matter that twenty charges are reduced to one, or even that the accused is found not guilty. According to law enforcement records it's still twenty crimes solved! No wonder those police stats look good when they want them to.

'Charge 4 is struck out,' says the mago. 'The rest?'

'Pleas of guilty, Your Honour,' sighs Cox sadly.

This is called the Mention Court. It's for those who are pleading guilty. No case here should take longer than ten minutes. It's like the express queue at the supermarket.

The procedure is this. The prosecutor reads an agreed summary of what happened. The mago pronounces the charges proven and, if the accused has prior convictions, they're read aloud or handed up. Then the accused or his counsel makes a plea for leniency and the magistrate imposes a sentence. It's how most criminal charges are dealt with. In the Magistrates' Court, about 95 per cent of accused persons plead guilty. There's a good reason for this: most of them *are* guilty.

The police summary is written by the informant, the police officer who laid the charges. It's supposed to be a fair account of how the accused broke the law. If the summary isn't fair and the accused disputes it, the case gets adjourned to a later date and the witnesses have to come and give evidence.

Now nobody wants that: not the informant who's got other work to do and isn't even here today, nor the prosecutor who's got her other 59 cases to get through, nor the accused, who's owning up and wants to put the whole business behind him. Not even the magistrate, who might be able to squeeze in some shopping if the list finishes early. So everyone has an interest in the summary being fair and balanced. It gives the accused's lawyer scope to negotiate a few changes.

Today's summary is typical. In its original form it went like this.

At 11.15p.m. on 18 July police were called to a disturbance in Reserve Road, Bundoora. The accused was in the company of four other youths and threw an empty stubby onto the roadway where it shattered. When spoken to by the informant, he replied, 'Why don't you fuck off? You're just a prick.' The accused was cautioned about his language and replied, 'Fuck off!'

The accused was unsteady on his feet, his speech was slurred, his eyes were glazed and he smelt strongly of intoxicating liquor. The informant formed the opinion he was drunk.

Without warning the accused swung a punch at the informant which failed to connect. Other police in attendance then attempted to restrain the accused, who struggled violently. Before he was subdued and handcuffed, the accused struck numerous blows with his clenched fists. He also kicked Senior Constable Murdoch on the left leg causing him extreme pain.

During this whole time he continued to use offensive language in a loud voice, including such expressions as 'You're dead, cunt', 'Fuck off' and 'Fucking pigs'. The accused was conveyed to Heidelberg

Police Station where he was lodged in the cells for four hours. Asked his reasons for committing the offences, the accused replied:

For offensive language: 'Fuck off.'

Drunk in a public place: 'You've got to be joking.'

Assaulting police: 'You cunts assaulted me.'

A few days earlier, Coxy had read through this summary and thought it was a bit one-sided. He'd arranged a case conference with the prosecutors' office. 'Look here,' he'd said, 'my bloke denies smashing the bottle; he reckons it was one of the other louts.' The prosecutor was dubious, but Cox had a point. After all, the accused wasn't charged with smashing the bottle; why should the summary say he did? So the wording was changed to read: 'A bottle was broken by one of those present.' Every little helps.

Then there was the bit about Senior Constable Murdoch's pain. In written summaries police always feel 'extreme pain' whether they receive a thump on the head or a slap on the back. There was no mention of the copper seeking medical treatment, nor details of his injuries. So 'extreme pain' gets deleted.

'And what about this offensive language?' asked Cox. 'My bloke was mouthing off, sure, but do you have to keep repeating it? Can't we moderate that part a bit? One "Fuck off" is enough, surely?'

By the time Coxy finished negotiating, the summary wasn't nearly as lurid. Toning it down like this is always worthwhile. Indeed, a defence lawyer who quibbles long enough can get dramatic improvements. Occasionally I've virtually written my own summary after the police have lost interest.

I once appeared for a parent involved in a fracas at a school council meeting. The internal politics had been simmering for a long time and one evening tensions came to a head. My man had a wrestling match with a female council member and the police summary was a classic. It had him rolling around the floor with the woman, shouting obscenities and ripping out tufts of her hair.

Now you can't always tell from appearances but my client was a bantam-weight who looked as mild and inoffensive as they come. He told me his opponent was twice his size and had got him in a stranglehold. He said he would have been a goner if the treasurer and vice-president hadn't come to his rescue. He conceded his language was on the strong side, but said hers was just as bad, if not worse.

What with the political in-fighting and the factions taking sides, the cops were sick of the whole incident. And, of course, nobody wanted bad publicity for the school. After lengthy negotiation I got the summary amended so the brawl became a 'disagreement', the obscene language became 'disparaging remarks' and the violent struggle was described as a 'brief scuffle'. Lucky the English language is so rich in synonyms.

Today's example, though, even in its modified form, doesn't sound too flash. 'Is the summary accepted?' asks the magistrate and Cox nods solemnly. Shortly he'll be assuring the court his client actually holds the police in high esteem and deeply regrets his conduct on the night.

Generally, evidence before a court has to be given on oath. Pleas of guilty are an exception. The police summary isn't on oath and is sometimes taken with a grain of salt. The accused's submissions aren't on oath either. Sometimes they're taken with several grains of salt.

So Cox stands to present his plea in mitigation. Courts take a dim view of assaults on police, and anyone with a previous conviction for violence might even be looking at a short holiday for an incident like this. Cox's job is to come up with a reason not to send this bloke to jail.

He tells the court of his client's personal background: good family, schooling to Year 10, started an apprenticeship – the usual stuff. The bloke's between jobs at the moment (they often are). He's got one lined up, starting next week (they often have) but nothing in writing from the new employer (they never do). I notice the kid's jacket is buttoned up now: the T-shirt doesn't show. Good move.

Another good move: the kid's mum is there with him, looking worried. A parent's presence is imperative for a young offender because you want the court to see there's some adult influence and concern. And it's always harder for a mago to send a kid to jail when his mum's sitting beside him on the point of shedding tears. I remember one young client of mine who was on bad terms with his parents. They were sick to death of his escapades and refused to come to court. He asked me, 'Can I bring along another lady and we just say she's my mother?'

Cox offers his client's explanation of how the incident happened. There are no surprises here. For street offences like this, an accused's excuses usually include any or all of the following:

(a) he was led astray by bad company;

(b) it was out of character;

(c) it happened on the spur of the moment;

(d) he panicked;

(e) he'd had too much to drink.

Drink plays a role in a lot of offending and of course it's no excuse.

Nobody rammed a funnel down this kid's throat and forced him to ingest those fourteen stubbies and the bourbon and Coke. He's the one who got himself into that condition. A man, sober, has to answer for himself drunk.

But Coxy's had the kid do his homework. The fellow has curbed his drinking and there's a letter from a drug and alcohol counsellor about the progress he's made. His mum is full of praise too; the boy's pulled his socks up and even loads the dishwasher these days.

The other important thing is to give the background to the incident. Coxy can't contradict the summary but he can offer additional facts which help account for the accused's actions. For instance, this lad claims he didn't mean to resist; he only started struggling after he'd had his jugular squeezed by a policeman's hairy hand.

But Coxy offers something even better, which puts the offending into a new perspective. The kid's girlfriend had just announced she was turning lesbian and breaking up with him! That very night! Heart-breaking it was; no wonder he sought solace in drink. The girlfriend was the one driving and she took off in the car without him, leaving him with a gang of roughnecks he'd never met before. By the way, he's got a new girlfriend now – very supportive, good influence, steadied him right down (no lesbian tendencies, one hopes).

So this young man gets comfortably over the line. A stern word from the mago but no jail. Community work and testing and treatment for alcohol problems. Coxy's earned his fee.

The plea of guilty was vital too. Owning up indicates remorse and entitles an accused to a discount on his sentence. Of course, remorse comes in two flavours: there's 'Sorry I did it' and there's 'Sorry I got caught'. But even when it's the second kind, an accused still receives a lighter sentence. Why? Because without an incentive to plead guilty, an accused might as well contest his charges. After all, he might win. He'd have nothing to lose by fighting every step of the way and we'd need about six times as many courts as we've got. Whatever the motivation, a guilty plea saves the community time and expense, and is something to be encouraged. The system depends on people copping it sweet.

Criminal barristers, then, spend a lot of time conjuring up extenuating circumstances. There's always something to be said for a guilty person and the barrister's job is to find it. A lousy upbringing? That's a reason for leniency: the accused has had to struggle to try and be a good citizen. A good upbringing? That justifies leniency too: the accused's already a decent citizen, he's just slipped up.

Accused persons are entitled to rely on their good character. They can draw on their credit in the community – if they've accumulated any. It's something the advocate always explores, though sometimes it's hard work.

'Have you made any contribution to the community?' I ask a client. I can see from his appearance he won't be a member of Rotary or the Lions Club.

'Like what?'

'Belong to the CFA? Help out at the Lost Dogs' Home?'

'Nuh.'

'Collect for the Salvos?'

'Nuh.'

'You a blood donor?'

'Nuh.'

'Rescued anyone from a burning building?' I try that one when I'm running out of ideas.

But this bloke's actually got a job. 'I pay my taxes,' he says, 'and I put my empties out for recycling.' Excellent! An upstanding citizen after all.

One important point: the advocate is there to present the facts, not to manufacture them. Often, of course, clients have an excuse for everything and won't shut up. But there's an opposite group who won't volunteer anything. Some are so unforthcoming it's like trying to draw teeth.

A colleague tells of a tight-lipped client charged with driving while disqualified. With his prior convictions, he's at risk of going to jail, but he won't offer any explanation at all.

The barrister says, 'We've got to tell the court something about the circumstances.'

'How do you mean?' asks the client.

'Why you were driving that day? Where you were going?'

'Can't remember.'

'Just give me something to go on.'

'Like what?'

The barrister remembers a recent example. He says, 'The other day I had a client on the same charge as you. His missus was away and he was at home with the kids. All of a sudden the youngest one took sick with an asthma attack. The kid was struggling to breathe and the bloke couldn't find the Ventolin. It was five minutes till the chemist closed and he figured he'd just have to take a chance and drive.'

The client listens in silence then gives a nod. 'Come to think of it, mate, that's exactly the way it happened.'

3

Hot Blood

Crimes of violence

Why do men fight? Is violence innate? Do real he-men enjoy a good punch-up? Such questions have baffled philosophers through the ages. What exactly *is* so enjoyable about getting three teeth knocked out?

Among normal men this pattern emerges. When they square up to each other preparatory to fighting, they, like the domestic dog, expect someone else will step in to separate them. It's what most of them are hoping. They'll put up a token struggle, then submit to being dragged away with their male pride intact.

Another breed of men shape up in earnest. This is where alpha-male rivalry comes into play. These fellows are at a different evolutionary stage – or, more likely, they've just had more to drink. When two such men encounter each other, the sparks fly. My client Brendan was of this type.

He was riding his mini-bike along a bush track which ran beside a tennis club. The track was shared by pedestrians and cyclists. Some of the tennis players thought the mini-bike was noisy; Brendan thought it wasn't. He told me he was riding peacefully along the track, causing no trouble whatsoever. Passers-by were smiling indulgently at him as they stepped out of his path.

Two tennis players, one male and one female, came out of the club and approached Brendan on the track. They took exception to the noise and clouds of blue smoke. He took exception to them. Words were exchanged and the challenge issued: 'Want to make something of it?'

My hero at once engaged the enemy male. Worse luck for him, both opponents were off-duty police, well-schooled in the martial arts. Brendan was no Sylvester Stallone and was behind on points even before the tennis-playing female joined the fray. As she later recounted in court, her contribution was to punch Brendan three times to the side of his head as hard as she could. It must have been pretty hard because she broke a bone in her hand!

After the third blow Brendan, slightly dazed, broke off contact and got away. He rode off some distance, parked his mini-bike out of harm's way and returned for Round Two.

'Why on earth did you go back?' I asked.

'I was still pretty sure I could beat them,' he said.

This time, though, he did no better. As he grappled with the male copper, the female used her tennis racquet in a slicing action and almost severed his ear. Brendan saw reason and called out: 'I give up.'

In addition to giving him a hiding, the police charged him. Brendan thought that was a bit rough. 'I wanted to call it quits,' he told me ruefully. 'I thought it was a draw.'

The rustic setting of the incident was unusual, as the traditional venue for a stoush is the pub. Indeed, the pub has given us the technical term: the 'pub punch'. The expression is always used with some other verbal modifier such as 'just' or 'only', as in 'it was *just* a pub punch' (broken jaw) or 'it was *only* a pub punch' (fractured skull requiring the surgical insertion of two metal plates).

Two clients of mine were accused of following a fellow out of a pub and starting a fight. They said the opposite, of course, that the victim followed them out and attacked *them.* I asked, 'So why were you lurking in the shadows in the car park, holding empty beer glasses in your hands?'

'We were planning to pinch them,' they said.

Mention of beer glasses brings us to another technical expression, the verb 'to glass', meaning to smash a bottle or glass and plunge the jagged ends into someone's face. These days glassing someone will send you to jail pretty much automatically.

Some light is thrown on the state of mind of violent offenders by looking at their own explanations. After interviewing an accused person, the police have to ask him his reason for the offending. Reasons I've seen include these:

> For glassing someone: 'Did I?'
> For assault by kicking: 'Everyone else was kicking him.'
> For recklessly causing serious injury: 'He looked at me.'
> For assault in company (by a Samoan): 'He was a Tongan.'
> For half-killing someone: 'I have no reason.'

I once got a brief which even the solicitor described as the 'Battle of the Low Life'. Two drinking mates had fallen out and went for each other like a pair of gladiators. My client was armed with a knuckle duster and a samurai sword; his opponent wielded a kitchen knife, with a cupboard drawer for a shield. My man didn't want a conviction because he was hoping to join the army! He thought his fighting skills were just what the military needed.

Some of these cases really make you wonder. Several years ago I arrived at court to be greeted at the door by a bloke in a suit who introduced himself as Simon Devlin. He informed me he was a follower of L. Ron Hubbard, the guru of Scientology, and mentioned in passing that he'd been reincarnated three times, first as a warrior in ancient Greece and then as a colonist in seventeenth-century South Carolina. (He didn't tell me about the third time.) It was then that I realised I was dealing with crazies because Devlin wasn't the client: he was the solicitor!

The client was Johnny Piggott, who was missing several teeth and looked as if he'd been reincarnated even more times. He was charged with a serious assault on a carpenter named Lopez. Piggott had a score to settle with Lopez because months earlier in a barney at a pub Lopez had thrown him backwards through a window, gashing his buttocks so deeply he hadn't been able to sit down for three weeks.

By chance, some time after his bum had healed, Piggott (with the emphasis on the 'Pig', joked the cops) spotted Lopez going into a shop in Fitzroy and waited for him to come out. Lopez emerged carrying a shopping bag in one hand and dry-cleaning in the other. Piggott called out, 'Hey, Lopez!

Remember me?' and as the bloke turned, whoompah, it was on.

Somehow in the course of the fray a hammer materialised. Piggott grabbed it 'in self-defence' and, holding it sideways, punched on. The cops said he struck seven blows, of which three connected fully. One of them smashed the bloke's mandible and almost took out an eye. Each blow left a tripartite impression, partly from the fist, partly from the handle and partly from the head of the hammer.

The cops had sixteen gruesome photos showing the outline of the claw, the indentations, everything. We'd been given black and white copies ahead of time and they were bad enough. When the prosecutor turned up at court with the pictures in colour, the effect was horrifying. And they weren't the size of old-time holiday snaps, of course. They were glossy A4 sheets, hot off the latest Xerox colour printer.

The case was adjourned for a month for sentence, and in the interim Piggott had a stroke of luck. He fell off a scaffold at work and shattered his ankle. So when he returned to court it was on crutches, looking frail and harmless. He also held one hand oddly with a white bandage showing.

'What's up with your arm?' I enquired.

'Nothing much.' He rolled his sleeve back and peeled away an elastic bandage. It was to hide his tattoos!

Devlin was with him in court again to lend a hand. I tried to elicit some good things to say about our mutual client and Devlin volunteered that Piggott held a First Aid Certificate.

'What,' I asked, 'specialising in broken jawbones?'

We all laughed, including Devlin. That was pleasing. I didn't know Scientologists had a sense of humour.

Reading back over this, I fear I may have conveyed the impression that violence is comical. It isn't. It's deadly serious. What's laughable are the excuses and justifications the assailants offer.

In that last example Piggott used a weapon, which is an aggravating factor, especially if the offender goes deliberately armed. Mostly, though, my clients' weapons turn up just by chance.

In the heat of battle, for example, another of my clients reached out and chanced to find an iron bar lying on a window ledge. A second just happened to have a chair leg in his pocket.

Another issue is the victim's injuries. When I ask my clients whether the victim was hurt, I'm usually told, 'A little bit.' They rarely notice blood, unless it's their own. Injuries are always minor when they're inflicted on someone else.

For instance, a client in the cells tells me he did nothing at all to hurt the victim. 'Well, maybe a tap,' he concedes. 'I'm not a violent person.' I challenge him with his criminal history, which includes wounding and causing grievous bodily harm. 'Like I said,' he winks, 'maybe just a tap. You know, now and again.'

On the other hand, injuries are often exaggerated in police reports. Blood noses turn into suspected broken noses then actual broken noses. In medical language a blood nose is epistaxis, a black eye is a periorbital haematoma, scratches are lacerations, grazes abrasions. Everything sounds worse in words from Latin or Greek.

Then there's the issue of self-defence. My clients are usually acting in self-defence, even when they deliver the first blow – it's a pre-emptive strike, you see. They think the other bloke is about to attack them, so they go the king hit. It's a common scenario; the blow is mostly delivered from behind and always at a moment when the victim isn't ready for it. It's the sort of blow that sometimes leads to tragedy. The victim goes down like a log and – if his luck's against him – he hits his head on a kerb, fractures his skull and they take him off life-support a week later. Somebody's dead and the assailant says, 'Sorry, I was pissed.'

I haven't had a case where someone's died that way, thank goodness, but it's more by good luck than anything else. I've had plenty where the victim drops as if pole-axed. Often I get to see how it happens because many of these incidents take place in pubs and nightclubs where there are security cameras.

The CCTV footage can be quite disturbing and the absence of audio makes it even more sinister. The scene usually opens onto a group of males, all drunk and aggro and ready to perceive an insult or threat in the mildest gesture. Yep, there's my client, the one with the shaved head, a picture of sullen, glassy-eyed belligerence. There's the victim, minding his own business or, occasionally, with his arms wide open in a gesture of appeasement. Suddenly a fist flies through the air and the victim drops. I watch the footage in the client's presence and he explains, 'I thought he was going to hit me.'

'How could you possibly think that?' I ask.

'Like, he was clenching his fists, but you can't see it on the video.'

It goes without saying that alcohol is the major factor in this sort of thing. It's rare for such an assault to occur without grog – and that applies not just to pub brawls but to violence elsewhere too – on street corners, in taxis, on public transport.

Here's an example of the last category. As a train pulls in to

Watergardens Station a bare-chested youth forces a door and climbs out before the train's fully stopped. Brandishing a can of beer, he stumbles onto the platform and almost falls. Some Protective Services Officers who happen to be there call out, 'Be careful, mate.'

Naturally, he responds as you would to any stranger concerned for your safety. 'Get fucked, you wannabe coppers!'

More drunken louts pour from the carriage and it's on for young and old. My client's the one in the dark hoody, forcing the head of one of the PSOs between the platform and the now stationary train. Of course if my bloke had been hurt it would have been someone else's fault: inadequate security, breach of duty of care or whatever. After all, someone's got to look after his safety when he's incapable himself through self-induced intoxication.

To be fair, once they've sobered up, a lot of these kids are relatively normal. It's the pathologically violent ones who are really scary. One client of mine was facing court for three separate bashings.

He'd only got two prior convictions – a miracle in itself – though one was for breaking his own child's arm.

He'd also breached a Community Service Order by missing an appointment. He hadn't made it because the police were interviewing him that day about his putting down an injured cat with a hammer. ('It was terrible, mate. Its eyes popped out and everything.') In the event, this bloke proved unfit to do community work. Chronic back pain precluded him from working in an op-shop, though it hadn't inhibited his pugilistic feats at the local boozer.

Some men with a propensity to violence, though, don't risk a barney in a pub – after all, the bruiser they tackle there might prove a better fighter. They have a softer target closer to home, indeed right at home: their wife or partner. Such men enjoy having a woman trembling at their slightest whim. It gives them a feeling of power and boosts their male pride. They think, 'I beat the shit out of her and she still loves me. I must be pretty wonderful.'

I have great sympathy for women struggling to escape an abusive relationship; often it calls for much courage and determination. But I cannot fathom the regularity with which some women, in a kind of contributory negligence, choose to *enter* relationships with men they know to be violent, egotistical thugs. Well aware their new sweetheart has bashed his last two girlfriends, they seem surprised when the same thing happens to them. They think their wilful blindness absolves them of any responsibility in their choice of partner.

But it's male behaviour and attitudes that are the real problem. Perpetrators of family violence come from all levels of society, including the middle class whose members don't like to think of themselves as criminals. Some excuse themselves – 'I can't help it if I've got a short fuse' – from any obligation to govern their own temper. On their reckoning, their behaviour is the woman's fault. If she hadn't pressed his buttons or nagged him, he wouldn't have lost his cool.

Such a man minimises his own behaviour. When he yanks three handfuls of hair from his partner's scalp, it isn't his fault, because she suffers from alopecia anyway. When he holds a screwdriver to her throat, she knows it's only a gesture and that he'd never dream of actually hurting her. When he shouts, 'You're gonna die, bitch!' she knows it's just the grog talking and that deep down he really loves her. When the police catch up with him he acts hurt and hard done by, and angles for a chance to contact her and try some emotional blackmail.

Attitudes towards family violence, though, have changed a lot, just as they did years ago towards drink driving. Courts now take violence against women very seriously – as, indeed, they should. When the fellow I speak of above cops 22 months jail, the penny starts to drop.

Police figures for family violence, by the way, increase year by year. I see that, paradoxically, as a good sign, not a bad one. International surveys support my optimism: countries that rate highest for sexual equality report the most abuse, while countries where women are the most downtrodden report the least. What the statistics are measuring, then, is not an increase in violence against women, but an increased willingness to report it.

4

In Combat

Who struck first?

Often, when a client pleads not guilty you know you're on a loser. Sometimes, though, you actually hope to win. That was my hope one winter morning as I pointed my old Renault east and headed for Gippsland with the sun in my eyes.

My colleague Madeline was defending a co-accused and when I reached the court house she was already there. She told me straight away her client, Murray Green, wouldn't be giving evidence. Sounded like he had something to hide.

My man, Trevor Wickham, was the opposite; he was busting to have his say. Stocky and fit, he was twenty-three but looked younger. You mightn't have picked Madeline's client for a Koori but Trevor clearly was. He was a cheerful bloke with a pleasant smile, though I guessed he'd be a handful with a few drinks in him.

He faced six charges, two each of intentionally causing injury, assault by kicking and assault in company. The case got started right on ten.

Barry Carter, the so-called victim, was the first witness. Overweight, with slicked-down hair and discoloured teeth, he was a surly type in his mid-thirties. He ran Carter Brothers' Security, which patrolled the town after dark for the Chamber of Commerce. He'd been cosying up to the police and looked pleased with himself as he stepped into the witness box. He was a bully-boy out to make a good impression.

Carter's account began at two o'clock one Sunday morning. He was patrolling the town with his two German shepherd dogs, he said, and slipped into the Railway Hotel to give them a drink. The pub had closed a while earlier so he went in by the side door. The manager and the crowd controller were chatting in the front bar and he joined them. He half-filled a bucket with water for the dogs. No prizes for guessing what fluid he was lapping up.

The blinds were drawn on the front window, he said, except for a couple of inches at the bottom. Through the gap, he noticed two pairs of eyes peering in. He went out onto the verandah to check and recognised Murray Green and Trevor Wickham. Trevor, he said, started mouthing off, then – without warning – hit him with a clenched fist to the side of his head. Carter said he hit back in self-defence. The fight was on.

They traded blows till he was caught off-balance and fell, pulling Trevor down with him. On the ground, Trevor was still landing punches until the crowd controller ran out and dragged Carter inside by his shirt.

Back in the bar, Carter realised one of his dogs was still outside. As he ventured out to look for it, Trevor pounced on him again and the fight resumed. The police were treating this as a separate incident; that's why they'd doubled up on all the charges.

Carter extricated himself from this second bout and made it back inside. He'd copped a broken nose, grazes to his face, plus bruising and soreness everywhere else. He embellished his evidence to put himself in a good light and peppered it with high-falutin' terms:

he 'observed suspects' and 'sustained injuries'. And what you and I would call a punch-up, he described as being 'in combat'.

Our side's version was very different, and I put it to Carter bit by bit in cross-examination. 'You had a grievance against Trevor's family, didn't you?'

'Nuh.'

'Because Trevor's cousin had fought with you the month before.'

'Nuh.'

'So this night you challenged Trevor to fight.'

'He just went for me, mate.'

'He accepted the challenge?'

'There was no challenge.'

'You thought you could beat him, didn't you?'

'I didn't think nothing.'

'But you were copping a hiding?'

'I wouldn't say so.'

'The crowd controller had to come and rescue you, didn't he?'

'He helped me.'

'You challenged Trevor Wickham because you thought you'd get the better of him, didn't you?'

'I didn't challenge him.'

'And you didn't get the better of him.'

It might not look so good on paper but the last bit came out pretty well. It wasn't really a question anyway, but Carter had no answer. He wanted it both ways, to be a victim and a hero at the same time.

I asked about the dogs. 'Were they your guard dogs?'

'No way.' He looked down for a moment. 'They were family pets.'

In the car park that morning, I'd seen the Carter Brothers panel-van, their 'command vehicle' as Barry Carter called it. Painted on the side was a picture of a snarling Alsatian and the words 'Patrols – Security – Guard Dogs'.

'If your dogs are so docile, how do you account for the picture and the inscription?'

'We've got two lots of dogs. Some are guard dogs; some are pets.'

'Really? So the pets were on duty that morning, were they?'

The crowd controller McAdam gave evidence next. He hadn't been in court to hear what Carter had said and he wasn't totally comfortable in the witness box. He agreed Carter joined him and the manager in the front bar. He said somebody outside banged on the window. 'They almost broke it. There was two of them. They stuck their fingers up at us. One was Murray Green. I know him well, I've had dealings with him in the pub before.'

McAdam said Carter went out to investigate. 'Then Trevor Wickham hit Carter and Carter hit him back. Murray Green was trying to get in on it, so I went and restrained him. The dogs were there too and Green threw the rubbish bin at them. Carter ended up on the ground, with those two both kicking him. I dragged him back inside. He was bleeding from the nose and mouth. That's when I rang the police.'

There were some interesting discrepancies. Carter had spoken of two separate incidents while McAdam recounted just the one. Carter had seen only eyes peeping through the gap in the blind, while McAdam said the men banged on the window and raised their fingers. The two hadn't compared notes beforehand.

I asked McAdam if he had a good view through the window. He said he had.

'So the blind was up?'

'Fully up.' Another difference. And he agreed he hadn't gone outside till the fight was under way.

'So you never saw how the fight started?' I asked.

'Not exactly.'

'You didn't see who struck the first blow, did you?

He paused before he answered. 'True.'

Then it was Madeline's turn. According to her client, Carter had set the dogs on Trevor.

Madeline asked, 'Wasn't Murray kicking the dogs to keep them at bay?'

'No, he was kicking Carter, not the dogs.'

'But what about the rubbish bin? Didn't Murray pick it up and throw it at the dogs?'

'That's right.'

'Not at Carter?'

'No.'

'Why would he throw it at the dogs if they weren't joining in the fight?'

McAdam hesitated. 'I wouldn't know,' he said.

The last witness for the prosecution was the informant, the policeman who'd laid the charges. He'd taken statements from Carter and McAdam, but when he'd approached our two blokes, he said, they wouldn't speak to him. Next day, though, they came to the station and made written statements. He produced copies.

I asked him about Trevor's injuries. Trevor had taken photos later the same morning and I passed them up. They showed two puncture wounds surmounted by semi-circular tooth marks. The policeman glanced at the photos.

'Were those the injuries you saw to his legs?'

'Yes.'

'Do you agree they resemble dog bites?'

'I'm not qualified to say what they resemble.'

We passed the photos up to the mago and he studied them carefully. You didn't need to be a forensic surgeon to see they were dog bites. Unless they were dingo bites.

I asked, 'Two men got hurt in a fight and they each blamed the other?'

'Yes.'

'And you weren't there yourself?'

'No.'

'So you don't know which version is the truth?'

'That's for the court to decide.'

'But you laid charges against my client, didn't you?'

'That's right.'

Did you lay any charges against Carter?'

'No.'

'Why not?'

'My superior didn't approve the brief for prosecution.'

'Do you know why not?'

'No.'

Madeline asked about the manager, the third man in the front bar: he must have seen some of what happened. She said, 'Is there any reason why the bar manager hasn't been called as a witness?'

'He refused to give us a statement,' said the informant. Interesting.

Now it was our turn. Trevor stepped into the witness box and took the oath. He came across well, with a bit of dignity. He admitted he'd been drinking earlier at another pub. He said he and his mate Murray Green were passing the Railway Hotel on their way home when Carter came out on the verandah and gave him a dirty look. He, Trevor, asked what the problem was and Carter answered, 'Do you want to make something of it?' Trevor accepted the challenge. He said Carter punched him first, and he hit back.

Trevor said he was getting the better of the fight till Carter whistled up his dogs. The dogs went for him so Murray joined in, kicking them away and warding them off with a dustbin. But even with the dogs' help Carter was getting the worst of it. That's when McAdam came out and dragged him inside. That was the end of the fight.

Trevor agreed he wouldn't speak to the police at first. He said, 'But I thought things over and next day I went to the police station to lodge a complaint against Carter. The police told me they couldn't do anything unless I made a statement. So I made a statement. Then they did nothing anyway.'

The prosecutor cross-examined and went in pretty hard. Trevor denied going up to the window of the Railway Hotel, but admitted somebody might have.

'Could the somebody have been your mate Murray?' asked the prosecutor.

'Could have been.'

'And could he have made an obscene gesture?'

'He did make it,' admitted Trevor. 'But that's no reason for Carter to look greasy at me.'

'What should he have done to a gesture like that?'

'A gesture should be ignored,' said Trevor. Good answer.

'You say Carter challenged you to fight?'

'That's right.'

'And you were happy to fight him?'

'I won't decline a fight with a bit of grog in me. Not if they're willing.'

'And once the fight with Carter was under way, what happened then?'

'Then,' replied Trevor cheerfully, 'I punched the crap out of him.'

The mago gave a wry smile. He was new to me and I couldn't read him. The smile was his first flicker of expression. An encouraging sign.

'And are you proud of that?' asked the prosecutor sarcastically.

'Yes,' said Trevor.

'And Green was helping you. He wanted you to win, didn't he?'

'Any friend would.'

The cross-examination ended with a nice exit line from Trevor. He'd said Carter had thrown the first blow and he was merely defending himself.

'Defending yourself!' exclaimed the prosecutor. 'I thought it all started over a greasy look.'

'I was still defending myself,' said Trevor. 'I was defending my pride.' Somewhere else it might have sounded corny, but at that time and place it sounded right. It wouldn't always be easy for a Koori to stick up for himself in a country town.

The mago adjourned to consider the evidence. Madeline and I went outside and stood in a patch of sun near the front steps. Our clients joined us, wondering which way the case would go. Murray lit a smoke and said he'd be willing to do community service.

'Community work,' said Trevor, 'I'll go for that too.'

'But we can't lose this!' I said. 'Shit, not on that evidence!'

'You get used to losing,' said Trevor. 'Living here, you have to.'

The PA system called us back. We went into court and held our breath. The mago started with the usual stuff about reasonable doubt. Then he pointed out the contradictions in the police case, even on issues which didn't matter, such as whether the blind was up or down. 'Mr McAdam said he saw Murray Green through the window making a nuisance of himself. So why doesn't Mr Carter agree? Why does Mr Carter say there were two incidents, when everyone else says there was one? The answer may be that Mr Carter wishes to conceal the fact that he was spoiling for a fight.'

So we'd won. Thank goodness.

As they often do, the mago finished up with a sop to the prosecution. 'I'm not saying Mr Carter is a liar or the accused are angels. I'm saying the charges aren't proven beyond reasonable doubt.'

The police looked sour and so did Barry Carter. I gathered up my papers, and Trevor and I headed outside. As we crossed the foyer I could see the informant and another copper waiting by the double glass doors. As we approached, the informant stepped into our path. 'Excuse me, Trevor,' he smiled. 'This is for you.'

Trevor took the papers, glanced at them and passed them to me. They were a new set of charges, a summons over another fight, well before the blue with Carter. They'd been issued that same morning, probably when the case against Trevor was starting to look shaky. Talk about bad losers. I stood there and shook my head. It seemed a lousy trick to play.

'That's what we have to put up with in this town,' said Trevor.

5

Demon Drink

Alcohol-related offences

Not many of my clients have a drinking problem. Most insist they're only social drinkers, especially the ones with three drink-drive convictions who've been picked up a fourth time. 'It's not like I'm a pisspot or anything,' they mutter.

Recently, one maintained he'd given up drinking completely. Knowing his record, I was sceptical. 'What, nothing at all?' I asked.

'Not unless you call half a dozen stubbies a drink,' he said ... then added, 'which I don't.'

And what's the problem anyway? Alcohol doesn't cause much trouble apart from fatal road accidents, street brawls, family violence, absenteeism, child neglect, cancer of the liver and urinating in public. Even the connection with liver disease is dubious. A client with cirrhosis once assured me he'd caught it in a boating accident! Some countries have tried prohibition, but it doesn't work. Heroin's already illegal, so why bother to ban a more dangerous drug?

Of course I'm being flippant: alcohol causes untold harm. Economists tell us it costs the economy $24.7 billion a year. Experts say alcohol contributes to 30 per cent of road accidents, 34 per cent of drownings, 16 per cent of child abuse cases and 10 per cent of industrial accidents. It's implicated in so many falls that I'm told some hospital records carry a standard abbreviation 'FOP', standing for 'Fell Over Pissed'. Alcohol is a factor in most offences of violence to come before the courts. If the stuff had just been invented, we'd ban it.

Lots of offenders think being drunk gives them a defence. 'I was pissed,' they say blandly as if it excuses everything. Intoxication can sometimes be a mitigating factor where it reduces someone's moral culpability. Mostly, though, it's no excuse. You can't say you're not responsible; your responsibility starts when you open the first bottle.

The notion of responsibility was foreign to my client Herman. I rang him the night before court and reminded him to meet me early the next day. Usually I'm delighted when my clients get to court punctually, but not this time. To tell the truth, I was the one feeling responsible – partly, at least. Herman had got there four hours early, not exactly to court, but to the cells of the police station next door.

Apparently, my reminder call had put the wind up him. He'd taken off for the pub and come home boozed. He'd clambered over the fence into the neighbours' yard and threatened them with an iron bar. The neighbours had put up with this sort of thing for months and were sick of it. So they called the police.

The cops arrested Herman and when they put him on a breathalyser he blew .32 per cent. That's absolutely blotto, more than six times the legal limit to drive – not that he was driving, thank goodness. He himself thought the reading unremarkable. He told me later his record was .41, a level at which most people would be in a coma.

The police deemed Herman too drunk to interview but gave it a whirl anyway. By the time I reached the police station he was flaked out on the floor of the interview room. I told him to say 'no comment' to everything so the interview would be short. Among the papers in my brief was a medical report stating Herman had been an alcoholic for twenty years. It pointed out one good sign though: he'd recently gone four days without a drink. Apparently that was a record too.

As the court's drug and alcohol counsellor was arriving to check him out, Herman took a turn for the worse. The cops called an ambulance and had him carted off to hospital. Besides his alcoholism, the medical report recorded hypertension, a heart murmur, anxiety, epilepsy and incipient diabetes. I got his case adjourned and arranged for a friend to feed his dog. Within 48 hours Herman would be out of hospital and back home, slaking his thirst once again on Carlton Draught.

People like Herman think nothing of incidents like this. Getting pissed, fighting, spewing up and being thrown into police cells are male bonding rituals. Drinking's their life and they have no wish to change it. If they gave up the grog they'd lose all their friends. And, by mixing only with other alkies, they judge themselves by them – among whom there's always someone worse. They develop strange ideas of what's normal. One bloke, for instance, fought for years in the Family Court to have unsupervised access with his children. When he was finally granted the kids for a day the only place he could think to take them was to Young & Jackson's for a counter lunch.

One of my drinkers had a stroke of luck last year. He was caught red-handed pinching a cask of wine and detained by the shopkeeper till the police arrived. In due course the police turned up, placed him under arrest and took possession of the stolen goods. Back at the police station they put him in an interview room. Before the interview could begin, the copper was called away for some reason and left my bloke unattended with the cask. He managed to guzzle the lot before the policeman got back. That's right, the whole two litres!

Booze artists like him take every opportunity that's offered. Late one Friday afternoon a client of mine was granted bail to return to court on the Monday. I'd got the Salvos to arrange a motel room for him over the weekend, but the police were concerned at the proximity of a Dan Murphy's bottle shop just a few doors away. To eliminate any risk, the magistrate imposed a bail condition that the man not attend the shopping centre, or indeed leave the precincts of the motel. What we all overlooked was that the motel room had a mini-bar! Say no more.

It's not only men who are hardened soaks. A worrying trend over the past ten years is the increase in female binge drinking and foetal alcohol syndrome. Last year the apprehension rate for female drunks went up 21 per cent. Male police no longer simply let the women off, as they once did. But that change still wouldn't account for all of the increase. You wonder about the liquor industry targeting women.

Female boozers reflect the same attitudes as their male counterparts. A twenty-year-old woman turns up to court with her mother. Her name is Shayvana; I know I've got the spelling right because it's tattooed on her mother's arm. Shayvana has a counsellor's report saying she's only a social drinker, yet she reeks of alcohol. 'Oh, can you smell it?' she asks. 'I only had a glass of wine this morning to steady my nerves.' I send her mother across to Shopping Land to buy some mints.

Clients sometimes turn up to court inebriated, and the women are even harder to manage than the men. Take Cindy, a thirty-year-old whose battered face speaks of a hard life. She's been told to meet me at nine. At ten she finally answers her phone to say she'll be there by eleven. During the course of the morning the bench clerk in Court 1 pages me several times, asking when Cindy's case will be ready. At 11.30 she shows up with a roughneck called Igor. He seems to have some influence over her, which is lucky because I have none.

Cindy's charged with stealing grog, smashing windows, fighting with security and resisting arrest. She's got a long record of this sort of thing – and worse. I speak to her briefly in an interview room and tell her to stay where she is. I dash down to Court 1 and let the bench clerk know she's finally arrived. I'm only gone two minutes but when I get back to the room Cindy and Igor have disappeared.

After twenty minutes they show up again. Cindy's speech is slurred and she's glassy-eyed and wobbly on her feet. She rambles on about her twin brother who died of an overdose when suddenly, in mid-sentence, she stands up, slips out the door and is gone. I remonstrate with Igor. I say, 'Why didn't you stop her?'

'Shit, mate! Don't blame me,' he shoots back. 'I can't control her. I'm sick of her. I'm going home.'

'No! Please don't go,' I beg. He's my only chance.

So Igor goes and finds her and coaxes her down to Court 1. She must be swigging vanilla essence because she doesn't actually smell of grog. I go and whisper to the clerk and ask if her case can be called on pronto. My intended spiel that she's overcoming her drinking problem won't go over too well if she collapses behind me in a pool of vomit. But just as it's our turn, the mago announces a short break and the court adjourns.

Cindy catches sight of some yokel in the back row and stumbles to embrace him. Next thing she's disappeared again. 'She's pissed,' nods the fellow knowingly.

Igor goes on strike so I have to head down myself to the smoking area. I can't spot Cindy there so I get security to check the women's toilets. I have her paged over the PA system and generally prowl around the foyers, but to no avail. Years ago at the old Melbourne City Court there was a pub diagonally opposite so you always knew where to look. Where do you look when you're out in the suburbs? There's no public bar in Shopping Land.

The case is called on again. It was first called an hour and 50 minutes ago.

I explain that my client's disappeared. 'So what's the go?' asks the mago.

'Well, it was going to be part of my plea that she's gaining some control over her drinking,' I say, 'but I'll have to omit that bit now. She told me she went to Alcoholic Anonymous yesterday and plans to go again tomorrow. Unfortunately she hasn't been today.'

'Do you want more time to look for her?'

'Your Honour, I honestly don't think I'm going to find her now.'

'I'll adjourn it off, then.'

At this moment the door to the courtroom bursts open and Cindy staggers in. 'Sorry, everyone,' she giggles, 'I thought it was lunchtime!'

Perhaps I shouldn't admit this in these days of gender equality, but I find female drunks sadder and more embarrassing than male ones. A drunken man can be a figure of fun, but less so a woman. Somehow for a female it's more undignified, more tragic.

Years ago I acted for a woman I knew by repute as sane, sober and respectable. Unknown to me she was an alcoholic who attended AA meetings a couple of days a week. But she stopped going to AA and hit the bottle.

She went carousing in pubs and was out till all hours. Her husband never knew where she went or what she got up to. Apparently, she made a male friend at a pub, then fell out with him. Feeling slighted, she took it into her head one day to pay him back. She got blotto and went round to his house to wreck the joint.

Drunk or not, she was thorough. She broke every window in the house and every mirror. With a pair of scissors she slashed all the curtains and cut up all the bloke's clothes. She went through the drawers and wardrobes and snipped pieces out of every single garment. She even found a few shirts in the washing machine and gave them the treatment. The damage was over thirty grand.

Her husband supported her at court, and I mean physically supported her. She kept going off to the Ladies and swigging something out of a scent bottle; after a few toilet breaks she could barely stand. We faced a mago who was a Methodist lay preacher in his spare time. He was a real wowser about alcohol and didn't like what had happened one bit.

Even so, my client was an otherwise respectable citizen with no criminal history. She ended up getting a community order with rehabilitation conditions and 200 hours of community service. She did three hours of the community work, then went on a binge. She crashed her car and killed herself, leaving her husband and two children. Simply awful. A complete tragedy.

Some of these boozers are barely older than children themselves. Cameron, aged twenty, had been drinking heavily for six years. In fact he'd celebrated his fourteenth birthday by having his stomach pumped. Whenever he had money he'd go out and get plastered. One night he staggered home to find his key wouldn't work in the front door. He went round the back and tried the glass sliding door but it was locked as well.

He hunted round for a way to get in and finally picked up a garden gnome and hurled it through the door. The glass shattered and he let himself in. He grabbed a bottle of sherry from a cupboard and settled down in an armchair to do some deep thinking. What mainly puzzled him was that when he'd left home there was no sherry in the house. Nor did his place have a sliding back door and definitely not a garden gnome. Then he sank into an alcoholic stupor.

Out in the street the courtesy van of the Ebbtide Old Folks' Club was just drawing up. There were a dozen passengers, all pensioners. They'd been celebrating the eighty-third birthday of one of their number and the youngest person aboard was the driver, who was seventy. As the mini-van rolled to a halt, dear old Gwen noticed her kitchen light on and knew something was amiss.

The senior citizens piled out of the van and armed themselves with a garden rake and barbeque tongs. Then they crept warily round the back, ready to do battle. They looked through the broken glass and saw my client sprawled unconscious in Gwen's new armchair, with its footrest extended.

When the matter came to court, Cameron was released on a bond to reside at an alcohol rehabilitation centre in Tasmania. His mother had arranged it and gave me a brochure about the place which featured glowing testimonials from school teachers, MPs and ministers of religion. Some of the treatments looked pretty unconventional to me and included bareback riding, whip-cracking and other rodeo skills. A photo in the brochure showed an inmate under treatment from some medical apparatus, with electrodes attached to his head and wires leading off to a control panel. That also looked unconventional. I asked Cameron's mother how she knew of the centre and she said, 'Oh, I send all my children there.'

Places in rehab centres are scarce and there are always long waiting lists. Even so, some of my clients have been through such programs three or four times, which makes you wonder how successful they are. I guess it depends how you measure success. One facility for elderly alkies seems to have given up entirely on the treatment aspect;

the residents love the place. They aren't allowed to drink on the premises but every pension day taxis queue up to take them to the pub of their choice. Ambulances bring them back the following morning and then it's all quiet again till next pay day.

Public drunkenness and violence, of course, tends to radiate out from hotels and other drinking spots. If you avoid the King Street nightclub strip at three in the morning your chances of being involved in a drunken fist fight are much reduced. However, there's one area in which alcohol-related offending puts all of us at risk, and that's on the road.

Courts are serious about drink driving because it's a matter of life and death. I've done cases where drunk drivers have killed someone. They're terrible cases. The parents are never the same after someone's killed their kid.

One client was a repeat drink-driver. He'd been disqualified from driving twice before but was re-licensed after persuading a court he wasn't a risk back on the road. Tearing home from the pub one night in his four-wheel drive, he swerved across the centreline and collected a Ford Festiva head-on. The young woman in the Ford died on the spot. Later, my bloke told me he hadn't had a drink since the accident. In a way that seemed almost an aggravating factor because it proved he was capable of controlling his drinking. If he'd stopped a day earlier the young woman would still be alive. As it was, he copped eight years' jail. He'll be due for parole in five but his victim will still be dead.

Curiously, even with a skinful, men like this retain an instinct for self-preservation. One of my customers was heading home from a country pub one night with his ten-year-old son in the front passenger seat. Witnesses in the car following reported seeing his car weaving all over the road. It drifted round a corner, hit an embankment, rolled once and ended up on its side. As the witnesses stopped to help, two figures climbed out a window and sprinted into the bush.

When the police arrived there was no trace of the driver or his son. The pair emerged later a few kilometres up the road. My client told me he'd been concussed and lost his sense of direction. He'd headed into the scrub to seek help and got lost in the bush for three hours. Yes, three full hours, exactly the time limit the police have in which to breathalyse someone.

When drivers are breathalysed, the operators have a standard set of questions to ask. Here's one operator's exchange with a driver who'd just returned a positive result to a preliminary breath test. It shows the sort of thing the cops have to put up with.

I said, 'Have you consumed any alcoholic liquor tonight?'

He said, 'What do you think?'

I said, 'What sized glasses, cans or bottles were you drinking from?'

He said, 'Fuck off, poofter.'

I said, 'What type of intoxicating liquor have you consumed tonight?'

He said, 'That's your business. You work it out.'

I said, 'How much intoxicating liquor have you consumed tonight?'

He said, 'Get fucked, you pissant.'

I said, 'What time did you have your first drink?'

He said, 'Stop asking questions that annoy me.'

I said, 'What time did you have your last drink?'

He said, 'Get fucked. Take a walk faggot.'

I said, 'I now require you to undergo a breath test pursuant to Section 55 of the *Road Safety Act.*'

He said, 'Pull your cock, mate.'

Drivers such as this often whinge when they lose their licence. 'How am I meant to get to work?' they demand, as if it's my fault. I should know better than to argue, but their petulance and lack of contrition really irk me. I tell them they should have thought of it before and suggest they check out the bus timetable.

6

Our Daily Bread

The food regulations

The *Food Act* 1984 runs to 242 pages. In addition there are Regulations made under the Act and Statutory Rules made under the Regulations. Among them are the Food Safety Practices and General Requirements which set out all kinds of surprising stipulations. For instance, food handlers aren't allowed to 'sneeze, blow or cough over unprotected food' or spit in areas where food is prepared. Or even 'urinate or defecate except in a toilet'. Amazing! Who would have thought it?

I appreciate that some pretty obvious things sometimes need to be spelled out in regulations, but this seems to be taking it to extremes. Talk about the Nanny State! Nowadays you even have to do a course on how to butter bread. My mum did voluntary work at a hospital kiosk for nineteen years till it was made compulsory for all the volunteers to do a food-handling course. Most of them were in their seventies and had been preparing lunches their whole lives. There were more than twenty ladies, so between them they'd been making ham and salad sandwiches for a thousand years. Yet they still had to do the course – and pay $130 for the privilege.

I honestly think we're over-fastidious about food nowadays. You can't build a strong immune system without exposure to dirt. Doctors recommend we ingest a kilo and a half of dirt a year to stay healthy – something like that. In my opinion penalties under the *Food Act* have gone berserk. You can go to jail now for up to four years just for poisoning a couple of hundred people.

Here's a true story. On my way home from court some years ago I called into a milk bar and bought a pie for lunch. The thing must have been in the pie-warmer for weeks, being heated up and cooled down again. The crust was as tough as terra cotta and when I broke through it, the meat was green. Honestly, green! I don't exaggerate.

I wasn't too impressed but I wasn't going to dob them in. It's hard to make a quid in a milk bar these days so I pointed out the colour of the meat in a friendly, non-judgmental way. They had to give me my money back as they didn't have anything edible in the shop as a replacement. If I'd been nasty I could have said, 'I'm saving you ten thousand bucks just by not dobbing you in, so what about a couple of grand and a Mars Bar?' It wouldn't have been a bad deal for the milk bar.

I did a case for a pie shop a while ago. The health inspectors had gone over the place and detected what they called 'a number of food safety risks throughout the premises'. They compiled a long report and, although some of the so-called risks were pretty minor, there *were* a lot of them: shelving cracked, exhaust canopy dirty, oven mitts dirty and worn, dirt on the underside of the milk-shake machine and so on.

My client was a dour, peevish individual, who you'd think would have heeded the warning. He could have solved the problem by organising a family working bee or shelling out for some commercial cleaners. Alas, things didn't improve. A second inspection was worse and on every follow-up visit the council found more to complain about.

By the fourth visit a section of the roof had fallen in due to subsidence, which wasn't my bloke's fault at all. It was obviously the landlord's responsibility but it 'created gaps through which pests gained entry' and got the inspectors finding even more things wrong. They included: rodent faeces in the store room, a kitchen-hand slicing tomatoes without wearing gloves, a melted plastic jug used to store sausage mince, a container filled with water and mildew stored under a bench, and bags of flour chewed by rats. What with word processors and cut and paste, there was no stopping them.

The situation got really bad the day the council made a surprise visit and checked out the client's food transport van. In the back they found ants, rubbish, mouldy bread, a spare wheel, gas cylinders, a circular saw and a blood-stained Esky.

'How could you let it happen?' I asked.

'They caught me on a bad day,' he grunted.

For good measure there was now a food analyst's certificate on a chicken sandwich which the inspectors had taken away the last time for analysis. The certificate listed details about its enterobacteriaceae, coagulase positive staphylococci and Escherichia coli.

I didn't really know how many E. coli your average chicken sandwich is meant to contain, but the certificate looked bad. It said, 'This sample indicates poor quality raw materials, inadequate cooking, poor hygiene or post-processing contamination and prolonged storage at temperatures conducive to microbial growth.' It didn't leave me much to say in mitigation except maybe that the sanger was nicely packaged in cling wrap.

Two weeks later council officers attended yet again. They noted that most of the items on the *Food Act* order had still not been complied with:
- The baking tray cupboard was dusty ('Big deal,' said the client);

- Rat droppings were sighted inside the flour cupboard ('Sighted? Not by me');
- The chest freezer was dirty and needed defrosting ('So what?');
- The wall in the corner of the storeroom was still grimy ('Which wall?');
- Rubbish was being stored in the rear yard ('We've always done that').

There was plenty more, but I won't go on.

By the twelfth inspection (seriously, the twelfth!) the premises were reported to be in a satisfactory state. Privately, the council officer told me things still weren't crash-hot but they'd got sick of forever going back and having to amend their reports. The mago was outraged the shop had been allowed to trade while these multiple inspections took place. I nodded sagely in agreement, as if everything was the council's fault.

The maximum penalty for each of the eighteen charges was $40,000. Theoretically the pie shop could have been up for almost a million bucks. He only copped ten grand. Who'd want to run a bakery?

I did a case once for a take-away Chinese restaurant. I called it 'The Case of the Stir-Fried Fly', which wasn't strictly accurate because the food wasn't actually being stir-fried at the time – it was sitting in a tub in a bain-marie alongside the tubs of honey chicken and sweet and sour pork. Above the tubs were some fluorescent lights, including one of that blue kind for zapping insects. What with a few flies buzzing around, some got zapped and fell directly into the beef and black bean sauce. Trying to 'control airborne pests' my clients were, and still got themselves into trouble. You can't win!

Colleagues have similar stories. One appeared for a cut-price restaurant in Chinatown. It catered for a student clientele but the court didn't see that as extenuating. There was a bird's nest in the upstairs hand basin! Maybe they were planning to use it for the soup.

At one suburban court a cake shop was charged over a mouldy piece of Black Forest cake. The local solicitor wasn't used to going to court. He turned up with a sample cake to present to the magistrate in a kind of 'show and tell'. It didn't help that the plate was cracked.

Another colleague told me of his worst case. The client was a fish and chip shop owner and the health inspectors sneaked a secret photo of him peeling potatoes. The trouble was, the bloke was sitting on the dunny doing it! My colleague swears this is true. Again, it didn't leave much to say in the client's favour except, perhaps, that he was a hard worker.

A barrister friend appeared for a Chinese businessman who was prominent in the food and restaurant industry. The fellow was a distinguished citizen and JP but his food premises definitely weren't up to scratch – full of bird droppings and weevils and so on. He got a big fright when the hygiene police came calling and closed his place down for a week to smarten it up. After the cleanup the kitchen gleamed like a hospital operating theatre. In fact it was almost too clean because it made the difference between the 'before' and 'after' photos so stark.

The man faced sixteen charges, including one of not having a clean tea-towel. My colleague adjourned the case once to avoid an unfavourable magistrate. When they came back a fortnight later they faced one who was even worse. The barrister's submission was for an aggregate fine. The mago said, 'I fine the defendant $10,000...' and everyone heaved a sigh of relief. Then he added, '...on each charge'. The total was $150,000, a crippling amount for just an ordinary suburban set-up.

'Is he a racist?' asked the shocked Chinese.

'No, he hates everyone,' explained the barrister.

But was the client right to suspect racism? In Victoria the Food Standards Register of Convictions is posted on the internet. At the time of writing, sixteen offenders are listed. Four of them have Anglo-Saxon names, though one of them runs the Old Rangoon Burmese Eatery. The other twelve are Chinese (five), Vietnamese (five), Thai (one) and Indian (one). Scope for an anti-discrimination claim there, surely!

One difficulty for ethnic restaurants is that some of the proprietors can barely speak English. While they were probably safe ignoring the red tape back in Chengdu, things are a bit different here. Another problem seems to be their fatalistic attitude. Councils give most restaurants at least one chance: if the proprietors clean up their act, they're off the hook. Yet lots of Asians in the food business don't take the opportunity, even the educated ones who speak good English. It's inexplicable.

I appeared for another Chinese restaurant and I've got to admit they really were below par. I'm not too squeamish, but even by my standards the place was crook. I travelled through Yemen a year later and never saw a kitchen that dirty.

In court the prosecution tendered a thick wad of photos. Worse luck for us, the mago considered himself something of a gourmet. He went through the photos one by one, drawing on the utmost resources of his vocabulary. 'Photograph number 17 shows slimy, grease-laden utensils ... Photograph 18 portrays the inside of an oven encrusted with grease and detritus ... Number 19 is disgusting! It shows a sink so filthy as to be nauseating! Any diner would be revolted to see such filth...' and so on.

My clients were solid middle-class people. They drove a BMW and had put their kids through Caulfield Grammar and Melbourne Uni. Their children were high-achievers – accountants or IT consultants. Pity none of them had done microbiology.

The conviction cost the business twenty thousand bucks. That figure isn't bad going on current levels but the family were pretty emotional about it. They didn't blame me, thank goodness. They paid my fee and even sent me a voucher for a complimentary dinner. Funnily enough, I haven't got round to using it yet.

7

Five-finger Discount

Shop theft

Children often go through a phase of stealing things from shops. I did so myself till I got caught. I was in a milk bar pocketing a White Knight, the chewy mint bar that pulls your fillings out and used to cost sixpence. The shopkeeper shouted, 'I know who you are and I'm going to tell your mother.' He actually didn't know me or Mum, but I nearly wet my pants with worry. The mere threat was enough to cure me of stealing. I was eight years old.

My clients are slower learners. They're also more ambitious and go in for pricier stuff than White Knights. Indeed, there's a clear pattern that people steal more expensive goods than they usually buy. In a way it makes sense: people on a low income succumb to temptation and pinch something nicer than they can afford themselves. Better to be hanged for a sheep than a lamb.

You can have some sympathy for a battler who tries to knock off something tastier than sliced bread and budget mince. But poverty isn't the cause of shop theft. For every battler I strike I find someone else who's simply brazen and greedy. One client of mine loaded up her trolley with smoked salmon and gourmet ice cream then wheeled it out to her late-model Mercedes. She was quite unapologetic. She copped a fine but probably paid it by selling stolen property from the stash I suspected she had at home.

I've learned that you can fit a lot of produce into a shopping trolley. Consider this. A bloke goes into Woolworths and a sequence of CCTV clips records his progress through the store. First he's in the dairy aisle, selecting cheese. Then he's at the deli counter, ordering pastrami. Next he's making his choice from the Asian sauces. Gradually, over an hour and a half his trolley fills to the brim. The final sequence shows him propelling the trolley at high speed out the liquor section exit. In the very last frames two dumbfounded shoppers are calling staff and pointing at the door as he gets away.

A few weeks later he's back. The trolley is chockers again and the management recognise him and call the cops. The police make the mistake of approaching him before he's left the store. He says he has every intention of paying for the groceries, though the fact that he's only got $4.20 on him doesn't help his credibility.

The shop tots up the groceries this time and they come to over $650. When the police charge him with the earlier theft they estimate the value at the same figure. We dispute it; we say the first trolley was filled with bulky, low value stuff like toilet paper. No-one can really tell from looking at the video so the cops reduce their estimate to $200. I haggle and get it down to $199. Sounds less.

Those who steal from shops reflect the customer base of the shop concerned. Males steal from Bunnings, females from Coles. This also makes shop theft the one crime where there's some gender equality and where I can start using female pronouns. According to Victorian statistics about 42 per cent of those sentenced for shop theft are female.

Of course women may form a bigger share – they might be cleverer at avoiding detection. No-one knows; there are no statistics for thieves who haven't been caught. The figures, too, record only offenders whose cases reach court. Plenty of culprits escape with warnings from the shopkeepers or police cautions or diversion programs that steer them away from the court system.

When women of good repute suddenly start pinching stuff from shops, there's usually an underlying psychological or physiological problem. Typically it's connected with menopause, and courts deal sympathetically with such cases, often by a good behaviour bond with a condition to seek treatment. I always look at what women steal to tell the genuine from the bogus. The genuine ones pinch things which are useless to them – spark plugs or six copies of the same book. Those who steal clothes in the wrong sizes probably aren't crooks.

Sometimes you just can't tell. I've had repeat business from an elderly migrant lady. Since she arrived in Australia in 1973 she's had at least one shop theft conviction every single year except one. On the last occasion I went to court for her, the magistrate looked at her record and noticed the gap. He remarked wryly, 'Well, at least 1989 was a good year.' I didn't let on it was the year she went back to Greece on an extended holiday.

Young Kristy was another case which clearly wasn't menopause. She went on a shoplifting spree in the Erotic Nights adult shop. Some of the merchandise I'd never even heard of. Nor had the mago, judging from his expression. Kristy's haul included crotchless panties, nipple grips and a 'vibrating cock ring'. Her explanation for the thefts was: 'Just wanted to give my man a good time.' She must have succeeded because the next time she was in court she was pregnant.

But don't think the females are all simply impulse artists or victims of their hormones. Far from it. One woman I represented, for instance, took more than a shopping list when she set out to do her Christmas shopping. Beforehand, she'd prepared a big cardboard box about the size of a microwave oven by covering it at home with Santa Claus gift paper. At the shopping centre she sat the box in her trolley and headed for her favourite stores. Anything she liked, she placed on top. The box had a flap in one corner and when she was unobserved she'd open the flap and drop the item inside. She'd almost finished – she'd been to ten shops – when she was spotted. Store security lifted the flap and $700 worth of stuff came to light.

It was also pre-Christmas when another client was leaving Big W and caused the alarm to sound. She told security she'd paid already but couldn't find the receipt. They didn't believe her so she moved onto her next excuse, namely that the stuff came from another shop and she'd shown it to the store greeter on her way in. The greeter was consulted and denied it. But my client had a back-up story. She remembered she'd intended to pay and had made an honest mistake by forgetting. 'See,' she told me later, 'I've got three defences.' People like her, I suspect, find stealing from shops so easy they don't think they'll ever be caught. They know, too, that hardly anyone goes to jail for low-level shop theft.

With another class of offender it simply doesn't register that pinching stuff from shops is actually stealing. Some while ago a client helped himself to a packet of mini chocolate eclairs in Coles and strolled round the shop eating them while he did the rest of his 'shopping'. Once he'd got his pasta sauce and Don salami he popped it all into the plastic bag he'd brought with him. Then he tucked a six-pack of Coke under his arm and headed out the door. The stakes were high because this fellow was on a suspended sentence and any offence would trigger four months jail.

When the police nabbed him in the car park he said it was all a mistake. He'd just gone out to his car to fetch his credit card (which didn't exist, incidentally). Why then, they asked, didn't he leave his purchases at the counter? Well, he'd only be gone a moment. And as for the chocolate eclairs, he explained, he was sampling them to see if the cream was off.

The police asked, 'Why did you need to eat four to see if they were off?'

'I couldn't tell for sure,' he said. 'Anyway, I only ate three.'

The bloke wanted to run a defence based on the credit card and his innocent intentions. I said to him, 'Never mind the other stuff, eating the chocolate eclairs is enough to sink you.'

'How do you mean?' he asked.

I said, 'They weren't yours!' and he looked baffled at the concept.

Liquor is a popular target for male thieves. Often they go in pairs so one of them can distract the shop assistant while the other does the deed. A client of mine was operating solo when he grabbed a bottle of Jim Beam and stuffed it down the front of his pants. He then walked past the register without paying. When challenged, he did a runner and made for the door. The staff gave chase, and as my man bounded down a flight of stairs three at a time he slipped and fell. The bottle broke and the glass cut into his upper thigh and severed the femoral artery.

The cop who charged him told me he got to the scene just as the ambos did and that he'd never seen so much blood in his life. 'I thought the bloke was a goner. He was pale as a ghost and the blood wasn't just a puddle, it was a lake.' The policeman went easy on my man in court because he thought he'd learn a lesson from his near-death experience. But no; he was knocking off bottles of bourbon again almost as soon as he was out of intensive care.

I represented another fellow pleading guilty to a series of shop thefts of liquor. There were three separate thefts, all to be heard on the same day. In the first incident he walked out of a shop carrying a whole slab of VB. In the second he pinched a six-pack, and in the third just a single can. Clearly, his offending was decreasing; indeed if you extrapolated the pattern, on his next visit he'd be returning beer to the store. Then, just in time, I noticed I was reading the papers in reverse chronological order. The bloke was getting worse, not better! It shows how careful an advocate needs to be.

Some of these thieves are real experts. They know the store layouts, the blind spots, the placement of the CCTV cameras, and which of them are operating and which are decoys. The lengths they go to! Here's how cunning they can be. First a bloke buys a food processor for $200 and a coffee maker for $80. At home he cuts the barcode off the coffee maker, goes back to the store and sticks it on another food processor. He then buys the food processor worth $200 for $80. Back home he removes the false barcode and takes the second food processor with the first receipt and gets a refund. Profit: $120. Not a huge amount, perhaps, but by the time he's done it twenty times it starts to mount up.

Another method: he alters a genuine receipt and inserts fake transaction numbers and store codes. Then he goes to the store, takes one item off a shelf and takes it to the refund counter using the bogus receipt. He receives a refund for something he never bought and gets to keep the doctored receipt on the grounds it covers other items. So the shop retains no documentary evidence of what's happened.

I don't mention these techniques so my readers can follow suit. It's to give an idea of the ruses to which ingenious thieves resort. It's on a very different level from snaffling a muesli bar on the spur of the moment.

Sometimes their audacity is breathtaking. A bloke walks into Harvey Norman, picks up a Sony LCD digital television (value $899) and carries it past the registers, cradled openly in his arms. At the exit to the furniture section he's asked to produce his receipt. He hasn't got one, of course, so he drops the television and does a runner. This time he's chased and caught by security and civilians. But how many times has he got away with a brazen stunt like that? 'A fair few,' he tells me.

Another of my clients faced 59 charges of shop theft, all from Target at a certain suburban shopping centre. He did it the same way every time, taking his own green shopping bag (at least he was environmentally conscious).

He'd fill the bag with computer games, up to 25 at a time. To avoid the cash registers he'd run down the Up escalator. Outside, he'd remove the tags and take them straight to his local Cash Converters. This went on twice a week for eight months. The total came to $38,000. Always the same Target, always the same Cash Converters. There's customer loyalty for you! How, you might wonder, did he get away with it for so long? Search me.

For scale and effrontery the Markovs take some beating. Their story begins about eight o'clock one night when Woolworths security staff notice André Markov leave the store holding something under his coat. They follow him to his car, a late model four-wheel drive (what else?) and see that he's pinched a video, some meat and some children's clothes. His wife and children are in the car and they all have to wait while the police are called.

When the police arrive they ask the couple for their names and addresses. At first the Markovs refuse, then they give their names but not their address. It's their big mistake. The value of the goods is about $60 and according to a check over the radio the two don't have police records. If they'd given their details the police would have let them leave and served a summons at a later date.

Instead, the cops arrest them and take them to the police station pending further enquiries. The children, all under ten, are hungry and tell the police they haven't had any dinner. The cops buy them a snack and something to drink. After an hour the parents divulge an address and the police take them there to check it out. It's an untidy rental property in Epping; no trees, no proper garden. The Markovs open the door and the police step inside and turn on the lights.

The joint is like Aladdin's cave! There are racks and racks of clothes, many with price tags still attached. Target, Myer, K-Mart, Big W, you name it. Every room is full: coats, pants, tracksuits, dresses, footwear, CDs and 1300 videos. There are few signs of anyone actually living there.

So the Markovs end up in court. They're pleading not guilty and I ask them how they're going to explain the presence of all this stuff in their house.

Donna, the wife, announces, 'I'm going to say I've never seen it before in my life.'

I turn to André. 'What will you say?'

'I'll say the same.'

On the first day the Markovs bring the kids to court with them. It's a school day but that doesn't seem to worry the parents. The kids are sweet little things with big round eyes. They run around the court foyer, approaching strangers indiscriminately; they're receptive to any adult interest. The youngest mite has bandy legs as if he's got rickets. He likes people in blue uniforms, I notice.

The case is an absolute loser. It opens with a succession of witnesses from the various stores who identify their merchandise, then undergo a lot of pointless questioning from me. The mago is a grim, plodding individual with the look of a funeral director. He doesn't like the kids opening the courtroom door and peeping in to see what's happening. I tell Donna not to bring them again. I dread having to explain to them later that Mummy and Daddy are going on a holiday.

On the second day there's no sign of the kids, thank goodness. By mid-morning I'm arguing the toss with a store witness as to how she knows that Bonny Blue brand girls' frocks are sold by Target, when a couple of policemen sidle in and approach the prosecutor. There's a bit of whispering and the prosecutor asks for a brief adjournment. He tells the court four unattended children have been found in a car parked near the court since 9.15! I make myself scarce while it's sorted out and after half an hour the case resumes.

The property is listed on an inventory that fills five pages and the Markovs are asked to concede its accuracy. They refuse and insist the police produce every single item before the magistrate. There's too much to haul into court so we all traipse up to the police station – mago, bench clerk, prosecutor, informant, plus me and the Markovs – and into the property room to go through the stolen goods.

The police property sergeant is sworn on the Bible and the rigmarole begins. 'I now produce Item 193 on the Inventory, two ladies' synthetic fur coats, size M' he intones and we all nod and tick our lists. 'I now produce five girls' halter tops, with a picture of a panda on the front.' He pulls them out of a marked bag and counts them out on a bench. We nod again. It's the death of a thousand cuts but the Markovs can't see that.

When we break for lunch the prosecutor lets me into a few secrets. According to him, the Markovs are big-time shop thieves who amass a truck-load of stuff, then drive it to Sydney to flog at markets there. They don't actually live in the Epping house, he tells me; it's just their warehouse.

When we get back after lunch the Markovs are missing. The magistrate asks me if I know where they are. 'Maybe they're out shopping,' I quip.

Twenty minutes later they turn up, entirely unapologetic, and we go through the last of the property. Then we reconvene back in court and it's their turn to give evidence. They say they have no idea who could have entered their house and deposited all that stuff. It's a total mystery! When the prosecutor gets to his feet to cross-examine them, the mago tells him not to bother. Their credibility is zero.

The magistrate launches straight into his findings. My pen can barely keep up with the flow of trenchant phrases. Their evidence is 'unbelievable', 'calculated to deceive', 'cunning and dishonest'; their explanations are 'simply rubbish'. The court will pass sentence the following day and His Honour warns pointedly that arrangements should be made for the children.

Next day, though, the kids are at court yet again! I dash round trying to find somewhere to leave them. The Salvos' office is closed so I approach the Court Network. These are volunteers who offer support to people attending court and make them cups of tea and so on. The children trot after me like baby chicks. 'These kids' parents are involved in a case,' I explain to the Network ladies. 'Could I please just leave them with you for a while?'

The ladies look worried. 'We're not meant to look after children That's not our role.'

'Only for a short time,' I beg. 'I'll be back in half an hour.'

They reluctantly agree and I race back to court where the Markovs each cop three months jail. I advise Donna to lodge an appeal, get out on appeal bail and look after the kids while André does his time. He'll be out before her appeal's heard and they can swap places. But they both want to appeal and apply for bail! There's some paperwork to fill in so they're taken to the cells over lunch.

Back at the Network office the kids are getting on fine. In fact, the ladies tell me how sweet they are. 'Can you keep them a little bit longer?' I ask.

'How much longer?'

'Three months,' I jest.

I go and buy the kids some lunch and the Markovs get out on bail in the afternoon. They're completely unrepentant – and uncomprehending, too, it seems. Anyway, I'm out of it.

A few months later I run into the cop who charged them. He tells me they somehow wriggled out of serving jail time. They're doing community work instead. 'Looks like they were smarter than all of us,' he says and I can't help thinking he might be right.

8

Behind the Wheel

Driving offences

They say that inside every car there's a pedestrian waiting to get out. Just don't bank on it! People love their cars; they're obsessed with them. Who knows why? Why not their fridges or their lawnmowers?

When it comes to driving, the ordinary rules of human behaviour cease to apply. It's like the Twilight Zone where everything goes haywire and enters the fourth dimension. Fast becomes slow, red lights are green, distances expand and contract. Otherwise law-abiding citizens fail to understand rules, boundaries or limits. They can't see reason; they deny the obvious. They refuse to accept they might actually have been in the wrong. And they definitely don't like accepting the consequences.

A driver takes a corner way too fast. He crosses the centre line, veers off the road and hits a tree. He's charged with careless driving and tells me he wants to plead not guilty! I wonder if I'm missing something. Did the tree walk into his path? How can it be other than lack of care on his part? Yet when I tell him this he acts baffled and offended.

Here's how irrational people can be. I was sitting in court the other day where a female driving instructor was defending herself on a charge of speeding in Bell Street, West Heidelberg. Her car, which she admitted no-one else drove, had been photographed by a speed camera. However she had documentary evidence, she insisted, to positively prove it couldn't have been her.

I was expecting her to produce an air ticket showing she was in Adelaide that day, or maybe Bangkok. But no, she tendered her work diary which showed that around that time she'd kept an appointment in Ivanhoe, about three kilometres away. Straight after that she'd been in Watsonia, about three kilometres the other way. Bell Street was directly between the two places. Far from proving an alibi, her evidence confirmed she was in the immediate vicinity. Yet she thought she was disproving the charge. Talk about barmy! And she was a driving instructor!

Many drivers dig their heels in like this. Just look at the lengths to which even distinguished people go, telling lies about their speeding tickets and getting busted for perverting the course of justice. Justice Einfeld in New South Wales and British cabinet minister Chris Huhne to mention two; both ended up in jail. Among my clients, many tell me of submitting false declarations to accept their wives' speeding tickets and vice versa. Everyone does it, they say. Everyone? Not me and my wife.

Drivers defend minor cases 'out of principle'. The principle usually means they've run out of demerit points and they'll be off the road if they lose one more. So they expect me to persuade a court that when they were clocked at 104 kilometres an hour they were actually doing 70. What are the chances of that? Buckley's.

The Regulations mandate a margin of error in any event: 2km/h is deducted off your reading automatically. It's expressed in the police summary as: 'Detected speed 105km/h; alleged speed 103km/h.' It *is* sometimes possible to get a further reduction where there's genuine potential for inaccuracy, for instance where the police have measured your speed by following you 'at an even distance' and watching their own speedo. There you might just succeed in knocking 105 down to 99. But you can't bring 105 down to 80.

Collectively, drivers spend a lot of money on lawyers to defend speeding cases. Most of it is wasted. When a solicitor sends me a brief to contest 89km/h in a 60 zone I tell him it has no chance. He replies, 'I know that! I just take their money.' And why shouldn't he? It takes hours to talk sense to some people. Let them have their day in court and learn the hard way.

The details they go into! They take dozens of photos all showing the same stretch of road and proving nothing. They brandish printouts from American internet sites, discrediting traffic lasers and showing radar doesn't work and light travels slower than everyone thinks. They ask pointless rhetorical questions: 'I knew the cops were behind me. Why would I speed?' They come up with ludicrous arguments: 'My car won't go that fast.' They get calculators and tape measures and come to outlandish conclusions.

The police said they pulled over one of my clients half a kilometre short of Rosewood Avenue. The client's muddled account made little sense, but he did give me some figures. I checked his maths and said, 'On what you've just told me you must have come to a halt 222 metres *past* Rosewood Avenue, not before it.'

'That's right,' he said.

'Have you measured it?'

'Not yet. But I will and it'll be 222 metres, believe me.'

He rushed off to take his measurements and ended up getting booked for speeding again!

When a client of this sort is about to lose his licence he wants to argue about everything. 'Shit, 66km/h! Why did they even book me!'

'Because it's over the speed limit,' I suggest.

'Over? Six k's! That's not over!'

'Actually it is.'

'That's bullshit.'

Now I'm not saying that driving 6 k's over the limit makes a person public enemy number one. Far from it; any of us can slip up like that. But I do say the laws of arithmetic still apply. Anyone who thinks otherwise can send me $66 and I'll send back $60 which, according to them, amounts to the same thing. We can do it in multiples, say $660 or $6600 and I offer the same deal. I predict that before long they'll get the message.

People come up with the most preposterous stories. Police charged one bloke with riding his high-powered motorbike at a dangerous speed in a 60km/h zone. According to him he was doing 40 and slowing down; according to the police, they were in pursuit at 130 with lights and sirens on, and couldn't gain on him. He insisted his bike couldn't go that fast, which seemed a bit far-fetched as the speedo dial went up to 240. 'Only if it's been tuned,' he explained.

When he finally did stop, he says the cops dragged him off his bike, threw him to the ground and rained blows on his head. (He was still wearing his helmet, so there was no brain damage.) His bike got scratched and he reckons the transmission's buggered.

I don't excuse the police, but the strain on them of attending horrific accidents can be severe. So, too, the job of informing a kid's parents that their son or daughter is dead on the road. No wonder they get stroppy with dangerous, smart-arse drivers. But even if this bloke did get roughed up it doesn't make any difference to the issue of his speed. Unless the police are so discredited by their alleged brutality (they won't be), their version will be accepted.

The kid's mother took offence at how rude and rough the police had been to her darling son. They called him an arsehole and handcuffed him! Terrible! If the cops had called round instead to break the news that he'd killed himself in a driving accident, she would have been the first to blame them for not catching him before he hurt himself (not others, mark you, but himself).

This bloke had taken 150 photographs which he wanted to show me but had forgotten to bring to court. He wanted an adjournment to prepare his case. 'What is there to prepare?' I asked. 'I've got your statement.'

'You've got to prove the cops are perjuring themselves, so we can win.'

I said, 'I've told you already. This case is unwinnable by you, me or anybody else.'

I hear a lot of clients whinge about speed zones and limits and enforcement. When they're booked they say the limit was stupid; there were no other cars and it was quite safe to go at the speed they were driving. They argue that if there's no other traffic they shouldn't have to obey the speed limit. If that's such a good idea why not apply it to traffic lights as well? If there's no other traffic we might as well drive through red lights too. And why not drive on the footpath if there are no pedestrians?

Often they call for variable limits which go up or down according to the time of day and the amount of traffic. In their next breath they complain about a stretch of road where the limit changes several times over a short distance. 'How are we meant to notice?' they ask.

They object to police hiding in the bushes to catch cunning drivers who slow down the minute they sight a police car. But why shouldn't the police do this to catch someone who endangers the life and limb of other road users? No-one objects to CCTV and store detectives to catch thieves.

The reason is that everyone who drives a car can find themselves caught out. Erring drivers don't see themselves as ordinary criminals and don't want to be treated as such – and by and large they aren't. Any normal driver makes mistakes, but there's a difference between an occasional misjudgment or lapse in attention and deliberate, persistent flouting of the road rules.

The lack of understanding and responsibility is sometimes mind-blowing. Here's an example. An Indian taxi driver was in a bad mood one rainy, stormy night when he picked up two couples heading off for an evening out. The weather was atrocious but he planted his foot on the accelerator and kept it there. He flew out the end of the Burnley tunnel into a rainstorm so heavy the traffic ahead was at a crawl and some drivers were pulling into the emergency lane till it eased off.

Mr Patel roared along at 102km/h. After all, as he explained to me, that was exactly the speed limit plus the police margin of error. Never mind that the windscreen wipers couldn't keep up and that no-one else was doing more than 30. His alarmed passengers hadn't wanted to antagonise him by criticising his driving. They'd only ventured occasional timid remarks such as, 'Excuse me, driver, I hope you can see where you're going.'

Up ahead, through the torrential rain, a line of red tail-lights came into sight and Mr Patel hit the brakes. The taxi started to aquaplane. How unexpected! It skidded into the right hand emergency lane, scraped a hundred metres along the concrete barrier and rammed itself into the back of a stationary truck. It finished up wedged under the tray.

No-one was decapitated, which was a miracle. Indeed, everyone was relatively unscathed except for Mr Patel who copped a metal rod through his shoulder. He was trapped in the car, though, and an emergency crew had to peel the roof off to get him out.

Mr Patel was charged with reckless conduct endangering life, which I succeeded in negotiating down to a charge of dangerous driving. The four passengers, all of them licensed drivers, were unanimous the speed had been far too high for the conditions, and several independent witnesses agreed. But Mr Patel couldn't grasp that he just might have been responsible for what happened. After all, he argued, he was travelling at the speed limit.

Dangerous driving, I told him, carries a minimum of a year off the road. 'How can I drive a taxi if I lose my licence?' he demanded. I suggested he find a job in a restaurant. After all, he was enrolled in some shonky college, allegedly studying hospitality.

'Tell the judge to let me keep my licence,' he whined.

'The judge hasn't got the power to let you keep your licence.'

'Ask him anyway.'

I read the section of the Act to him: '...on a finding of guilt the court *must* cancel the offender's licence and disqualify the offender for not less than twelve months.'

'Ask him to make it six,' he begged. This I ignored.

In court he got a fine and the minimum time off the road. It was the best we could have done. As we walked out he asked what had just happened, as if he hadn't been in the courtroom and heard it all himself.

I said, 'You got the minimum.'

'How long is that?'

'As I told you. Twelve months. You cannot drive for twelve months or you face going to jail.'

'Can he make it three months?'

I began to lose patience. I held up the *Road Safety Act* and said, 'This is the law. It was made by the Parliament of the State of Victoria. It applies to you. It applies to everyone.'

'What about six months then?'

I turned to the index. 'Okay! Let's check for your name ... letter P ... here we are: "...Parking ... Parliamentary reserve ... Passenger transport..." No, there's nothing under Patel there. Looks like they haven't made an exception for you, Mr Patel. So the law applies to you too.'

Stone the crows, he still wanted to argue! I didn't know how to explain it to him any more clearly so I made sure he had the notice cancelling his licence and warned him again not to drive. When I got home there was a phone message from Legal Aid saying Mr Patel wanted to appeal. I rang back and said, 'Tell him to go ahead if he wants to. Maybe he'll get more time off the road, because he can't get less.'

The moral of all this is that when it comes to driving, people simply aren't rational. According to surveys 80 per cent of drivers rate themselves above average. They can't be persuaded otherwise, especially those who drive for a living. Professional drivers, of course, cover more kilometres than the rest of us, but it still astonishes me how often truckies, taxi drivers, mechanics – people who depend on their licences for their livelihood – end up with them suspended or cancelled.

My former mechanics, for example, always seemed to be getting theirs suspended. I had an arrangement with them: they'd service my car and I'd represent them in court. At one time their driving suspensions overlapped and none of them had a valid licence. I asked, 'How can you give my car a road test?'

They said, 'Don't worry, we'll find a way.'

I didn't like the sound of that, but after they'd serviced my brakes I asked if they were safe and got the answer, 'We hope so.' I liked that even less.

Now everything I've written so far is about relatively normal people. When you get to the anti-social element – with whom we all have to share the road, don't forget – things become alarming. I'm seeing a biased sample of course, but the attitudes I encounter make me despair.

A drugged-up girl with her druggie boyfriend in the passenger seat ploughs into the back of a parked car. That car careens into the one in front and both are total wrecks. The girl's car is caved-in at the front but it still goes. The only trouble is the bonnet's been squeezed open and won't go down. So the boyfriend drapes himself over it to hold it down. The girl gets back behind the wheel and drives five kilometres with him spread-eagled across the bonnet. The car hits a bump and all of a sudden the bonnet springs up and the bloke is catapulted onto the road and half killed.

When I say half killed, I'm overstating it, but he gets gravel rash over his entire body, various lacerations and a gash to his head that needs 40-odd stitches. The police informant, who's been a traffic cop for seventeen years, tells me the girl was the most drug-affected driver he's ever encountered. Of course her main preoccupation at court is how soon she can get her licence back and resume driving. Even before we'd left the court the girl's mother was on the phone to someone, whingeing about her daughter's loss of licence.

Then there's the kid who's held a licence for twelve days. He was driving his friends round town from one night spot to another. He flew round corners at high speed, swerved between lanes, did 120 k's in a 60 zone and roared through red lights. After a petrol stop, he went the wrong way up a divided road to avoid having to make a U-turn. This account of his driving came from his passengers, who said they'd been terrified by it the whole night.

The evening ended when the fellow noticed one of his passengers had fallen asleep and started swerving sharply from left to right to wake him up. On the wet road he lost control, hit a post and they all ended up in hospital. According to him, he hadn't been drinking so he'd done nothing wrong. His moronic parents agreed.

The kid was convicted of reckless conduct and got four months of community work and two years off the road. I thought it a reasonable result but he and his parents held a different view. According to them, since nobody got killed, it was all a storm in a teacup. So the fellow appealed.

While the appeal was pending he reoffended and copped eight months' jail for driving while disqualified and drink driving. He appealed that too and got appeal bail. A week later he was caught doing 126km/h in a 100 zone with alcohol in his blood again. Somehow the cops gave him another lot of bail and the very next day he was drink-driving yet again. After that he was locked up. The parents asked me if there was any chance of bail. When I said no, the mother said, 'Goodness, you're a hard man!'

Parents like this make you almost give up hope. Instead of teaching their kids caution and responsibility, they do the exact opposite. Parents with money are often the worst. Knowing their spoiled children to be selfish and immature, they buy them dangerous, high-powered cars. They inculcate the kids with the attitude that you don't have to stop at red lights if you drive an Audi convertible with personalised number plates. Such parents do their children and the community a great disservice.

In Victoria driving while disqualified used to carry a mandatory jail sentence for a second offence. The idea was to defend the integrity of the legal system and ensure court orders were obeyed. But even jail didn't deter a lot of disqualified drivers. So many ended up in prison that Parliament had to relax the law to prevent the jail system from being swamped.

I've had clients caught driving months into their disqualification periods. They'd tell me, though, that it was the very first time they'd driven since they lost their licence. That's right, the one and only day they chanced it, they got caught. Extraordinary police efficiency!

I say, 'Listen, the court won't buy that.'

'Why not? It's the truth. I was only driving to work.'

'So how've you been getting to work, then, for the last six months?'

'Bus.'

'What number bus?'

'Um, couldn't tell you the number. It goes along Stud Road.'

'Stud Road? Wouldn't you have to change at Knox City?'

'Would I? I don't think so ... anyway, er, sometimes I go by train.'

I tell them, 'Of every ten people who say it's the first time, nine are bullshitting. Even if you're that one in ten, you still won't be believed.'

Driving while suspended is such a prevalent offence, I always recommend my clients get to court early. It's important to get the case heard before all the usual excuses have been used up for the day. With so many accused claiming their driving was a 'one-off' it helps to offer an explanation that's a bit out of the ordinary.

The police said one of my clients claimed to be driving because he'd got rabies and was going to the chemist to buy some cream. At court the man enlightened me: 'Those cops were deaf! I never said rabies, I said scabies!' That at least made sense and gave me something to work with. Yes, knowing how contagious the scabies mite is, and how excruciating its itch, this fellow had nobly refrained from taking the bus. Talk about public-spirited!

Another of my clients had eight prior convictions for driving while disqualified. He'd even been to jail for it three times yet he drove himself to court! I was indignant when I found out. I said, 'That's a bloody insult.' I must have been feeling especially moralistic that day because at other times I've turned a blind eye to such things. One client, for instance, had been driving without a licence since 1997. His car was parked in the Shopping Land car park but he told me a 'friend' had driven it. I enquired no further.

You'd think catching disqualified drivers might prove difficult. If they obeyed the road rules the police would have no reason to pull them over and check their licences. But do they drive responsibly? No such luck. They continue to draw attention to themselves and speed, drink-drive, cross double lines, tailgate and use mobile phones much as they did before they lost their licences.

Often, they fail to wear their seat belts, a certain way to attract the attention of the police. You lose three demerit points for failing to wear a seat belt. You also signal your utter lack of responsibility. Seat belts are for the protection of the wearer, no-one else. If drivers don't even care for their own safety, how likely are they to consider the safety of others?

Seat belts have been compulsory in Victoria since 1970, decades before most of my clients were born. Yet some still forget to buckle up – or more to the point, couldn't be bothered. In the year they became compulsory there were 1061 traffic deaths in Victoria; last year, with three times more cars on the road, there were 211. Australia-wide this law (together with random breath testing) has probably saved about 50,000 lives. It represents a great achievement, a triumph of collective wisdom over individual stupidity.

But getting away with disqualified driving now is harder. These days the police have digital recognition cameras which read number plates and are connected to a central database. The system alerts them when a car comes up as being owned by a disqualified driver and the cops pull it over, no matter how the good the driving. Sometimes, of course, the person at the wheel proves to be not the owner himself, but a fully-licensed friend or partner borrowing the car. How often? Traffic cops tell me about one time in ten.

9

Not My Fault

Too old to drive?

Ernest Doble was getting on for eighty. He was a dapper, cocksure little man who'd taught in primary schools and ended up a principal. Though he'd been retired for years, something about his demeanour suggested his earlier career. I could picture him the petty despot, wielding the strap in the good old days. He epitomised the saying about schoolmasters: a man among boys and a boy among men.

Mr Doble ran a small business cutting lawns. He played it down when he spoke to me, saying he only did favours for a bit of pocket money. Probably he was worried about getting his pension docked. At any rate, he had three mowers and a whipper-snipper rattling round in the back of his Holden ute one unlucky April day.

It was mid-morning as he headed for home up Raglan Road, keeping a safe distance from the car in front. When the car's brake lights came on, he guessed it was intending to turn right. He checked briefly in his side mirror and by the time he looked back he was rather close to the turning car. He swung the steering wheel sharpish to pass it on the left. A bit of an emergency manoeuvre, you understand, just a bit sudden.

As Mr Doble straightened up, his Holden overshot; both wheels on the passenger side mounted the kerb. The ute bumped along the nature strip for about ten metres then regained the roadway. The mowers clanked as they shifted in the back, but that was all there was to it. Mr Doble continued blithely on his way.

About a kilometre ahead there was a level crossing. The boom gates were down and Mr Doble joined the queue of waiting cars. As the train was passing, another car drew up behind him. The driver ran to his window and called out, 'You just hit someone! You'd better go back!'

Mr Doble shouted, 'No I didn't!'

The other driver insisted: 'You did! You've got to go back.'

Now Mr Doble knew he hadn't hit anybody but it crossed his mind to go back anyway, just to check. To gain some clearance to make a U-turn, he engaged reverse. As his car edged backwards he heard a crunch and realised he'd hit the car behind.

By now the train was through and a stream of oncoming cars prevented him making his U-turn. So Mr Doble moved off with the flow of traffic and kept going till he got a chance to turn back. All told, it took about fifteen minutes to return to where he'd swerved onto the nature strip. On his right he saw a small crowd gathered round an ambulance.

He drove past then made another U-turn so his ute was heading north again, his original direction of travel. He passed the ambulance and stopped at the kerb. By chance he parked at the very spot where his car had regained the road, where the tyre marks came off the grass.

People were attending to whoever was hurt, so Mr Doble didn't volunteer any help. He noticed the driver whose car he'd bumped at the level crossing and exchanged names and addresses with him. When two police arrived, Mr Doble approached one and gave him his details. Then he left.

About a month later, the police called him in for an interview. Soon after that, he was 'flabbergasted', he told me, to receive a summons. He was charged with recklessly causing injury and a string of driving offences, including leaving the scene of an accident and failing to render assistance.

Today Mr Doble was sitting in my chambers, cocky and unapologetic. He'd done nothing whatever wrong, he protested. He'd held a licence since 1955 and never committed a single driving offence. Not ever! He simply didn't understand what all the fuss was about – at least, he pretended not to.

I asked how badly the pedestrian was injured. 'A few bruises,' he said, shrugging. 'It was her own fault.'

'Her own fault?' I queried. 'But wasn't she standing at a bus stop, waiting for a bus?'

'She was on the nature strip. She was too close to the edge.'

'But your car went up on the kerb.'

'That wasn't my fault.'

Mr Doble was pleading not guilty to all charges. He maintained he hadn't realised there'd been an accident, and if that was true he did have a defence for failing to stop. As for causing injury, he said he hadn't been reckless; another vehicle had created an emergency and he'd done the best he could. Possibly he had a point there too.

'What about unsafe reversing?' I asked.

'What about it?'

'How can you plead not guilty to that?'

'It was nothing,' he sniffed. 'Twelve hundred dollars damage to the other car. My insurance has already paid for it.'

'But you hit him. He was stationary.'

'But why should they charge me? It's been repaired! It was nothing.'

I said, 'It's still an offence to reverse into someone.'

'I don't see why!'

On the day of the hearing Mr Doble turned up with a teenage grand-daughter for moral support. His brother was expected later in the day and so was his son, a teacher. Mr Doble's wife wasn't coming; she had bad nerves.

The case got under way and the first witness was the victim, a drab, disgruntled woman in her mid-fifties. She recounted how she'd been waiting for a bus. She noticed a car intending to turn right, with other traffic passing to its left. The next thing, a car was heading straight for her. The driver looked directly at her and she saw his jaw drop. She recognised the man as Mr Doble.

A moment later she felt a blow and when she came to, she was in an ambulance on the way to hospital. She suffered concussion and bruising but no broken bones. After a few hours the hospital discharged her, but she spent the next few days on her back in great pain.

'She's lying,' muttered Mr Doble behind me.

'Which part?' I whispered.

'All of it.'

The next witness was the driver who'd caught up with Mr Doble at the level crossing. He was middle-aged, a technician of some kind, absolutely your average bloke. He'd been following Mr Doble up Raglan Road and agreed he was keeping to the speed limit. But from 400 metres back, he said, a stationary vehicle was visible ahead with its right-hand indicator flashing.

He said he'd seen the ute head straight for the turning vehicle, then swerve at the last moment. He saw it bump onto the kerb and noticed a coloured object rolling along the ground. He thought something had fallen out the back of the ute.

I felt a tap on my shoulder. Mr Doble was leaning forward. 'He's lying,' he whispered.

'What?'

'He's lying about the indicator,' he hissed. Not wrong or mistaken or incorrect, but lying.'

'Why would he lie?' I shot back.

'I don't know.'

The witness said he then realised there was a woman lying injured on the ground. Other people were stopping to help her so he chased the ute and caught up with it at the level crossing. His version of the exchange with Mr Doble tallied with ours. I wondered what the mago was thinking.

Last for the prosecution was the policeman who'd spoken to Mr Doble on the day and interviewed him later. He'd inspected the ute at the scene and found one of its tyres flat and the passenger side wing mirror shattered. He said a plastic bumper bar on the nature strip matched the ute. I felt a tug at my sleeve. 'Ask him why it took him four weeks to interview me!'

It wasn't a good idea, but I asked.

'That,' explained the policeman, 'was because I didn't realise the accused had driven off and then come back. When I first spoke to him, he was standing by the wheel marks on the nature strip. It was only later when I compared notes with my offsider that I realised he hadn't stopped.'

It was our turn and Mr Doble went into the witness box. He gave his evidence well. His answers were sharp and to the point. He maintained he simply didn't know he'd hit a pedestrian; he'd been distracted by the noise of the mowers and the jolting of the ute. As for the turning car, it had not indicated, he was adamant about that. Mr Doble didn't concede anything. He was a man who brooked no contradiction. And you could see it in his manner that he expected to be believed.

The magistrate adjourned and half an hour passed, then an hour. Was the delay a good sign or a bad one? Or was the mago just having a cuppa?

While we waited, the rest of Mr Doble's entourage arrived, including his school-teacher son. I'm not alone among lawyers in finding teachers uncongenial as clients. Opinionated and complaining, Mr Doble's son was true to type. 'What are we waiting for?' he demanded belligerently. 'My father was telling the truth.' Not that he'd even been in court to hear what his father had said.

The PA system called us and we filed back in. The magistrate gave his findings. He mentioned the damage to Mr Doble's car and the eye contact with the victim. He ruled that Mr Doble knew very well he'd hit a pedestrian. He found him guilty of all charges. You could hear the family gasp at the back of the court.

I addressed the mago on penalty. Mr Doble had a fair bit in his favour: a long, unblemished driving history, war service, advanced age, the fact that he did go back to the scene in the end. I asked for a moderate fine. The Dobles lived on a pension; their only assets were their car, the ute and their war-service home.

None of this cut any ice. The mago was savage. He sentenced Mr Doble to six months jail, suspended for a year. On top of that he fined him $10,000 and disqualified him from driving for five years. I thought it was an outrageous sentence. The old man wouldn't be back on the road till he was eighty-three. It was tantamount to disqualification for life.

Mr Doble was shattered. 'Why didn't he believe me?' he bleated till it was difficult to remain polite. The son blamed me, not having heard a word of the prosecution evidence. We lodged an appeal against the severity of the sentence and I left for home with recriminations ringing in my ears.

It therefore came as a surprise to be briefed for the appeal. At first I was told it was the time off the road that Mr Doble most wanted reduced. Then he said it was the stigma of a jail sentence, then the size of the fine. I couldn't tell what rankled most. Probably not being believed.

At the County Court three months later Mr Doble looked overwhelmed by the formality: the purple-robed judge, the wigs and gowns, the uniformed tipstaff. He seemed to have shrunk in the intervening weeks. His shirt collar was loose around his scrawny neck and he seemed a sad, pathetic, vulnerable figure. Again, his wife hadn't come.

The judge was elderly himself, not that much younger than Mr Doble. I'm sure that helped, but so did the other factors and the many years serving the community in the teaching profession. In fact, everything went our way.

'How old are you, Mr Doble?' asked the judge, not unkindly.

'I'm seventy-eight, Your Honour.'

'You might have to think about how much longer you should be driving at all.'

'Yes, Your Honour.'

The judge was spot-on. He said, 'You're getting on in years, Mr Doble, and your reflexes aren't what they were. You didn't notice that car turning right and when you swerved, you hit a pedestrian...' he paused, '...as you were well aware.'

I heard a sharp intake of breath from the old man.

'You panicked, Mr Doble, and it wasn't till another motorist ran up and pricked your conscience that you returned to the scene.' My own surmise is that he may actually have made it home and been told to go back by his wife. It explained the fifteen minutes delay and perhaps, too, the wife's absence from court. You never know.

The judge allowed the appeal and quashed the suspended jail sentence. He slashed the $10,000 fine to $1000. He reduced the disqualification from five years to one month and backdated it to the Magistrates' Court hearing. That meant Mr Doble was back on the road then and there. We couldn't have got a better result.

As we left the courtroom I turned to speak to Mr Doble. Before I could exchange a word, though, the son took his father's arm and shepherded him away. They didn't say thank you. They didn't say goodbye. They took off without a backward glance.

10

VCAT

Tenancy dispute

VCAT stands for the Victorian Civil and Administrative Tribunal. It's pronounced Vee Cat, as in 'she-cat'. It was formed by merging a dozen separate tribunals to offer a one-stop shop that deals with everything from domestic building to freedom of information. 'VCAT provides Victorians with a civil justice system which is modern, accessible, efficient and cost effective.' That's how the website puts it.

It's not a tribunal I have much to do with. In some of its divisions it really does deal with important matters, but not when I'm involved. Over the years I've done a few cases for pawnbrokers who've had their licences cancelled. A couple of times I've turned up for planning appeals as an objector myself, or to help out friends. It's a disheartening experience. Some hideous development gets knocked back by the local council and the developer appeals. The residents sign petitions and the developer recruits a team of expert town planners who explain how 'sensitive' the design is and how 'respectful' of the built environment. After three days in a panelled room, VCAT gives the scheme the go-ahead, subject to a few more parking spaces and some extra shrubbery. Depressing all right.

Today I'm in VCAT out in the suburbs. It's a dispute over a rental bond and my clients are two Indian ladies. They're on the receiving end of a claim from their former tenant, and I'm on the receiving end of their convoluted explanations. The ladies are nice people, but they won't answer a question in five words if they can use fifty-five.

I can scarcely remember how I got roped into the case, except that I'm doing it as a favour. Mrs Gupta is a friend of my ex-wife and Mrs Pillai is a friend of Mrs Gupta. I won't be able to charge them anything like an economic fee – and anyway, no amount is worth what I'm about to go through.

I've shelled out $45 to buy a copy of the *Residential Tenancies Act* and the only bit I've read is the part that says lawyers aren't allowed to appear in this kind of proceeding unless the other side agrees or the tribunal grants permission. So I shouldn't have been taken by surprise when, the minute I enter the hearing room, the Tribunal Member asks why he shouldn't kick me out on the spot.

I start to answer when the Member turns to the tenant and says, 'Mr Singh, you'd feel disadvantaged, wouldn't you, if there was a lawyer on the other side?'

Naturally Mr Singh agrees. He's a big, powerfully-built man. He's clean-shaven and doesn't wear a turban. He's the kind of Sikh who smokes cigarettes and drinks whisky.

The Member turns back to me. 'Hear that? Why should I let you appear?'

The ladies have brought me along because Mr Singh claims to work as a bodyguard and has told them he's got a gun. I tell the Tribunal Member they feel intimidated.

'Have you informed Security?' he demands.

'No, sir.'

'Have you arranged for the PSOs to be in court?'

'No.'

'So again, why should I allow you to appear?'

I'm starting to feel intimidated myself. I say, 'I'm not suggesting the applicant will produce a gun in court, but my clients have been bullied and they feel inhibited in the presentation of their case.' So I'm allowed to stay. Only just.

Now, both my ladies have taken a day off work to come to the hearing with their armfuls of folders. They've brought condition reports, tenancy agreements, bond receipts, sets of unnumbered photos, quotes for repairs and a long essay recounting the history of their rental unit since the dawn of time. Out in the foyer we've just spent an hour pulling the papers out of plastic pockets and trying to arrange them in sequence. But we're sort of organised now.

The story is that Mr Singh was the sole tenant. After a year he installed a few relations in the unit without the ladies' say-so. Then he cleared off, leaving the relos there. Mrs Gupta only found out he'd vacated when the water company wrote and told her. When she and Mrs Pillai inspected the property they were horrified at the state it was in.

The trouble is, the case really isn't about the condition of the place. There's only one application before VCAT: Mr Singh asking for his bond back. The ladies are withholding it because of the damage, but according to the Act they've missed the bus. 'If they want to withhold the bond they should have applied to do so,' snaps the Member. 'The Act gives them ten days; it's now been four months!'

I fumble with my copy of the Act, hoping an answer will spring out at me from among its 533 sections.

'We didn't know he'd left,' comes a voice from behind me. The ladies had assured me they'd be too tongue-tied to utter a word, but now they're recovering the power of speech in a big way. 'The water company told us.'

'When was that?' demands the Member.

Me: 'October, sir.'

'That's still three months!'

Mrs Gupta: 'But we ourself didn't know, Your Highness.'

The Member ignores her and addresses himself to me. 'Your clients had agents.'

'The first went out of business and the other was remiss,' I argue. 'My clients shouldn't be disadvantaged by the incompetence of others.'

'They're landlords.'

Another voice: 'But he did all that damage, isn't it.'

I say the ladies' expectation was to raise the issue of the damage when Mr Singh applied for his bond.

'Their expectation!' splutters the Tribunal Member. 'It's sheer ignorance! I have no sympathy for them. He's entitled to his bond!'

At this, Mrs Gupta gives vent: 'He put in tenants without our knowledge, he paid late always the rent, he told them they could take over his bond, that they paid him for it already. I've got a stat dec from them.' We pass it up.

'So you've already got your money back, Mr Singh?'

'Well, er...'

The pendulum swings our way. 'So you want to be paid twice! That's outrageous! You can't do that, Mr Singh. I'm going to dismiss your application!'

A rumble of protest, 'But they got...'

'Yes, I'm going to dismiss it! The landlord's entitled to a bond! You can't leave the landlord without a bond.'

'But they got it from my cousin.'

The tribunal member turns on us again. 'What! So you *have* got a bond?'

The voice again: 'We got only $600 Your Majesty but it's not enough. They are paying a bit every month but they aren't paying it.'

A torrent of words issues forth. The cousins are afraid of Mr Singh. He cut the lemon tree down. The tiles in the bathroom leak. He spoiled the carpet of the second bedroom, the one where he tore the fly-wire after he forgot his key and forced the window when he was drunk.

The Tribunal Member sags under the barrage. He says, 'I'm going to adjourn this case.'

Strewth! I don't want to have to come back a second time. This is costing me a day's real work. 'Adjourn, sir?' I ask. 'For what purpose?'

'To get all the parties here, the cousins. Find out who's paid what.'

I start to panic. I object to the adjournment.

Then the Member adds, 'And since your clients are holding a bond, I'm ordering the return of Mr Singh's bond immediately.'

Cripes! That's even worse! It means we lose our case today a hundred per cent. All of a sudden I *am* in favour of an adjournment. 'Sir, if we join the other parties my clients can issue for compensation. Everything can be adjudicated together next time.'

'No, Mr Singh's entitled to his bond.'

Mrs Gupta calls out again: 'Can I say something?'

'Very well,' says the Member, frowning.

She climbs into the witness box and launches another torrent – nay, a tidal wave – of words. 'He overcharged his cousins, he put the rent up and kept the extra for himself and he never used the exhaust fan when he was cooking and all the fumes discoloured the ceiling and now we've got to get it all repainted yes and it was in the very first-class condition when he moved in and the last tenant she was a lovely lady with two cats and she looked after everything so beautifully and look at these photos Your Honour look at all the grease isn't it.'

We've been passing papers up from the floor of the hearing room, but Mrs Gupta in her excitement bounds out of the witness box and actually joins the VCAT Member behind the bench. She tries to stand at his shoulder to go through the pictures, but he flicks her away and orders her back into the witness box. Luckily, though, he does glance at the photos and he doesn't like what he sees. 'Mr Singh,' he growls, 'this doesn't look good at all.'

Mr Singh says, 'Well, er, my cousin...'

'If they bring an application for compensation you'll be in trouble!'

'Er...'

He turns to me: 'Mr Challinger, do the parties want to settle this matter? Well, do they? Are you willing to have a word with Mr Singh?'

'Yes, sir,' I answer, quick as a rabbit.

So the case is stood down and we go out into the foyer with Mr Singh. He's got more to say for himself out here than he's managed in the hearing room, but he does concede the knee-high grass and busted kitchen cupboards aren't too flash. He offers us $150 and the ladies look as if they're going to faint at the impudence of it. They demand $800 and they and I and Mr Singh shout figures at each other as if we're haggling in a Bombay bazaar. After ten minutes we go back and tell the Tribunal Member we can't agree.

'What! Can't agree!' he explodes. 'Why can't you split it fifty-fifty? I can make the order straight away.'

I turn to the ladies. Even if they come back a second time and win some compensation, they'll have the devil's own job getting Mr Singh to cough up. This way it comes out of the bond so at least they get something. They're not looking happy but Mrs Pillai blinks, which I interpret as agreement. I say, 'With reluctance, my clients consent.'

'All right, Mr Singh. What about you?'

With bad grace he shakes his head, which I believe means yes in Indian body language.

A voice behind me starts to say something about carpet shampoo and the curtains turning yellow, but it's all over now. As we flee the hearing room the Member grunts dismissively, 'Well, Mr Challinger, it seems you were *some* use after all.'

We go upstairs to collect the order. The ladies look relieved. They ask me if I like vindaloo because they've got it in mind to invite me for dinner to show their gratitude.

Upstairs the clerk has five copies of the order already printed and waiting for us. I ask if five copies is normal.

'We don't know what's normal for Mr Holloway,' says the clerk.

'Mr Holloway, was it?' I stammer. 'I hope I never strike him again!'

The clerk nods. 'That's what everyone says.'

11

On the Hop

Juggling the workload

In 1777 Dr Johnson wrote, 'Depend upon it, Sir, when a man knows he is to be hanged in a fortnight, it concentrates his mind wonderfully.'[3] Nobody faces the death sentence at Dandenong Magistrates' Court, but the same principle applies. The prospect of six months in the slammer also serves to concentrate a man's mind.

---

[3] The quip was made about the Rev. Dr William Dodd, a fashionable preacher sentenced to death for forgery. His case generated enormous controversy and 100,000 people signed petitions asking the king to grant a reprieve. A 'victim of the greed of lawyers and the malice of judges', Dodd was out of luck and was hanged. See The Macaroni Parson by Gerald Howson, Hutchinson, London, 1973 – a terrific read.

Recently, one of my clients there was facing a string of theft and dishonesty offences. He was contesting some of the charges and the prosecution witnesses were out in the foyer, ready and waiting. If we lost, they'd all claim a day's pay for witness expenses; if he changed his plea to guilty they could go home early and would probably forgo their loss of earnings. More importantly, since my man's odds of winning were minuscule, pleading guilty would earn him a sentencing discount and an outside chance of avoiding jail.

As usual, I hadn't been told exactly what his defence was. One of the charges was going equipped to steal. I said to him, 'The solicitor tells me you've got a lawful excuse for being found at midnight carrying a hammer, bolt-cutters, a glass breaker, screwdrivers and tape.'

'Yes,' he said.

'What's the excuse?'

'I haven't thought of it yet.'

On my count, he had five minutes to come up with it, and we both knew that wasn't going to happen. Common sense started to impinge. At last.

It's not as bizarre as it sounds. Weeks earlier the solicitor could have spent a morning trying to extract the full story and talk sense to this fellow. The client wouldn't have listened; back then, jail would have been only a distant possibility. But right now we were at the door of the court and he was minutes off getting locked up. Only now did he start facing facts. A criminal's mind works best when it's almost too late.

I hope I don't sound precious; in many occupations people work under pressure. Trauma surgeons and air traffic controllers must have it worse, but no doubt all jobs have their stressful moments. Even librarians must feel pressured when five customers arrive at once to borrow the same bestseller.

Borrowers in libraries, though, are usually polite, which isn't the case with some of my clients. Last month, for example, I encounter Jake, a man of many tattoos but limited vocabulary. The word 'fuck' constitutes about fifty per cent of everything he says to me. He uses it in its various grammatical forms as noun, verb, adjective and adverb, not to mention interjection as in, 'Fuck you, pal, you're meant to be my fucking lawyer!' Not an appealing client; a nasty bit of work in fact.

Customers in libraries also normally help the librarian to meet their needs. Mine often do the opposite. They come late or not at all. They change their minds. They fail to listen. They ignore advice. They try to pull the wool over my eyes. They make promises they don't keep. Not all of them, of course, but enough to make my day harder than it need be.

Here's a typical day when the pressure's on. I have two clients and I've told one to be punctual so I can get his case out of the way first. Worse luck, he's running late, while the second arrives unexpectedly early and subjects me to a long, involved, irrelevant monologue. His defence to being unlawfully on premises at midnight, incidentally, is because he wanted to check out the architecture. The clerk in Court 1 pages me and asks if I'm ready with Client A. I say no and ask her to put the case on hold till he turns up.

Though Client B is sitting there with plenty to say, nothing else about his case is ready. His father hasn't arrived yet, nor the youth worker, nor the psychological report I've been promised. The prosecutor meanwhile has mislaid the police brief, and when he finds it, the 48 charges have swelled by 23 extra ones that nobody's told me about. At this point Client A sashays in.

By now they're paging me in Court 7 for Client B's case. I run downstairs and tell the bench clerk I need more time. She says the mago won't wait and wants to start immediately, so I dash up to Court 1 and tell Client A there'll be a delay. Back I go to Court 7 where the clerk now says the mago *will* wait till I'm finished in Court 1 after all. But by this time I've lost my place in the queue there and the client's wandered off for a smoke.

Juggling cases like this is a strain. Some barristers claim to enjoy the pressure; they like to do everything in a crisis; they say it's more energy-efficient. I'm the opposite; I find it puts too much wear and tear on the nervous system.

Most colleagues feel as I do. The clients and their families are on edge and the waiting makes it worse. The waiting is unavoidable because courts can't run to a timetable like the Swiss railways. Sometimes a case ahead of yours settles and a court suddenly becomes available. More often the case ahead takes longer than predicted and everybody has to wait. Besides, there are plenty of other snags: witnesses get stuck in traffic, people fall sick, drugs haven't been analysed, interpreters fail to arrive, emails aren't received, time estimates go awry, adjournments are asked for.

The cops are always sceptical when an accused calls in sick and asks for an adjournment. So are courts. Generally you won't get an adjournment unless the client faxes in a medical certificate. Sometimes the client says he's too sick to go to the doctor. Courts are sceptical about that too.

In the past, medical certificates used to contain useful information and specify whether the patient had broken his leg, say, or contracted measles. These days, out of misguided notions of privacy, they often just say that he's 'ill' or suffering from a 'medical condition'. Mickey Mouse certificates like that are likely to be rejected out of hand. So too, are ones such as a client of mine recently produced. It stated he'd be unfit for three months due to 'dyslexia and poor concentration'. The mago told my man that if he claimed to be sick again he should bring 'a proper certificate from a real doctor'!

Most adjournments are sought by the accused, who's generally the one trying to put off the evil day. Just occasionally the prosecution are short a witness and the boot is on the other foot. That's when I try to pay them back. A prosecutor recently applied for an adjournment because the police informant had been injured in an accident and broken both arms. I said, 'So what? His tongue isn't broken; he can still give evidence.'

The prosecutor said, 'I'll remember that, Challinger!'

I smiled sweetly. 'Just kidding.'

The availability of witnesses is a crucial factor because sometimes my clients don't exactly have the strongest defence. They just hope the witnesses against them won't turn up – which sometimes does happen. One week I was in a contested hearing in which there were to be three witnesses against my man. None of them turned up: one was dead, one was in jail and the third had lost interest. The case collapsed, the client got off and I had an early day. Nice to have a lucky break occasionally!

A while ago another client had a stroke of luck along similar lines. He was accused of failing to stop after a bingle in a shopping centre car park. A passing shopper had taken down his rego number and was the star witness for the police. They served a subpoena on her, together with a ten dollar note. The cash was what's called conduct money, an amount to cover the person's cost of getting to court. Without conduct money the witness isn't obliged to turn up.

It transpired the witness was now living 160 kilometres away in Gippsland

and failed to show up. That was fair enough because you can't get from Traralgon to Melbourne for ten bucks. Without her, there was nothing to connect my client and his car with the incident, so the police got an adjournment and had to pay our costs.

The second time round the cops did their homework. They checked the fares and train timetable, then served the witness with $29.50 conduct money. But she didn't attend this time either. It turned out she was now in Dubai, and I know for a fact you can't get from Dubai to Melbourne and back for $29.50. The police gave up and this client too went scot-free. A bit of luck is always helpful.

You'd hope your client's own witnesses would cooperate, but that's not always the case. One young bloke absolutely hates the cops. His mother, who's my client, has had an almighty stoush with them, but he's such a half-wit he won't come to court voluntarily. We have to subpoena him to give evidence on behalf of his own mother! You'd have thought, too, that he'd try to make a good impression but he slouched in, oozing resentment from every pore. I don't know how, but he was holding down a job as an apprentice painter. He turned up in paint-spattered overalls, security having confiscated his paint scrapers and other tools of trade at the court entrance.

In the witness box he referred to the police informant as 'that fat cunt' and nobody turned a hair. Either the magistrate hadn't heard him or – more likely – decided it was expedient not to have heard.

Incidentally, in England at least one judge is equally uninhibited in her language. In 2017 at Chelmsford Crown Court Judge Patricia Lynch sentenced a man to 18 months jail. As he was being led away to the cells he called her a cunt, to which she shot back, 'You're a bit of a cunt yourself'! The Judicial Complaints Investigation Office later ruled that her language was inappropriate, but didn't amount to misconduct or warrant disciplinary action. That's England for you.

Sometimes it's not the witness who's unavailable but the magistrate. A while ago I wasn't going too well in a case of car theft. There were some legal complications, but basically my man had hung onto a hire-car for months; he'd tried to return it but found the office closed – or, as he claimed to believe, closed down. The mago was going on leave and the case was adjourned part-heard for four months. The prosecutor said to me, 'That's ridiculous, the magistrate will forget everything about this case.' I thought to myself: let's hope so.

But getting your own client to court on time can sometimes be the hardest thing of all. A colleague told one to be at court at ten to nine and the fellow asked, 'What's that in digital?' Last week I told my own client to meet me at nine and he turned up at 10.45. He didn't offer a word of apology; to his way of thinking getting there before lunch amounted to being early.

Even when they're on bail and obliged to come, clients have to be reminded and cajoled. Allan, for instance, promises to meet me at nine, but at 10.15 there's still no sign of him. Half an hour later he answers his mobile. Yes, he'll be leaving home any minute now; he's just got to go and pick up his methadone first. 'Why didn't you get it earlier?' I ask. 'The chemist opens at eight.'

'I didn't have the four dollars till my missus came home.'

I was running a County Court appeal one day. I phoned the client at 10.30 and he said he was stuck on the freeway. That was strange, as I didn't think he still had a driving licence – or a car that was registered. I got through to him again an hour later, just after the judge had given me one last chance before she struck out his appeal. The client said he was in the lobby on the ground floor and was coming straight up. Eight minutes passed; I counted them. The tipstaff was just calling the bloke's name as he sauntered out of the lift clutching a half-drunk can of Pepsi he'd bought on the way. We spoke for exactly one minute before we rushed into court. At least his instructions were to the point: 'Mate, get me an adjournment!'

Clients like him cost me money as well as angst because Legal Aid pay you less if the case is adjourned. Still,

I was entitled to extra for a conference with him at the rate of $162 an hour. I did the arithmetic and calculated I could charge an extra $2.70 for our one-minute exchange. It didn't really make up for what he'd put me through.

Even when clients do arrive on time they don't always make it easy for you. One day I was at court, trying to locate my client. It was a very busy day: the foyer was crowded, all the seats were taken and the queue for the registrar's counter extended down the stairs. The client's phone wasn't answering so I had him paged, then weaved through the milling crowd calling his name. 'Shane Reid? Shane Reid?' No response, though I noticed a young fellow about the right age glance up then look away.

I checked my papers and noticed there was an alias in brackets on one of the documents. I tried that instead. 'Hudson Flockhart?'

The bloke got up and ambled over, the one who'd raised his eyes earlier. 'That's me,' he said.

'You're Shane Reid?'

'Don't answer to that any more. I'm Hudson Flockhart now. Changed it by deed poll.'

'But I'm your lawyer, for crying out loud! I was trying to find you. You saw me.'

'I thought it was a trick.'

'Why the new name anyway?'

'I'd never get bail if I used my old one.'

Out of curiosity I asked, 'So where does Flockhart fit in? Your mother's maiden name or something?'

'No, mate. Just made it up. Sounds good.'

Once your client's arrived other pressures come into play. Popular wisdom, incidentally, is that in the Magistrates' Court no case is certain and no case is hopeless. The saying isn't entirely accurate, though, because there *are* cases which are certain losers. Those cases, naturally, are ones you're resigned to losing. By the same token, you're relieved to win the ones you should win and delighted if you fluke a win in one you expect to lose. But losing the one you ought to win is the thing that spoils your day.

It's therefore a relief to get cases that really are either unwinnable or unloseable. Then the pressure's off. Doing the job badly or doing it well won't affect the result. And I should mention that whatever the standard of advocacy, courts do get things right most of the time. Not every time, of course. You don't get Rolls-Royce justice in the Magos' Court; it's more like a Holden Kingswood. And don't forget, the case isn't about whether the accused has done something, it's about whether the prosecution can prove he has.

Some of my clients have no idea of what's realistic. They think the case against them is like a house of cards and that if there's a slip, no matter how minor – a name mis-spelt even – the prosecution falls apart. It isn't like that. A case is more like a jigsaw. It doesn't matter if a few pieces are missing or in the wrong position, so long as the pattern emerges clearly.

Some also don't understand the role I play. My job is to act on their instructions. I'm not being paid to believe them, but to present their case. They can't tell me one thing and say they'll swear the opposite in the witness box. I say, 'I'm not here to tell lies for you, or to help you tell lies.' With that proviso an accused has the right to put the prosecution to proof. After all, every citizen is entitled to the presumption of innocence – and to the services of a lawyer for as long as he can afford it. On that last point, cynics say justice is what you get till your money runs out. Realists say it's what you get *once* your money runs out!

Many of my clients, of course, can't afford a lawyer. They apply for legal aid, which works like this. If they're battlers, struggling to support themselves and their family from some ill-paid job, legal aid will knock them back because they're employed. Conversely, if they're heavy crims committing serious offences who've never done a day's work in their life, they'll qualify. The more crimes you commit and the more likely you are to go to jail, the more certain you are of getting legal aid.

Legally aided or not, there are things a client can do to help his case. For pleas of guilty, for example, character references can help. I tell the client what's needed and sometimes give him a pro forma. Yet many references I receive are ludicrous. They say the accused is 'of high moral character', though it's his fourth time to front the court for dishonesty. Even adult family friends come up with strange remarks: 'His home is full of love and lifestyle.'

Sometimes my clients find religion and enlist a priest or clergyman to put pen to paper for them. Something sensible would definitely help but some of these preachers think church attendance is all that counts. A client who'd stolen $23,000 produced a pastor's reference which said nothing of his propensity to steal and cheat, but recorded that he attended church 85.7 per cent of the time (six of the last seven Sundays, I gather). Even if the arithmetic was right, what of it? What's 85.7 per cent of $23,000 – or more to the point, what's 85.7 per cent of nine months jail?

Adoring girlfriends are always keen to volunteer a reference. They think the strength of their love will carry the day.

A recent one gushed on for two full pages. As a friend, the accused was 'amazing', as a plasterer he was 'amazing' and as a fiancé he was also 'amazing'. I reached the end of the first page, which addressed his qualities as father of the children he'd sired by his last two girlfriends. I expected he'd be amazing at that too, but I turned the page and learned he was 'awesome'. Such eloquence.

Parents' references can be powerful, provided they show some balance and objectivity. One mother wrote an excellent one, saying her son had finally seen the light and mended his ways. Unfortunately, her confidence proved misplaced and the kid kept reoffending. In each successive case, though, I was able to tender the same reference; all the mother had to do each time was change the date and reprint it.

Though I tell clients quality is more important than quantity, one fellow turned up with seven references. They were all on A4 paper in the same type-font, and almost identical in content and style. I pointed out that they looked as if one person had written the lot. 'Yes,' he said, 'that's because my nan wrote them all.' It's noticeable, incidentally, that handwritten references from grandmothers are invariably more legible and grammatical than those of the mothers; and both are better than anything the client can write. A commentary on the standard of modern education.

Sometimes the client fancies himself a wordsmith. He wants to write something 'from the heart' to sway the magistrate. Such efforts are mostly unimpressive; they tend to be rambling and too obviously self-serving. Needless to say, spelling isn't their strong point either. In expressing his determination to go straight, one wrote, 'a nuf is a nuf'. Another conceded he wasn't 'inner sent'.

A third fellow insisted he'd write something but didn't know how to start. I suggested he imagine himself back at school writing an essay on the topic, 'Why I did an aggravated burglary and shouldn't go to jail'.

He asked, 'What's an essay?'

12

Mother England

A lawyer in London

Mention of England in the last chapter reminds us that the Australian colonies inherited the English legal system. We adopted not just statutes, but also the English Common Law, the ancient law of the land made by judges over the centuries. Getting back to basics is always educational and I've done it twice myself by working in the law in England.

The first time was in 1972 soon after I graduated. I travelled overland to Europe, taking six months to get there. I'd asked my brother to send my one and only suit by post, but when I reached England the suit hadn't arrived. A shipping strike, said my brother.

I rang the Law Society and they offered me a job over the phone. It was lucky they didn't want to interview me in person because I was going through my hippy phase. My best clobber included a waistcoat I'd bought in Afghanistan, embroidered with gold thread and with a whiff of hashish and camel urine about it.

The Law Society is the professional body which regulates solicitors in England and Wales. When sole practitioners die without a successor, the Law Society takes over their files. At the time, the archives weren't kept at the society's headquarters in Chancery Lane but in a nearby office building called Fenham House. There I joined three other young Australian law graduates on working holidays.

Our job was to go through the accumulated files of defunct legal practices, sorting out what documents needed to be kept and what could be thrown out. Criminal files had to be kept for seven years, conveyancing files for fourteen years and so on. It wasn't demanding work. I didn't know much but I could tell the difference between a letter dated 1968 and a parchment two centuries old, festooned with ribbons and sealing wax.

The four of us seldom worked at full pitch. Indeed, often we weren't all there at the same time, as the British Museum was nearby as well as pubs and wine bars and other distractions. Every day one of the others bought *The Times,* the second the *Telegraph* and the third the *Guardian.* I contributed a tabloid if I could find one in a rubbish bin. We spent the morning reading the papers and doing the crosswords; in the afternoon we slacked off.

The files were an eye-opener into the English way of doing things. Everything seemed so fussy and formal. The typewriter had been invented in 1867 yet I came across thirty-page documents from as late as 1930, painstakingly written by hand in perfect copperplate – possibly with a quill for all I knew.

The files were stored in the basement of Fenham House, while our office was on the third floor. To carry them up we had a uniformed flunkey with Law Society insignia on his lapels. His name was Dudley, though we never found out whether that was his first name or his surname. He was like some Cockney character from Dickens, cheerful and chirpy, and even lazier than us. On the rare occasions we actually needed him, Dudley was impossible to find. Just as our day revolved around the morning papers, his revolved around a betting shop where he spent hours agonising over bets of twenty pence, a pitifully small sum even in 1972.

Our work was supervised at long distance by some Law Society toff in Chancery Lane. I occasionally overheard him as one of the others reported our progress over the phone. 'Not long now. Yes, yes, definitely halfway.'

'Good show!' came the muffled reply.

'Should finish the lot within about three weeks.'

'Splendid!'

Alas, we were speaking only of the files Dudley had dumped on the third floor landing, while our boss had in mind the entire contents of the basement, an enormous dungeon piled to the ceiling with yellowing papers. At our rate of progress the whole job would have taken not three weeks but about seven years.

One day the boss paid a surprise visit and realised how badly he'd misunderstood us. Our careers at the Law Society came to a sudden end. By then, however, my suit had arrived and I paid a call to head office and bought a Law Society tie to enhance my employment prospects elsewhere.

The tie came in handy in 1984 when I braved England again for another stint. This time I got work through an agency doing locums, where I stood in temporarily for solicitors on holiday, sick, dead or – in one case – in jail.

My first locum was in Wembley, famous for its stadium and the FA Cup Final, but in reality a dump. Wembley High Street alternated between boarded-up shops and tattered film posters in Hindi. It was a cross between Mumbai and the bombed-out part of Belfast. To get into Godfrey Cohen & Co, you had to ring a bell and wait while they checked you out through a spyhole, then unlocked the door.

Godfrey Cohen was an amiable man, but completely under the thumb of his blonde, middle-aged female 'assistant', the abrasive Mrs Rock. Both were chain smokers, and to enter their shared office was to step into a fume cupboard. The atmosphere was tense as well as smoky, because a crisis was always threatening – or actually taking place.

The firm had a branch office in the genteel suburb of Kenton, where their former employee solicitor had been in cahoots with an Arab and embezzled the trust funds. Mr Cohen needed a stand-in to hold the fort at Kenton. While the conveyancing clerk there made the money, I was to keep a lid on everything else.

The clerk was a strange, unattractive fellow. He spoke in a whining, low-class Pommy accent and sprayed spittle with every syllable. He was obsessed with his feud with an Indian grocer in the shop next door. Whenever the Indian's footpath display of mangoes encroached onto our frontage he'd run out and shove the crates back, shouting, 'Wot are them fings anyway?'

The clerk was also something of a sneak and used to secretly report on me to Mrs Rock. (It was he, too, who slyly showed me a paragraph in *The Times* about my predecessor's arraignment at the Old Bailey.) Several times Mrs Rock got to hear of something or other I'd done and burst in unexpectedly like a hurricane. Since I wasn't officially admitted as a solicitor in England, she was paranoid I'd get Mr Cohen struck off and the firm ruined.

On one occasion I did a favour for a client who happened to be Irish. His son had broken up with his girlfriend and I let him leave a bag at the office for her to collect. The clerk reported this to Mrs Rock who, equating Irish with IRA, pressed the panic button and notified the bomb squad. Over the phone we were ordered to leave the office and we stood around on the footpath while the Indian hurriedly shifted his tropical fruit out of shrapnel range. After half an hour some suburban bobbies turned up and together we ventured into the office and gingerly cut the bag open with scissors. Inside we found a cardigan and some Mills & Boon paperbacks.

But Mrs Rock had plenty of real things to panic about. The files at Kenton were in a terrible mess. Important letters had gone unanswered and judgments had been signed against our clients because we hadn't delivered defences in time.

One balls-up was entirely my fault. Our client's factory had burnt down in mysterious circumstances and the insurance company, suspecting fraud, had refused to pay. On behalf of our dodgy client we were suing the insurer.

One day a court document arrived. The terminology was unfamiliar but I should have twigged that '14 days final' meant something nasty. Worse luck, I waited till the fifteenth day to figure out that the insurer had applied to strike out our claim. We'd been given one last chance to come up with certain paperwork and now the deadline had passed. Mr Cohen took it rather well when I broke the news, but Mrs Rock flipped her lid. The client was bound to sue us for professional negligence unless we could get the claim reinstated.

I swotted up the applicable law. It was contained in a mammoth two-volume *Manual of the Law of Civil Procedure,* universally called 'The White Book', a masterpiece of legal scholarship which runs to 1800 pages of small print. I prepared a set of documents explaining why our claim should be reinstated and promising to pay any costs the other side had wasted through our delay.

The application was listed before the Master-in-Chambers of the Supreme Court, a judicial officer one notch down from a full judge. He presided in Room 492 of the Royal Courts of Justice, a monumental edifice in the Strand, opened by Queen Victoria in 1882. The vast building has 63 courtrooms, five kilometres of corridors, and over a thousand offices numbered out of sequence. The Master's room adjoins an area called the Bear Garden.

To find my way to the Bear Garden I had to buy a guide book, which detailed a short cut I could take called the 'Chicken Run'. From the Carey Street entrance I followed these instructions: 'Turn right up stairs to Inns of Court library; continue up straight flight of stairs and past Room 716. Enter unmarked door opposite messengers' room and cross stairwell into Chicken Run corridor. At end, cross stairwell and emerge at extreme northern corner of Taxing Masters' corridor in Centre Block. Turn right, cross over bridge at lift and enter northern end of Chancery Master's Corridor.' From there it would be a cinch to count backwards to Room 492.

On the morning of the application I was a bit on edge and when I reached the Kenton office I noticed I was wearing one black shoe and one brown. I dashed across to the local shoe shop and bought a pair of bovver boots, the only footwear they had in black that were vaguely my size. They were a lousy fit and with all that walking along the Chicken Run corridor, they chewed up the skin at the back of my heels something cruel.

I limped in to face the Master and he chewed me up too. He gave me a ticking-off and told me the application would have to go to a judge in open court. So the following week we briefed a barrister who relied entirely on my research and breezed in the result we wanted. I'd done the hard yakka and he got the two hundred quid. Perhaps that's what subconsciously inspired me to go to the bar.

That was only one of many crises at Godfrey Cohen's; others were popping up all the time. Often I'd have to dash down to the County Court to try to pull our chestnuts out of the fire. Since I still wasn't officially admitted to practise in England, I used to ask for leave to appear. I'd explain I was an overseas practitioner whose admission was pending. The judges all looked ancient and spoke with posh accents. Some were nice: 'Or-stralia! Splendid! Leave is grahn-ted with pleasure.' Others were arrogant snobs.

One morning the clerk at Kenton showed me a file, spluttering, 'I fink you better 'ave a look at this.' The case was listed at the Willesden County Court that morning. I had about twenty minutes to get there through London traffic. On the way the clutch cable snapped in my clapped-out Vauxhall and I had to drive the rest of the way in second gear without stopping at traffic lights. When I reached Willesden there was nowhere to park so I drove up onto the footpath and rushed straight into court.

I should have been in wig and gown but I scurried in wearing my suit. The judge was a pompous stuffed-shirt who looked at me down his nose. 'You are not admitted in this country,' he drawled. 'You are not robed. You are not on the record.' After that I never mentioned the fact that I wasn't actually qualified to appear in an English court. On leaving the court house, incidentally, I found the Vauxhall had been cordoned off as a suspected car bomb, but I said sorry to the police and they let me drive it away.

I lasted six weeks at Kenton before I told the agency I couldn't hack it any longer. They congratulated me on my tenacity. Of the five locums they'd sent, I'd lasted the longest. 'None of you chaps seem to hit it off with Mrs Rock,' commented the fellow in charge as he handed me a Christmas bottle of sherry as my reward.

After Kenton I went up in the world and did a stint at a classy solicitor's in South Kensington. The local Crown Court there was directly behind Harrods department store and its famous food hall. Waiting litigants congregated in the street near the shop's rear entrance. It was a handy location if you felt like buying one last jar of caviar before you were declared bankrupt.

While I was at South Kensington, Iran and Iraq were at war. One file I handled involved a dispute between two Saudi princes over a personalised Rolls-Royce. In the course of mutual mudslinging, each accused the other of arms-trading. A contract came to light for the supply of surface-to-air missiles. It stipulated that the shipment was to be delivered to Teheran in an unmarked Boeing and, on delivery, every tenth SAM was to be shot off to make sure the consignment worked! I thought of applying for a part-time job with MI5.

Instead, I moved to working-class Edmonton, helping out a lovely man called Lawrence Brass, a solicitor who'd stood for Parliament three times against Margaret Thatcher. The citizens of Edmonton inhabited a different world from their betters in upper-class Kensington. To give a minor example, Lawrence took on a black girl from a local school for work experience. She was so innocent of the ways of the outside world that when she was sent out for milk for morning tea she didn't know to ask for some petty cash. She thought she was expected to use her own money and, having none, went into a shop every day and just pinched a bottle.

The local Magistrates' Court at Tottenham was bizarre. The Cockney defendants, white or black, barely spoke the same language as the magistrates, who were honorary justices – members of the Conservative Women's Association or toffs from the County Hunt. When my client was asked whether he consented to having his indictable charges dealt with summarily, he answered, 'Wot's all that abaht, guv'nor?'

After I appeared at Tottenham the first time, Lawrence Brass received a call from the court and called me in. I thought they'd discovered I was an unqualified impostor but it turned out I was being commended. It's something of a pattern in England that Australians are well received. The goodwill evaporates if we get too good and beat them at their own game, but that was a pitfall I avoided.

On one occasion I had a client from Camden, a few kilometres away, who failed to turn up to court. He was charged with breaking into a pet shop and stealing a valuable parrot. I phoned him at home but he couldn't afford the bus fare so I drove to Camden in the Vauxhall and picked him up. It would have been unacceptable for a middle-class Englishman to do the same but for an Aussie it was fine; somehow we transcend the English class system. Everyone thought I'd shown great compassion and initiative but I'd only wanted to get home early.

By this time my admission as a solicitor in England really was pending and I needed only to pass an exam in a ghastly subject called Accounts. England had turned cold and I'd already decided to leave. I sat the exam three days before I flew out and wouldn't have bothered except that I'd already paid the fee. The exam was held in a large Victorian hall opposite Westminster Catholic Cathedral. It was crowded with earnest public-school types. I took my camera and took a snap as a souvenir.

Years later, out of curiosity, I wrote to London to see whether I'd passed. Always pedantic, the Law Society wouldn't tell me whether I had or not. All they could divulge was that a candidate with my name and an address in Royal Crescent, Ruislip, appeared on the pass list. They had no knowledge of whether he and I were one and the same person. Honestly!

I sent forty quid and received a certificate signed by the Master of the Rolls. Unknown to me, there was also an annual fee and over the years I got letters demanding ridiculous sums in sterling to keep me up to date. I didn't pay. Finally I received a notice from the Law Society telling me my name had been removed from the Roll of Solicitors. I suppose my file's turning to dust now in the depths of Fenham House.

13

Greeks and Others

Ethnic clients

Just as migrants have spiced up Australia's culinary scene, so do they enrich the professional lives of criminal barristers. Different nationalities have brought their delightful customs with them: forced marriages, genital mutilation, cock-fights, vendetta, eating dogs. These supplement our own traditional customs of drink driving, road rage, dole-bludging and family violence.

Dealing with these cultural differences adds challenge and variety to my working day. Nothing beats a blue at a Greek wedding when the tradition of pinning money on the bride's dress goes awry. Or a punch-up among sixty-year-olds at the Iranian social club when they play the national anthem from the Shah's time instead of the present Islamic Republic one. Or a peeping Tom who's half Greek, half Irish and totally mad!

In our wonderful ethnic diversity there are differences that deserve to be celebrated. George Orwell once drew up a table of national characteristics as portrayed in English boys' magazines ('Spaniard, Mexican: sinister, treacherous', 'Negro: comic, very faithful' etc).[4] A barrister of my acquaintance has done the same from a forensic viewpoint. Here are his preliminary findings:

Chinese: obsessed with saving face. Slight problem with the Chinese gambling gene.

Greeks: incurably disputatious, though their fish and chips are pretty good.

Vietnamese: drug traffickers or plastic surgeons (unless they're running bakeries).

Serbians: surnames end in IC, which stands for 'I'm Crazy'.

Jews: very law-abiding, apart from occasional multi-million dollar frauds or unlucky warehouse fires.

---

4 'Boys' Weeklies' (1939) in The Collected Essays, Journalism and Letters of George Orwell, Penguin Books, 1970.

Pacific Islanders: two main types: violent thugs or training to be pastors.

Racial stereotyping, of course, can be prone to error. My colleague concedes his table is subject to revision – especially if he cops a complaint for racial vilification. He says it's just that after six or seven examples of the same thing he notices a pattern emerging.

Nobody's suggesting all members of any particular nationality are criminals. Far from it. My pal Madeline reckons that of every migrant group a third become law-abiding citizens, a third become criminals and the last third become interpreters for the other two. She could be right; more research needed!

Among international contests, I've had two Iraqis versus an Egyptian and a Lebanese (fizzled out), an Italian versus four Greeks (a win for Italy) and an obnoxious Sri Lankan versus a transvestite Filipino (a draw). The Sri Lankan, by the way, had worked for three weeks in the previous five years, a real asset to the country. Another tussle was a Turk versus a dinki-di

Aussie. I know the latter isn't yet an ethnic minority but he was a former Digger with an RSL badge and they're a dying breed. The badge didn't do us any good though, and the Turk won hands down. Gallipoli all over again.

The Italy-Greece match concerned an elderly Italian charged with assault. He'd been at his garden plot and was driving home with shovels and rakes in the back of his station wagon. As he turned into a main road he accidentally pulled in front of an approaching car. The car changed lanes to avoid him and tooted its horn.

At the wheel was a young man of Greek background, with three of his cousins as passengers. When both cars stopped at some traffic lights the young blokes got out and approached my client with a view to discussing the shortcomings of his driving. A battle ensued. Even though Mr Benedetti was in his seventies and outnumbered four to one, he vanquished the Greeks by twirling a couple of garden stakes around his head. At that, the Greeks raced off to the police station and got him charged.

At court, two 'independent' passers-by materialised, saying they'd seen it all and that the old boy was definitely the aggressor. Curiously, they both had Greek surnames. In the end, the mago thought it unlikely a septuagenarian would take on four young toughs just because they'd tooted him. So the Greeks lost the court battle too. There's a Russian expression that covers the situation: 'To lie like an eye-witness'. Maybe it's a saying in Greek as well.

Intervention orders give rise to the most exotic permutations. There was the slippery Russian, a former major in the Red Army who'd staged a mental breakdown to avoid being posted to Afghanistan, then posed as a Jew to emigrate. He battled it out with his new Filipina wife.

A Syrian sent his Lebanese wife mutilated photographs, an erased wedding video and a champagne bottle filled with urine and semen. Charming.

One day I appeared for a Romanian woman applying to kick her elderly Australian husband out of his house. She'd once been the mayor of a town in Romania and produced a photo of herself conducting civil marriages beneath a portrait of President Ceausescu. At court, a pack of shady-looking males hovered in the background, waiting for their share once the old bloke was evicted from his home.

The case preceding ours involved three Macedonian women. As the magistrate gave his decision, the first began sobbing and shouting insults, while the second glared and rolled her eyes. Security escorted them both out while the third, the winner, called out, 'Thank you, Judge, God bless you!'

I appeared for two Moroccan brothers in another intervention order case. Their younger sister was a university student – and lucky to attend uni at all, given the brothers kept her under such close control. The elder one used to drive her to classes every day and pick her up the minute they were over. He was so loving and protective it was his full-time occupation.

During her brief moments of academic freedom the sister met an Indian boy. A secret romance blossomed. As soon as the girl turned eighteen the lovers eloped and got married. She must have had an inkling it wouldn't go over too well with the family because she went to a police station and got the cops to phone her father to break the news. Then the happy couple vanished.

The family tracked them down and spent the next three months making the girl's life a misery. They reported her as a missing person and told the police she'd been abducted. They wrote a scurrilous leaflet, forged the girl's signature on it, and distributed it at the local supermarket. They dobbed in the Indian to the police as a rapist, a drug dealer, a gangster and a pedophile and tried to get him deported. There was no evidence of any criminality – apart from the drugs the first brother himself planted in the Indian's car.

Finally the couple applied for an order against the brothers. The elder one sat in court sobbing his eyes out to show the mago how caring and broken-hearted he was. The younger delivered a violent diatribe from the witness box. None of it went over too well with the mago, who ordered the brothers to keep away from their sister and her husband for the next ten years.

Africans are the most recent additions to the mix. Madeline mentioned a Somali client of hers who arrived at court to find that not only were his solicitor and barrister female, so were the prosecutor and the magistrate. Madeline said the fellow freaked out. Too bad; this is Australia.

I remember doing a case years ago for one Sudanese bloke. He had a strange, distracted demeanour; no doubt he'd been through a lot. He brought his Bible to court and sat in the foyer studying it till his case was called on.

He was charged with assaulting four railway ticket inspectors after failing to produce a valid ticket. He said they'd attacked *him* and that he hadn't known who they were anyway. On the day of the incident they'd been dressed in civilian clothes, not the smart public transport uniforms they wore to court. When I cross-examined I asked them why they hadn't been in uniform if they were checking tickets from the travelling public. 'Operational reasons,' they said, whatever that meant. 'The supervisor told us not to wear our uniforms.'

My man had been dragged off the train and pinned down on the platform for an hour till the police arrived. When searched, he was found to have a valid ticket! Indeed, in the witness box he produced a thick wad of Metcard tickets, one for every train trip he'd taken since arriving in Australia. No passengers were called as independent witnesses and the CCTV footage had been 'accidentally' erased. That case we won. So we should have.

Another time I arrived at court, looking for my Sudanese client. I noticed a tall African man, introduced myself and sat him down in an interview room. His English was rudimentary and we weren't getting far. I said, 'I think we'll wait for the interpreter.'

He said, 'I *am* the interpreter.'

I knew then I was in trouble! I don't mean to be unkind but he was the most inexpert interpreter I've ever worked with. Once, in Papua New Guinea I needed two interpreters simultaneously, one from English into Enga, the second from Enga into a language spoken by just a few hundred people in some isolated valley. This fellow was worse than the double interpreting. Luckily my client's English proved better.

Another Sudanese client pleaded guilty to assaulting his wife. He was pretty unrepentant, though; he thought she was his to beat. He said, 'I paid five cows for her.' I told the court there were 'cultural issues'.

It does take time for people to adjust. It can't be easy being a Sudanese in Australia, though I suspect it's easier than being a Sudanese in Sudan. The Migrant Support Centre puts on weekly sessions for Sudanese men. They light a fire in a cut-down 44-gallon drum and sit around discussing their roles as males and fathers and breadwinners. My client got a bond to attend for twelve weeks. Hope he learned something.

As for Greeks, a barrister of Greek background himself once warned me: 'With Greeks all reason flies out the window.' I knew it already from experience. Getting a straight account of anything from them is hard yakka.

They can drive you up the wall. It's no surprise the Greek phrase for give and take is 'take and give'. Nor that Greece is the only country in the world that celebrates a public holiday for 'No Day'.[5]

Greeks mostly turn up to court accompanied by large numbers of family members. I remember one where the father was on sickness benefits, the son was on Newstart and his sister was on compo. (I'm meeting a biased sample, of course.) The mother spoke the best English and seemed okay, but it turned out she was on a disability pension. I asked her, 'What's your disability?'

'You know...' she mumbled, 'I don't-a-feel too good.'

My client Stavros brought his father, his brother and sister-in-law, his younger sister, a friend called Agnes and some others I didn't speak to except to tell them to get rid of their chewing gum and take their sunglasses off in court.

---

[5] October 28. It commemorates Greece saying No to an ultimatum of Mussolini's in 1940.

Just as a preliminary, I looked over Stavros' list of prior convictions. One was for robbery, but the family insisted that Stavros had never robbed anyone. He'd just paid someone a visit one night to suggest they take a stroll to an ATM.

'And this threat to kill?' I asked.

'Stavros never threatened anyone,' said the father.

'Well he's got a conviction for it.'

'That's wrong. Tell the judge that's wrong.'

'I can't tell her that. It's on his record. He's stuck with it.'

'That's not fair.'

'If it wasn't fair he should have appealed.'

'Okay, he'll appeal now,' said the father.

'He can't.'

'Why not?'

'It was eight years ago. He's out of time.'

'How long did he have?'

'Thirty days.'

We moved on. 'Obstructing police,' I read.

'I never obstructed no-one,' protested Stavros. 'They just thought I did. Like there was this car accident, see, and one of the drivers couldn't talk English. And like, I'm Greek and I just tried to help him. And the police, they told me to go away, see, and they kind of misunderstood.'

As for Stavros' prior for driving while disqualified, that was wrong too because he didn't receive the notice telling him not to drive. In that case, I asked, why had he pleaded guilty?

'Well, the policeman at court was Greek too,' he explained, 'and he goes, "Stavros you better plead guilty because I don't want to come back to court after lunch." So that's what I did.'

All this was just background, much of it peppered with interjections and side talk in Greek. We hadn't even started discussing the case in hand. As I said, it can drive you up the wall.

I was once representing another Greek-Australian on driving charges. Looking at the court lists, I noticed he had an additional case listed a week later, a road rage incident. When I rang him, his mother answered and told me they knew nothing about it.

Yet when I got the paperwork about the road rage, it detailed how the mother was at home when the police had called. She'd heard them discuss the incident and heard her son say, 'That bloke hates me because of my Greek heritage.' She'd also watched him fall to his knees, cross himself and beg the police not to handcuff him. She'd been at home too, I learned, when her son got back from the police station with his charge sheets and the CD of his interview. So she knew as well as her son did that he'd been arrested, interviewed and charged. Yet the two of them had been insisting they had no knowledge of any road rage charge.

When I remonstrated with them they said, 'Oh, we didn't know you were talking about that.'

Honestly! It was my job to handle the man's legal problems. Why not help me? It was like refusing to tell the dentist which tooth hurt.

Chinese can be annoying too, though in a different way. China is a low-trust society, and it shows. Chinese clients are often suspicious and argumentative. They treat Legal Aid as their automatic right: 'The government is paying you,' they say. They demand Rolls-Royce treatment – and outcomes.

Saving face also presents difficulties. There's a type of Chinese who can be caught red-handed but still not admit to anything. He'll plead guilty only so long as the court's told he didn't actually do anything wrong and nothing's noted on his record. He's willing to pay a small fine provided he can get a receipt for tax.

Superstition plays a role too. Mr Zhang tried to blackmail his former girlfriend and demanded she pay him $7000. He had debts of a lot more than that and I asked him why he'd demanded that particular figure. He said, 'Seven is my lucky number.' I thought: not any more it isn't.

On the other hand, many Chinese are good to deal with – and so polite. Mr Li, for example, was on a drink driving charge, an uncommon offence for a Chinese. 'You're going to lose your driving licence,' I told him. 'The court's *got* to disqualify you.'

'Thank you, thank you,' he smiled and nodded.

'Plus you'll get a fine.'

'Ohhhh, thank you.'

'I mean a *big* fine.'

'Thank you, thank you.'

Either his English wasn't as good as I thought, or he was the most agreeable client I've ever had.

Language was also an issue with my client Feng Weng. He might have been putting it on but his command of English didn't seem crash-hot either. He and his brother had been nabbed flogging pirated DVDs at Pipeworks Market. I was only representing Feng; his brother, Heng Weng, had had his own case adjourned.

Feng was caught wearing a walkie-talkie headset, keeping a lookout for the police. If they turned up he was meant to raise the alarm so his brother could pack up the stall and do a runner. Feng chose the wrong moment to take a toilet break and missed the cops' arrival. Both brothers were arrested.

The police later got a warrant and searched their flat. They found a mountain of empty DVD packaging (Feng said it belonged to his brother) and several computers and burners (also the brother's). The production method was to download stuff off the internet (the brother's work) burn it onto discs and package it.

Before court I suggested to the cops it was just an innocuous cottage industry, but they reckoned $10,000 a month was going through the bank account. Feng was very surprised to hear that. As you might guess, the money was all going to his brother and Feng's share was only $20 pocket money and an occasional tank of petrol.

I asked Feng, 'Where is your brother anyway? Why isn't he here today?'

'Ah, Heng in hospital.'

'He's sick?'

'Ah, heart attack.'

'Really? At his age? Is it serious?'

'Mmm, serious.'

'You must be worried.'

'Very worried.'

'Well,' I said, 'the judge might be worried too. Because when your brother gets well, he might come to court and say it was all *your* fault.'

'Ah, I don't know.'

It was hard to know what the court might do with Feng. Fines for selling pirated goods can be phenomenal these days, tens of thousands of dollars. In the event, we did amazingly well. Feng ended up with a fine of a few hundred. I said, 'Feng, this is your lucky day! You ought to buy yourself a Tattslotto ticket.'

'Tattslotto no good,' he replied. 'Just have lunch then go casino straight away.'

I wondered if I'd said the wrong thing.

14

Unsocial Distancing

Intervention orders

Courts in the past weren't oblivious to family violence; newspapers dating back into the 1800s report such cases. The trouble was that courts rarely dealt with family violence because the perpetrators were seldom charged. Laying charges was in the hands of the police, and an assault on a female at home was, in the parlance of the times, 'just a domestic'. It wasn't thought to be any concern of the criminal law; it was something for the parties to sort out themselves.

These days there's specific legislation to protect women and children from family violence – and to protect people from harassment by strangers. In Victoria they're called intervention orders, in other states apprehended violence orders or restraining orders. Their aim is admirable but in every state, it seems, the system is out of control and bringing the law into disrepute.

When I say out of control, here's what can happen. My client was Victor, and when his marriage to Ingrid broke up their three children stayed on with her in the family home. Over time she kicked them out one by one and they moved in with him. As each child swapped from mum to dad, the parents traded insults and the sparks flew. In support of Ingrid, her new partner John stirred the pot and so did her parents, Janet and Aldo.

When Victor applied for an intervention order against Aldo, Ingrid's side fired back with a couple of cross-applications. It happens all the time; tit for tat. Victor gave me a history of the previous orders and I compiled this table:

In 2013 (when Ingrid kicked son Raymond out at the age of 12):

Victor v. Aldo

John v. Victor

Ingrid v. Victor

In 2015 (when Ingrid rejected son Tony for coming out as gay):

Tony v. Ingrid
Tony v. John
John v. Tony
Ingrid v. Tony
Victor v. Ingrid
Victor v. John
John v. Victor
Ingrid v. Victor

In 2019 (when Ingrid kicked daughter Samantha out after she turned eighteen and her family payments stopped):

Aldo v. Victor
John v. Victor
Ingrid v. Victor
Samantha v. John
John v. Samantha

I tried to spot the pattern in all this but I couldn't quite see it. I wrote all the names in a circle on a sheet of paper and marked the applications as connecting lines. It came out looking like a map of the East Berlin railway network and raised more questions than it answered. For instance, Raymond and Janet hadn't applied for orders against anyone. Why not? Were they pacifists or something?

You may think I've made all this up, but I haven't. Sixteen separate orders! It was grotesque, the waste of time, money and court resources, all to indulge a tribe of squabbling adults. But once the process had got going there was no stopping it.

I was involved this time round because at the last hearing, Victor had mouthed off at Aldo in the foyer of the court: 'You better follow the orders, you fucking wog.' He'd been charged with using threatening words in a public place and I was briefed to represent him. Just as the case was due to start, the police prosecutor informed me I'd appeared for Aldo at some earlier stage in the saga.

It was news to me. I honestly didn't recognise Aldo or remember anything about the case – an authentic instance of repressed memory! I made a hurried call to the Bar Ethics Committee to see if I had to relinquish the case. Since Aldo was only a witness this time, not a party, I stayed in it. Victor copped a fine, by the way, and had to write a letter of apology to the court staff for creating a scene.

My point is that you absolutely lose count with these things. That they take on a life of their own is but one of the problems. Police and courts issue Safety Notices and Interim Orders at the drop of a hat. But after that first step, the way the wheels turn is the legal system at its most creaking and clumsy.

I offer these remarks as a barrister who represents female applicants as often as male respondents. Violence against women has been a huge and hidden scourge for a long time. Something had to be done and intervention orders were the first and most important step. Education is another and so are changes to community attitudes.

There's no doubt some men are complete bastards. They need to be restrained, and their compliance enforced by immediate sanctions. But many men are not bastards; many are decent, ordinary blokes who love their kids and deserve to be treated fairly. It shouldn't be a case of 'one size fits all'.

The law defines family violence so broadly it includes the sort of friction that occurs occasionally in even the happiest household: raised voices, a slammed door, unkind words, the silent treatment. For a determined female this can make for open slather. It's not misogynistic to write 'female'; the preamble to the Victorian Act specifically spells out that family violence is predominantly committed by men, and that the victims are predominantly women and children.[6]

Casting the net so widely is intended to provide maximum protection, but it creates the potential for trivial incidents to be magnified out of all proportion. I realise that these days, even to use the word 'trivial' in this context is to invite criticism; the current mantra is that

---

[6] Men are also victims of family violence. While a woman in Australia is killed by her partner on average every nine days – a shocking statistic – a man is killed by his on average every 29 days. Australian Institute of Health and Welfare: Family, Domestic and Sexual Violence in Australia, 2019.

every incident of family violence is 'serious'. I disagree. As in any offending, there's a continuum that ranges from minor to heinous. Slamming a cupboard door and swearing isn't nice, but it's very different from terrorising a woman, threatening to kill her, then half-choking her and breaking her arm. We should not equate the two.

Cases of physical violence are the straightforward ones. Mostly, the facts are indubitable; often there's evidence of injury. The response should be unequivocal. The men should be charged and Safety Notices issued on the spot. It's mainly what happens now, thank goodness.

But other forms of family violence are less clear-cut. Bullying, insults, put-downs and controlling behaviour leave no visible signs. They can cause psychological harm, but behaviour like this is harder to define and measure, and the truth harder to come by. With allegations of this kind there are always two sides to the story; verbal exchanges are mostly a two-way street. But when it's a woman's word against a man's, how easy it is to always believe the worst of the male.

Intervention orders are heavy-handed and one-sided, and the bias against men is now built-in. Police protocols require them to take the woman's side every time. And courts, through lack of time, err on the side of caution. The default position is to issue an order no matter what. The unspoken reasoning seems to run: 'If these allegations are true, the court's got to restrain this man. If they're not true and he's not violent, then an order won't affect him.'

But orders do affect men. They prevent a husband communicating with his wife, they separate him from his children and frequently evict him from his home. There are meant to be safeguards but often, once an Interim Order is made, months pass before the man gets a chance to give his side of the story. Some claims wait almost a year before they're adjudicated. The delays are outrageous.[7]

Almost all first hearings now are held *ex parte,* meaning in the absence of the man affected. The man on the receiving end isn't there and doesn't even know it's happening. The original intent of the *ex parte* procedure was to avoid giving advance notice which might endanger an applicant. Now it's used routinely. If a woman tells a good enough story – and believe me, it doesn't have to be very good – an Interim Order will be issued on the spot.

So in a man's absence and without his knowledge, an order is made that turns his life upside down. Often the first he knows is when the police arrive at his house or workplace and serve the order on him. He gets twenty minutes to pack his bag and vacate his home. A new status quo is set which gives a spiteful mother a court-sanctioned opportunity to alienate

---

[7] Some courts now have a 'fast-track' system, which creates a different set of problems.

his children from him. He gets no real opportunity to challenge the order for months. And when he does, his word is rarely accepted because courts are so risk-averse. Many men feel they haven't had a fair go.

A colleague tells of a couple whose argument in their kitchen turned physical. He said she was the aggressor; she said he slapped her first, though if he did it left no mark. What was indisputable was that she threw a saucepan of boiling water over him.

He drove himself to a police station suffering second-degree burns. The police were heading out to arrest the wife when they received a call from a neighbouring police station where the wife had got in first. Her version was accepted without demur and he was the one who ended up under arrest, charged and ordered out of the house.

Occasionally, after months of delay, a final order is actually refused. The man on the receiving end is expected to pick up the pieces and just move on. There's no sanction against a woman guilty of exaggeration or downright lying. To my knowledge, no-one has been charged with perjury for lying in an intervention order application, though I suspect it happens almost daily. A woman who makes a false accusation runs no risk whatsoever.

Getting an intervention order is a common tactic in family law disputes. It's the way to go if you want to get your man out of the house. Family lawyers know this and advise their clients accordingly. Provoke him to smash a coffee mug, stand in his way so he can't get past and 'causes' you to fall, and the problem's solved. Call the cops and he's out of the house in no time. Just remember to get the locks changed the same day.

Intervention orders are also misused for immigration purposes. If a woman comes to Australia on a spouse or fiancée visa and the relationship ends, the man who sponsored her has to notify the Department of Immigration. The woman's visa is at risk of being revoked unless she finds grounds to avoid it. The simplest way is to be a victim of family violence. If she can establish that, she gets to remain in Australia *automatically*.

Here's an illustration. My client, Marina, was a woman from Moldova in her early forties who met Gordon, a widower, on the internet. He travelled to Moldova where the romance bloomed and the two got married. Gordon then returned to Australia and set about arranging a visa for her and her daughter to migrate. This took several years of hearings and appeals, and by the time the visas were granted Marina's daughter had grown into a sour, discontented teenager, though she'd earlier written a letter to Immigration saying how much she adored her new papa.

Within a year of their arrival in Australia, mother and daughter had fled to a women's refuge where they were now living on public charity. Marina applied for an intervention order. Her allegations of domestic violence were that Gordon had criticised her cooking and slammed a glass door.

'Did he break the door?' I asked.

'No.'

'Did he break anything?'

'No.'

'Has he ever hit you?'

'No.'

'Has he ever pushed you?'

'He pushed past me.'

'But actually pushed you?'

'Once.'

'How did it happen?'

'I pushed him first.'

We waited all morning for court time and I warned Marina her application was light-on. When she came back after lunch she reported that Gordon had approached her daughter outside the court and made her cry. This sounded helpful and I extracted the details from the daughter. No, Gordon hadn't been offensive or threatening; he hadn't caused her fear, but he'd told her something that made her cry. And what was that exactly?

'He said the cat was missing me.'

In the course of negotiations with his barrister I heard Gordon's version of events. According to him, the mother and daughter had turned difficult only when he started refusing their demands for money and new smartphones. My colleague pointed him out to me on the far side of the court foyer. Gordon was a smallish man with a visibly withered arm. But his age was the thing that struck me most. 'How old is he?' I asked.

'He's seventy-six. Didn't you know?'

Incidentally, Gordon was still paying off Marina's $1200 phone bill and now she was on Centrelink, he was liable to refund her benefits under his Immigration Assurance of Support.

If the case had gone before a magistrate Marina might actually have been refused a final order. But, like most such cases, this one wasn't decided by a court. The endless delays drive respondents to cut their losses and give up. This was the third court date and we were likely to be adjourned off yet again. Gordon was worn out and consented to an order without admitting Marina's allegations. Men do this all the time when they can't spare repeated days off work or afford the legal expenses.

I have no doubt some of these Immigration cases involve collusion. If the man consents to an intervention order – even with a denial of the allegations – the woman attains her end. Under the *Immigration Act,* the

Order is conclusive of victimhood and the woman wins permanent residence. Does money change hands in some of these cases? That's what I hear.

Applications for intervention orders are made in writing. They're meant to spell out the conduct that constitutes the family violence but they seldom contain the full case the respondent has to answer. Indeed, some border on the unintelligible. The allegations are unnumbered and the parties referred to in the third person to make it hard to work out who's done what to whom. They're written in reverse chronological order and words in inverted commas aren't direct speech, they're just whatever the clerk 'feels like inserting'. To make the whole shebang unreadable it's typed in capital letters, often with weird spacing and numerous typographical errors.

Here's an example. AFM stands for Aggrieved Family Member.

THE RESPONDENT IS THE EX-DE FACTO OF THE AFM'S SISTER. HE DOES NOT ACCEPT THE BREAK-UP OF HIS RELATIONSHIP WITH THE AFM'S SISTER AND BALMED THE

AFM AND THE AFM'S BOYFRIEND WHO IS HIS BROTHER. ON 23 NOVEMBER THE RESPONDENT CALLED HIS BROTHER AND SAID 'HE WILL GET MY BIKEY MATES' TO FIX HER UP IF 'SHE DOESN'T PULL HER HEAD IN.' THE AFM BELIEVES HE IS ASSOCIATED WITH A CRIMINAL GANG AND HAS ACCESS TO FIREARMS. ON THE 19 NOVEMBER THE AFM RECEIVED SIX HANG-UP CALLS FROM A PRIVATE NUMBER AND THE AFM'S BROTHER TOLD HER 'THAT'S DARRELL' BUT DENIES IT NOW BECAUSE HE HAS HAD A FALLING OUT WITH HER IN SEPTEMBER AND OCTOBER THE AFM HAS HAD HER TYRES LET DOWN THREE TIMES AND THE RESPONDENT HAS DONE WHEELIES AND DONUTS IN FRONT OF HER HOUSE. THE AFM IS IN FEAR AND DOES NOT WANT ANYTHING TO DO WITH THE RESPONDENT AND HIS BROTHER.

Got that straight?

I was chatting to a court registrar the other day, a very sensible, competent and experienced lady, and asked her what proportion of intervention order applications she thought were without merit. I expected her to say a third (my estimate) – or even half. Without batting an eyelid she said, 'Ninety per cent', and I think she meant it. I was appalled, but perhaps she's right. I do these cases from time to time, whereas she's seeing them day in and day out. When I mentioned her opinion to a fellow barrister, she said, 'Well, ninety per cent of the ones *I* do are bullshit.'

In Victoria, intervention orders are regulated by two different Acts, one for family violence and the other covering violence or stalking by strangers. The personal safety ones are even more bizarre, and not just in Victoria.

In New South Wales householders have got them against tradesmen to avoid paying their bills. Criminals have taken them out against police, with one drink-driver taking one out against the policeman who arrested him. During a municipal election campaign in Victoria a councillor got an order against a supporter of a rival candidate. Weeks later the court dismissed the application.

Most unusually, it awarded legal costs against the applicant, who simply passed them on for the ratepayers to meet!

I once represented three bus drivers, all with surnames beginning with the letter B. An applicant had wanted an intervention order on behalf of her daughter against every bus driver on a particular school bus route. The court registry would only let her apply against the first three on her alphabetical list of 27 names. Her complaint was that the drivers were harassing her daughter by being rude and nasty and wanting to inspect her ticket! It was utter nonsense but it cost the drivers time and money to defend themselves.

The present situation regarding costs orders is an invitation to mischief. In most litigation, legal costs are awarded against the unsuccessful side. This helps filter out claims that have no merit. With intervention orders, costs are awarded only for 'frivolous' applications or those brought in bad faith, which in practice means almost never. While no-one should be deterred from protecting themselves for fear of financial risk, I do think respondents who successfully defend spurious claims should be compensated for the expense they've been put to.

Lawyers cost money, but in this jurisdiction they're indispensable. Negotiations between the two sides are essential; if every case went to a full hearing we'd need five times more courts and magistrates. To function at all, the system depends on parties coming to terms, and the lawyers dart back and forth bearing offers and counter-offers while the delays wear the parties down. There's nothing so productive of compromise as a three-hour wait.

I warn my clients they're facing a long day at court and tell them to bring something to read. Mostly, though, they want to talk. So I sit and listen patiently to the travails of their personal lives. '...I told Lisa that Chloe's cat gave Bianca an asthma attack and she went and told Chloe and the fat bitch just barged into my unit and I'm like, "Bianca plays with other cats and they never give her asthma and anyway I was talking to Lisa," and she's like, "Get fucked" and I'm like, "Get fucked yourself" and then...'

'Mmmm,' I murmur. 'And are there any witnesses?'

'I've got six witnesses and they all know Chloe's the troublemaker and they want her out of the flats.'

On this occasion I'm even given the names of the witnesses, which is unusual in this sort of case. More unusual, too, is that when I speak to my opponent she tells me her side's also got six witnesses, all of whom will say *my* client was the troublemaker. Six each; it seems a coincidence. We compare names and – you've guessed it – they're the same six!

Goodness knows what the witnesses would have said, but we never find out because the case fizzles out. On the day of the full hearing neither party turns up. To them, as to many, the case was just a form of entertainment. I've seen a young couple blocking the court stairs, embracing and pashing on, before going into court and getting orders to keep each other away! The contempt with which orders are treated worries me.

Having an intervention order gives a woman a weapon. If she reports that an order's been broken, the police are obliged to act. They arrest the suspect, take him to a police station and charge him. He faces a maximum penalty of $22,000 in fines plus two years jail.

It's a weapon that can be abused. First a woman gets an intervention order to keep a man away and prohibit him from making contact. Then she rings him up and invites him round. Men are stupid to take the bait, of course, but they do so in the hope of reconciling or seeing their kids or having sex. If the couple have another falling-out she phones the police and it's the man alone who faces the music. Women who incite a breach of an intervention order aren't charged. The crime of aiding and abetting a breach of an order was abolished a couple of years ago.

Here's a typical example: a wife took out an order against her husband. Despite being 'in terror' of him, she made a practice of inviting him round to mow her lawn, baby-sit while she went night-clubbing and to fix the ducted heating, as well as for occasional sessions in bed. When her mood changed she rang the cops and got him arrested. It seems outrageous to me that she can get an order, connive at its breach and then complain. But that's how it goes.

Women now enjoy greater protection from violence than ever before. What a good thing that is – though the job is far from over. But part of it has come at a cost. There's another value called justice. One good has been bought at the cost of daily unfairness. The system needs to work better.

15

Dicing with the Devil

When neighbours clash

Gus and Wilma Clark were a retired couple with a very nice home. From their front patio they looked down onto a green, well-kept garden. Much of the road was screened off by rhododendrons and camellias, but visible through the shrubbery was a little bit of number 27 on the other side of the road. I know all this because I saw the photos.

Living at number 27 was Harry Brenker, a heavy, bearded fellow who looked a bit of a bruiser. Harry owned about twenty cars and most of them were parked in the street opposite the Clarks' place.

The cars didn't just spoil the view; they annoyed the Clarks as a matter of principle. With their own lawn well-trimmed and their paths swept, they held strong opinions about tidiness and good order in their patch of suburbia. They approached Harry about removing his cars, but rubbed him up the wrong way. When they got nowhere with him they started complaining to the council.

The council put up a 'No Standing' sign near the corner. This restricted Harry's parking options and he got booked a few times. When he took to parking his cars on the nature strip he got booked for that too. He felt kind of pissed-off with the Clarks.

Now it so happened that Harry held strong opinions himself – in his case, about religion and politics. By religion he was a Satanist (a convert, I presume); in politics he was also a Satanist, indeed an active one. He was the secretary of the newly-formed Satanist Party which intended fielding candidates at the next state election. Whenever Harry saw the Clarks, he warned them he was a powerful, dangerous man.

By way of emphasis, he started directing a few nasty gestures their way. He would hold up his right hand with index and little finger extended, which in Satanistic circles means something unpleasant. He made the gesture whenever he saw Wilma Clark putting out the rubbish bins or watering the camellias.

Poor old Wilma started to crack up. She worried about being on the receiving end of all those satanic curses. So she and Gus applied for an intervention order to make Harry desist. They engaged me to represent them.

I did some homework and checked out Harry's political activities. I heard he'd been written up in the *Herald Sun* and, as it was before the days of online searches, I trudged out to the newspaper room at the State Library. I tracked down the article on microfiche and took a photocopy. The article said the Satanist Party was well under way and already had eleven members and three policies. The party was pro-drugs, pro-Satan and anti-immigrant. There was also a photo of Harry which made him look kind of sinister. It must have been the lighting.

By the day of the hearing I was feeling pretty pleased with myself. I kept my copy of the newspaper article under wraps, ready to produce in the middle of my cross-examination. I was all equipped to show just what sort of a citizen Harry Brenker was.

I was waiting in the foyer of the court with the Clarks when Harry arrived to check in. He was easy to pick. He was wearing black leather trousers and a black leather jacket. The jacket was unzipped to show a black T-shirt with Satanist Party wording on it and their logo, a goat. (More research: *Brewer's Dictionary of Phrase and Fable,* 3rd edition states, 'From early times the goat has been associated with the idea of sin and devil-lore'.) Unfortunately Wilma noticed Harry too. She got an attack of the shivers and was ushered away to be hugged by the court support workers.

At the counter I introduced myself to Harry in the hopes of sounding him out on any common ground. I needn't have been so secretive with the newspaper cutting. Harry had his own copy, nicely laminated in plastic like a place mat. He flourished it at me and was delighted when I told him I'd read it already.

Harry and I exchanged views. He told me he was pissed-off with my clients. He said he intended to continue to exercise his rights of free expression, motor vehicle ownership and religious worship.

'Maybe you should lay off the fingers and the curses,' I suggested.

'That's my democratic right.'

'Not if the court orders you to stop.'

'I don't give a stuff what the court orders.'

I asked, 'What if the Satanist Party wins office at the next election and you're appointed Attorney-General? Wouldn't you want court orders obeyed then?'

This got us into deep philosophical waters about authority and the rule of law. The possibility hadn't occurred to him and he gave it some thought and grudgingly agreed. 'Yeah, I suppose so.'

Mainly, Harry wanted to talk about religion. He thought the community wasn't according his religious beliefs proper respect. He pulled out a paperback book, *The Satanic Bible,* and offered it to me for a read. Out of politeness I skimmed through a couple of pages and noticed it had enough 'thou', 'thee' and 'thine' to resemble a fair dinkum Bible – or at the very least *The Book of Mormon*. Published in California. Where else?

Harry struck me as a good-natured sort of bloke and I tried to talk him round, to get him to agree to shift his cars and stop giving the Clarks the evil eye. He wasn't interested. He had other ways, he told me, of dealing with troublesome neighbours. He said, 'I paint your client's face on a pumpkin and then I kick it round the room.'

'Do you eat the pumpkin later?' I asked.

'Listen, mate. When I go home I'll get my little voodoo doll out and start sticking a few pins in it.'

I said, 'I hope you won't put a curse on me.'

He said, 'No, mate, I've got nothing against you.'

That was a relief.

We went into court. The magistrate was an old-timer: dour, humourless, very formal. Harry's manner didn't go over too well in the preliminaries. He tried to make a speech first-off and talked over the magistrate. In fact, he antagonised the mago from the word go. It suited us fine.

Our side went first and Gus gave his evidence with great precision in a clipped, intense voice. He had meticulous notes of various outrages, especially relating to car parking. Wilma, trembling, sat surrounded by a protective cordon of court support ladies.

Harry asked some probing questions in his cross-examination, such as: 'Why did you dob me in to the council?' and 'What's wrong with youse two?'

Then it was Harry's turn to give evidence. He stepped into the witness box and was immediately at cross-purposes with the magistrate.

'Raise the Bible in your right hand,' said the bench clerk.

'No.'

'Raise the Bible,' ordered the magistrate.

'I refuse.'

'You won't be sworn?'

'I'll be sworn.'

'Well, do as you're told.'

'I've got my own Bible. Why should I be persecuted just because my beliefs are different?' He waved the sacred paperback.

'Put that away. Raise the Bible.'

'No! Not that one.'

In the front row of seats Wilma broke down in choked sobbing.

Now if he'd only known it, Harry could have given his evidence by affirmation – a solemn promise – instead of on oath. I could have let him know but I didn't. It's an old rule: never stop an opponent from making a mistake. The magistrate thought Harry was taking the mickey. 'Sir, this is a court, not a circus.'

'This is persecution!' responded Harry.

'Stand down.'

After a few more cross words, Harry gathered up his papers and place mat and stalked out of the courtroom.

I asked for an order. We'd wanted Harry not to threaten, intimidate or approach the Clarks, but the magistrate, who was well-known for his intricate orders, added some extra terms on his own initiative. One was to exclude Harry from going within 200 metres of the Clarks' house – which effectively prevented him living in his own home! We even got an order for Harry to pay our costs, something almost unheard of.

Gus wasn't exactly grateful. He seemed aggrieved he'd had to come to court at all. In his opinion it was someone else's job to sort Harry out – the cops or the council or the thought-police. He also thought an order was a magic wand and that all his problems were over. I told him there were no magic wands in this jurisdiction. I warned him too, that he might have trouble collecting his costs from Harry.

It wasn't long before Harry lodged an appeal. Two months later we were in the County Court for Round 2. A fellow barrister came along to spectate. He was one of those way-out schismatic Catholics, and had volunteered to give me his opinion on whether Harry Brenker was possessed by demons. (His verdict: 'Definitely!')

Harry seemed to elicit one of two reactions in people. Some were repelled and angered: the Clarks, magistrates, Tridentine Catholics. Others were amused and charmed. Perhaps I was in the second category; the judge certainly was.

His Honour was a crusty example of the old school, but susceptible to Harry's ingenuous manner. Harry described how he'd been treated at the first hearing. 'That magistrate, Your Honour, he didn't like my shirt.'

'Why was that, Mr Brenker?'

'It was my Satanist Party T-shirt, you know, with our party symbol. I reckon he was prejudiced against my politics.'

The judge looked at our photos of the cars. They made Number 27 look like a wrecker's yard. 'Not too flash, Mr Brenker,' he commented.

'No, Your Honour, but I can deal with that no worries. I'm going to move them all out once we get our big project going.'

'How soon can you move them?'

'Maybe six months.'

(Me, interjecting: 'They've already been there eighteen months, Your Honour.' The judge, angrily: 'Sit Down!')

He turned back to Harry. 'That's not soon enough, Mr Brenker.'

'I might be able to do it in five.'

'I'll give you a month.'

'Your Honour, I need more time than that. I'm moving to twenty acres at Fish Creek. A few of us are going to start a worm farm.'

'Twenty acres, eh?' mused the judge. 'Mmm, you can get a lot of worms on twenty acres.'

'Yeah, it's a real big project, Your Honour...' And so on.

The upshot was that we kept our order but in more restricted terms. It was a win for us but Gus was still dirty on me. He hadn't liked my speaking to Harry before the case; he hadn't liked the judge's light-hearted attitude. He'd been wanting Harry to be hanged, drawn and quartered.

I never met the Clarks again, which was a pity because they didn't pay their bill for the appeal. Strangely, I've run into Harry twice. Once was soon after the case, but the second time was years later when I was taking a short cut through the foyer of the Sofitel Hotel in Collins Street. We spotted each other at the same moment but I got in first: 'What are you doing in a fancy place like this?' I quipped.

He said, 'Mate, I was going to ask you the same thing.'

'How's the neighbourhood situation?' I enquired.

'Still going.'

'And the worm farm?'

'Pretty soon now. Like, once we buy some land.'

'All those cars of yours?'

'Still there,' he smiled.

We didn't get on to religion or politics.

16

Not by Chance

Gambling and poker machines

Here's some ancient history. In 1983 the Victorian Government appointed a Board of Enquiry to consider whether to introduce poker machines. Among other things, the Board looked at the experience of New South Wales. Its report[8] ran to 800 pages and it recommended they NOT be introduced. The NOT was in capital letters and appeared on the first line of page 1. Maybe it wasn't prominent enough; Victoria legalised pokies a couple of years later.

Before then, Victorians gambled on other things. Problem gamblers did, of course, exist and some of them turned to crime. Some lied and cheated and

---

8 Board of Enquiry into Poker Machines (Murray Wilcox QC) Report, Victorian Government Printer, Melbourne, 1983.

stole to punt on the horses or play cards. It happened, but it was relatively rare. It isn't rare any longer. With the pokies it's common.

Over the years I've represented a bank teller with a pokies addiction, an accountant, a bookkeeper, shop assistants, a personal care attendant and a member of the armed forces. They gambled their own money away, then their family's, then money they stole from employers or friends. As thieves, they had to answer for their own behaviour, but to my way of thinking the community bore some responsibility too.

That's because the enquiry found, not a risk, but a *certainty* that poker machines would make gambling addicts of certain susceptible people, those who otherwise wouldn't gamble compulsively, or perhaps not even at all. The effects on people who fell prey to the pokies, and on their families, were likely to be catastrophic. That fact was known all along, well before the community, through Parliament, deliberately placed temptation in their way.

Poker machines are addictive because they're designed to be. A rapid succession of stake and play is interspersed with frequent small payouts. Lights flash, bells ring, jackpot winners are announced over loudspeakers. Unlike discontinuous forms of gambling – there are intervals between horse-races or the spin of the roulette wheel – the pokies never stop. The 1983 enquiry found poker machines to be the most pernicious and addictive of all forms of gambling.

The most extreme case I've struck was a mother with four children. She had a drug habit too, but her gambling addiction was the stronger. The usual pattern of drug addicts who commit a desperate crime is to spend the money immediately on their next fix. This woman committed three serious armed robberies but didn't spend any of the proceeds on drugs. In each case she went straight to the pokies and blew the lot in record time.

When I became involved in her case she was already on bail for an armed robbery committed with a blood-filled syringe. Her husband was struggling to keep tabs on her, but she woke at four one morning while he was still asleep. She got dressed, snuck out to a nearby 7-Eleven and held it up at knife point. She netted $335 and headed straight for the local hotel gaming room (naturally, it was open at that hour) and put it through the pokies.

Eleven minutes later she'd lost the lot. On her way out she ran into her husband and the police, each of whom were independently looking for her. Allowing thirty seconds to enter and leave, she went through the money in ten minutes, a rate of over $2000 per hour! And she only stopped when she had no money left.

The job of government is to avoid avoidable ills. So for a government to have done the opposite and saddled its people with an evil whose results were entirely foreseen was unforgivable. You don't need to be a wowser to find it disturbing that in order to enrich the few you visit ruination on thousands of others in the form of poverty, fraud, crime, broken homes and suicide.

Those are my thoughts whenever I represent a poker machine addict in court. I even used to quote slabs of the report but it never did my clients much good. After a few years a magistrate remarked, 'Mr Challinger, the horse has well and truly bolted.'

How times change! I can still remember that white-bread world where gambling was officially frowned on. Yet these days no social restraints against gambling remain. Nowadays it's not only legal but patriotic to squander your money. Indeed, it's not even called gambling any more. These days it's 'gaming', provided you lose your money on a state-sanctioned rip-off.

In my early days at the bar the terrible crime of gambling was dealt with at the old City Court in Russell Street. In the afternoons long lists of names would be called, mainly Italian and all mispronounced. 'Antonio Jiggly-yotti! ... Antonio Jiggly-yotti! ... No appearance, Your Worship.' These were criminals who were undermining civilisation by playing cards for money in their own homes. None of them ever turned up and the court would just fine them in their absence.

Before my time, I'm told, gambling was a nice little earner for crooked police. I've heard of raids on two-up schools by appointment. The manager would announce the raid and ask the customers to wait in the street till it was over. Anyone willing to earn two quid by being arrested was invited to stay on. When the cops rushed in they'd arrest the volunteers, growling, 'Give us your names – and make them short ones.' Then they'd take them down the police station while the two-up manager followed with the money to bail them out. On the court day nobody turned up and the bail was forfeited. End of story.

On the subject of pokies, though, I once did a case where the boot was on the other foot. Jimmy was an intelligent bloke of Asian background, but a bit of a battler. He was charged with deception of a poker machine. I had to look up the law to see if you can deceive a machine at all. You can. For example, you can deceive a weighing machine. You put in a coin and get yourself weighed, then your mate climbs aboard, you step off and he gets weighed. A third joins him before he steps off and a whole string of you get weighed for the price of one. When I was a kid it cost a penny and I used to take part myself, though I didn't know I was committing a felony.

One day Jimmy visited the Monte Carlo Room, went to machine number 22 and put in a dollar. The machine showed a credit, but his coin dropped back out through the chute. He thought the machine was giving him a bonus spin. He put the dollar in again and the same thing happened. So he kept doing it. Why wouldn't he?

The credit didn't show every time, nor did the coin drop back every time. Sometimes the machine kept the coin. That's why Jimmy thought the machine was still running correctly.

'How often did you get the coin back?' I asked him.

'Hard to say.'

'But more often than not?'

'Oh yes.'

'So what proportion of the time did you lose the dollar? Half the time?'

'Less.'

'Ten per cent?'

'Mmm, less.'

'So ninety times out of a hundred you'd get your money back?'

'Ninety-nine.'

This bit was important because the issue was whether Jimmy had the necessary criminal intent. If he believed he was winning, then he wasn't acting dishonestly. If he thought the machine was defective he was committing an offence by continuing to take advantage. You would know a Coke machine was on the blink if it dispensed a can then gave you your money back. But how do you tell with gambling machines? Sometimes they do refund your stake.

Everyone I discussed the case with was sympathetic to Jimmy and pleased to see the tables turned. Even the cops were understanding, though they thought he'd taken it to extremes. 'Come on!' they said, 'he knew the machine was out of order!'

'How's he meant to know?' I asked.

'A couple of hundred bucks, okay, good luck to him. But he went overboard.'

'He made the most of it,' I agreed. 'He thought he was on a lucky streak.'

The copper laughed. 'What, for twelve hours straight?'

A statement on the prosecution brief explained what had happened. The coin hopper hadn't clicked back into place when the machine had last been cleared. Whenever a coin passed a trigger it registered a credit but instead of falling into the hopper it mostly came out the chute again. When they did the reconciliation it turned out Jimmy had put a coin in 11,212 times.

'Strike!' I said to him, 'you would have got RSI!'

'I did,' he told me. 'My whole arm swelled up.'

During the course of the twelve hours Jimmy had gone to the cashier 45 times to pick up his winnings. Nobody had queried him, though he was at the same machine the whole time. We argued that if the management didn't question a string of wins from machine 22, why should Jimmy?

We called for the video surveillance: twelve hours of tape of Jimmy at the machine to work out how often the coins came out; and twelve hours of the cashiers' desk to see how many changes of personnel there'd been. But the Monte Carlo Room didn't want us seeing their secret, behind-the-scenes footage of the cashiers' desk. They objected to producing the tape, which put the police on the spot to justify their refusal.

In the end the police got tired of protecting the Monte Carlo Room's trade secrets and did us a deal. Jimmy pleaded guilty to a single charge and we got the summary sanitised. The police also agreed not to ask for an order that he repay the money. He'd already blown it on the pokies elsewhere, of course.

The mago was sympathetic too. Jimmy got a bond with a condition he attend counselling for problem gambling. He sent me a bottle of whisky later as a present, not that I drink the stuff. Nice bloke; I hope the whisky hadn't fallen off the back of a truck.

I've had some sympathy for other clients, too, like the cleaner who used to suck spare coins up with his vacuum cleaner. Admiration was more the feeling for another bloke whose method of financing his habit was new to me.

He started with his last $10 note and attached about 30 centimetres of sticky tape to one end. Then he got another 30 centimetres of tape and stuck it to the sticky side of the first length. That gave him a $10 note with a long, smooth ribbon of tape hanging off it.

He fed the note into a money-changing machine which disgorged $10 in coins. Then he tugged on the ribbon and eased the note back out of the machine. After repeating this a few times he went and changed some of the coins into $20 notes, one of which he doctored the same way. That doubled his productivity. I can't remember if he graduated to fifties but he went through the process till he'd pocketed about $800.

He only got caught by spending too long at the machines. His comment to the police was that his activities were harmless. He said it was a victimless crime: nobody suffered – nobody deserving, that is. Just the pub, the owner of the poker machines and the State of Victoria. I could see his point.

On the subject of tape, security footage before the digital age used to be recorded on videotape. I represented a client charged with using a stolen credit card to take money out of an ATM at a pokies joint. There was video footage of someone making a number of withdrawals, whom the police asserted was my client.

Well it did look like him, but I wanted to be sure. When I watch security video, I find I have to go over it repeatedly to take it all in. Sometimes, for example, I've watched a fight sequence a dozen times before noticing something important I'd missed – a gesture by someone in the background, for example. This time I viewed the tape by appointment at the police station a couple of days before court. With every playback and rewind the quality of the tape deteriorated.

On the day of the hearing the clerk set up the TV and video player in the courtroom and the prosecutor and I ran the tape through a couple more times. By the time I'd asked, 'Can I watch that bit again?' for the eighth time the picture had lost all definition. It looked like ectoplasm floating in outer space. Finally, the machine gave out a noise

Khhhhhhhh and chewed the tape up completely.

The magistrate came into court and said, 'I understand there's to be video evidence.'

'Not any more!' I smiled.

Sad to say, that sort of thing doesn't happen with DVDs.

On another occasion the CCTV system at the pokies wasn't compatible with the equipment the cops had. I went to the hotel with the police informant. All those flashing lights and noises, the air of cheap sophistication and the suckers sitting there getting fleeced. I really can't see the attraction; you might as well stand in the sun and feed money into a parking meter.

The policeman and I had to go into the cashier's office to view the tape on a monitor. From time to time attendants carried in buckets of coins and we had to hold our hands over our ears as they were poured down a chute. The noise was deafening. What a horrible place – though I hear they do a good smorgasbord on a Sunday.

Still, it was democratic; the pokies take anyone's money. I looked around and saw a couple of old dears, some men in suits, a young tradesman, some office girls. By the law of averages one or two of them would lie, cheat, steal and defraud even their families. Which ones? I couldn't pick them.

Of course, it's not just the pokies. We've got a casino now – or more correctly, a 'World-class Entertainment Complex'. My client Vincent used to frequent the place. He was a qualified accountant and worked for a small manufacturing company. When he'd been interviewed for the job, he didn't mention that wee bit of a gambling habit he once had. And that fraud conviction a few years ago slipped his mind, too. His new employer went off to a trade fair in Europe. He left Vincent in control of all the bank accounts, including access to credit cards, which were used for buying stock for the business.

Vincent drew a couple of unauthorised cheques but failed to strike lucky at the baccarat table where he'd planned on solving all his financial problems. As the boss's return drew closer, he got more desperate for a win to make good the missing funds. He drew $5000 on the boss's credit cards and blew it all. He did it again and again, another four times. That's right, $25,000, at which point the boss in Hanover wondered why his Visa card wouldn't cover his hotel bill.

The twenty-five grand of course was all lost. Vincent fled his company flat, pocketed the bond and even hung on to the company car. On his return, the boss had to do his own detective work to track Vincent down to a house in the northern suburbs.

Vincent pleaded guilty but he didn't go to jail. He was assessed as suitable for an Intensive Corrections Order. In those days the order counted as a jail sentence, while letting him do his community work and serve his time at home under strict conditions. The assessment report had rated Vincent's risk of reoffending as low. Work that one out! A nice man but an incorrigible gambler.

Another bloke, Anthony, was issued with a company Diners' Club card. It was intended for travel expenses only, but it accumulated a lot of mysterious cash withdrawals, all $1000 apiece. Anthony knew nothing about them; he said someone had stolen the card. The withdrawals were from ATMs in Moonee Ponds (near Moonee Valley racecourse), Flemington (near the racecourse) and South Melbourne (near the casino). He claimed he'd never been to any of those places till the police produced his mobile phone records showing calls made from all three around the times of the withdrawals. Suddenly he remembered he did occasionally have a flutter on the horses or try his luck on the pokies.

Anthony didn't go to jail either. He stole over $10,000, but apart from gambling, he was a decent citizen with a clean record. By the time he faced court he'd got himself another job, was paying taxes and supporting his family. What was the sense in sending him off to mix with criminals at public expense? None the court could think of.

17

Bearing Witness

Problems with witnesses

Some clients plead not guilty. They have every right to do so; in our system no accused person has to admit to anything. By pleading not guilty they're availing themselves of their right to have the case against them proven. They're simply putting the prosecution to proof.

In the bad old days some honorary justices thought otherwise. One was famous for calling out: 'Those pleading guilty to this side of the court. Those who want to waste the court's time and plead not guilty to the other side.' That doesn't happen these days.

Magistrates now are trained lawyers, most of them pretty shrewd and intelligent people. But how often do even shrewd and intelligent people get things wrong? The answer is: sometimes. Most of us think we're pretty cluey but we all still make misjudgments and occasionally get ripped-off. How easy is it then to make the right call every single time? It's hard. Magos get it right most of the time, but not always. Yet in saying this, I'm expressing my own opinion. How do I know where the truth lies? I'm making a judgment myself and I might be wrong.

That uncertainty answers the question often asked of barristers: how can you defend someone you know to be guilty? The answer is that we don't know they're guilty – not unless they tell us so. And even if we've got our suspicions, the accused is entitled to the court's judgment, not ours. It's for us to put the defence case as well as we can and for the court to do the judging.

When clients contest their charges witnesses are called to give evidence. Sometimes my clients act surprised at this. 'I won't have to say anything, will I?' they ask. They're surprised; I'm astonished. Surely they've seen courtroom scenes on television? Surely they realise the prosecution witnesses will come and testify against them? And surely they realise that if they want to give their own version of events, they'll have to do it from the witness box?

To some, the prospect is about as welcome as climbing into a dentist's chair. In the higher courts there are some formidable barristers, very clever men and women who get paid a lot of money to make a witness look stupid or dishonest. In the lower courts there are police prosecutors, some of them skilled and forceful.

Magistrates in the lower courts and juries in the higher courts are the finders of fact. They decide what happened. They form their opinion by listening to the witnesses – and observing them. They rely on their experience and intelligence and common sense. The other day a young bloke in the witness box was insisting he was telling the truth. He said, 'Your Honour, I'll take a lie detector test or anything.' The mago replied, 'Son, I *am* the lie detector.'

Some people reckon they can tell if somebody's telling the truth just by watching their demeanour in the witness box. Not everyone would agree, Lindy

Chamberlain for one. Smarter lawyers than me think the ability of magistrates or juries to judge the truthfulness of witnesses is greatly overrated. Some say it's sheer delusion to think you can tell when people are telling the truth.

Gaps and inaccuracies in people's evidence tend to weaken its strength. Yet no-one can remember everything. Memory has evolved to do the job of getting its owner successfully through life. Perfection isn't needed, only adequacy. Selective forgetting of useless information is as important as selective remembering of the useful. The trouble is we can't always tell what's going to be important or useful in the future.

Most witnesses, too, have a bias, sometimes an unconscious one. They tend to support the side that calls them. If they're giving evidence for the police they want to help the prosecution case. If they're the victims of a theft or burglary they're especially partisan. The more they repeat themselves and the more they're challenged, the more certain they claim to be. They're honest witnesses but they talk themselves into it.

Some witnesses, though, *are* dishonest. Some are smooth-talking liars who are out to hoodwink and deceive both you and the court. A practised liar can be very persuasive. Sometimes the witnesses on both sides look shifty and unreliable. The question then becomes, which liar do you believe?

On the other hand, truthful witnesses can be unimpressive. In their desire to be accurate they can seem nervous and uncertain. Some are pompous and long-winded, others look as if they've got something to hide. Some people, too, are just plain unappealing in their appearance or manner. With witnesses of this kind, less likeable means less credible.

Early in my career I defended a chap charged with indecent assault. He was a sad, scrawny individual who lived in a Salvation Army hostel. He was accused of touching a girl's breasts in Myer's. The teenage victim said he'd looked straight at her and leered as he groped her. The store was crowded but no-one else saw what happened, not even the girl's school-friend beside her.

The lass went straight to a policeman in Bourke Street and complained. My client was still nearby, having made no attempt to get away. When the police spoke to him he said he knew nothing about a girl in Myer's. He agreed he might have accidentally bumped someone in the crush.

It was one person's word against another's. I should have handled it better. I didn't make anything of the fact that the man had no criminal history. I didn't go in hard enough with the complainant, who burst into tears at my first question. I had to hang fire while she was offered a tissue and a glass of water. Then she got into her stride and wouldn't give an inch.

By contrast, my bloke was shy and hesitant in the witness box and avoided eye contact with the magistrate. He was convicted and got a good behaviour bond. It was a low penalty but it still went on his record. These days he'd possibly go to jail and certainly be placed on the Sex Offenders Register.

The girl's father, who'd been in court, came up to me later and expressed sympathy for my man. His daughter wasn't a very pretty girl but she was well-developed. Maybe she had some hang-up about her physique. Who knows? The father gave me the impression he knew something I didn't. Maybe his daughter had been over-imaginative in the past, maybe she'd made other similar complaints.

Personally, I think if my fellow bumped the girl at all it was an accident. I don't think we should have lost, but these days such a case would be even harder to win. The 'victim' would have a cheer squad of support workers. And if the mago dared dismiss the charge it would 'prove' the court had disbelieved her and thereby 'disempowered' her. The lesson from this is that a young, middleclass female from a private school makes a better impression than a dero.

I'm not alone in thinking impressions count. Some of my clients think so too.

'Shall I put these glasses on?' asks one.

'Of course, if you want.'

'Yeah, they make me look brainy.'

Something makes me ask: 'Do you normally wear them?'

'Nuh, they're my brother's actually. I can't see a thing now.'

'Take them off.'

Over the years I've found witnesses unpredictable. I'm not meant to coach them but I give them a pep talk. I say, 'You're here to tell the truth and tell the court what you saw and heard.' I warn my client not to glare and grimace at the other side's evidence or nod approvingly when his side has its turn. Those I expect to do well in the witness box sometimes get tongue-tied or suffer stage fright. Those I fear will be hopeless sometimes come up trumps. Of course I always tell my schizophrenic witnesses to keep taking their medication till the hearing date.

Clients are mostly keen to make a good impression in the witness box. I tell them to listen to the questions and answer only the questions. 'If I want more, I'll ask you for more,' I say. But people love talking! They can't help volunteering extra details they think are helpful. I asked one witness an innocuous question and he blurted out, 'Are you talking about the time I went crazy with the nail gun and ended up in the County Court?' Another time my client had no convictions and I wanted him to rely on his good character. I asked him if he had a clean record and he answered, 'Yes, I beat the murder charge.'

In another case I called a neighbour to give evidence of what she knew of an alleged assault in the flat next door. Before court I went through her statement with her. She said, 'I heard a commotion through the party wall. Bangs and piercing shrieks. A woman's voice rang out. Distressed! Anguished! A plea for help!'

'Go on,' I said.

'My husband and I sprang to our feet. We ran for Vicky's front door. Another scream rent the air.'

It sounded too pat and contrived. I asked, 'What do you do for a living?'

She said, 'I write crime fiction.' Truly!

Neurotic witnesses can be very convincing. They think they're telling the truth, and self-deception makes it easier to deceive others. The hope that a devastating cross-examination will simply demolish a witness the way it does on TV isn't borne out in the real world. It happens rarely – very rarely when I'm cross-examining.

Some witnesses argue and quibble and refuse to give you a straight answer. They talk like politicians and beat around the bush. Some are uncontrollable. They give cheek and respond to a question by asking one back.

In an assault case I ask the alleged victim, 'Did you take a step forward?'

'Well, what was I meant to do?'

'I'm asking you whether you stepped forward.'

'How am I meant to remember everything I did?'

I put on a stern face and remind him he's a witness. I say, 'You're not here to ask me questions, you're here to answer mine.'

'Is that a question?' he asks.

'No.'

'Well I can't answer it.' A point to him!

Young children rarely give evidence, but when they do some are brilliant. The belief that children will always be truthful is quite wrong, in my opinion.

You only need to think of the practice they get every day telling fibs to teachers and parents. In my time I've called a couple of child witnesses who came across in court as if butter wouldn't melt in their mouths, whereas I knew the reality was very different.

It may be unfashionable to say so, but I find women more skilful liars than men. I warn my male clients of this when they're up against their former wives or girlfriends. I'm diplomatic and tell them that a convincing liar may be believed. 'She'll be convincing, all right,' they say grimly.

I'm not saying women tell more lies than men but I think they're more successful at it. And when they're hard-pressed in the witness box they always have tears to fall back on. It's probably natural selection at work again: being physically weaker than men, women have developed other survival skills, verbal ones. Women are more audacious in what they say and more tenacious in sticking to it. Some, of course, are too clever for their own good. The more they deny the obvious the more clearly they show they've got an axe to grind.

In the course of one case I asked, 'Do you agree your husband is a good father?'

The wife could have agreed and displayed a bit of fairness, but she didn't want to give any ground. 'The kids sometimes seem to enjoy their time with him.'

'But do you agree he's a good father?'

'I suppose he's not a bad father.'

'Well, the Family Report says he's a good father. Do you disagree with that?'

'I don't know whether I do or not.'

'The Family Report says you're a good mother. Do you disagree with that?'

'No.'

'So the report got it right about you and maybe wrong about him?'

I think that's the way it went. I hope it flowed as well on the day but I may have done some unconscious editing to make myself look good. Your best cross-examination is the one you go over in your mind driving home.

Personally, I'm not always sure how I'm going in cross-examination. I can't tell whether I'm kicking goals or not. I take a peep at my opponent and if he or she is looking serious I reckon I'm on the right track. Some experts, incidentally, say you shouldn't ask a question unless you know the answer the witness will give. I think this is rubbish. How can I know what the witness will say? I don't even know what I'm going to say next!

When it comes to lining up their own witnesses, clients often don't understand what's relevant and what isn't. Sometimes they bring crowds of well-wishers to give evidence, who know nothing of the facts in issue. I ask them why they've come to court and they say they have no idea. 'John just asked us to come.'

The typical family violence incident happens in private, with no-one present except the husband and wife. In one such case I remember an accused, the husband, turning up to court with two male witnesses in tow. Neither had been at the incident nor seen anything of it. Yet my client wanted them to give evidence. I asked him, 'What are they going to say?'

He said, 'They're going to say my wife's a fucking moll.'

Unexpected responses from your own witnesses aren't always detrimental. I was running a civil claim before a jury. My client had been injured and was now restricted in various jobs on his hobby farm. A neighbouring farmer was giving expert evidence on which tasks were now beyond my bloke's capacity. One such task was castrating sheep and he was describing how the sheep have to be lifted and operated on. I naively asked, 'And while this is happening, do the sheep cooperate?'

The farmer looked thunderstruck and said, 'Would you?'

Everybody got a laugh at my expense but it didn't do us any harm when the jury came to decide the case and assess my man's damages.

Witnesses have to remain outside the court and beyond the hearing of the court until it's their turn. This is to stop them hearing what the earlier ones have said and tailoring their version to fit. Collusion is suspected if an earlier witness is seen talking to another who's yet to be called. When a court adjourned at 1p.m. the current witness was told not to discuss the case, but was seen in animated conversation with another witness over lunch. On the case resuming at 2 o'clock, I asked him: 'Did you have lunch with Witness X?'

He said, 'I can't remember.'

Better is the exchange a colleague once elicited in a similar situation.

Barrister, cross-examining the new witness: 'Do you know the person seated in the middle of the court?'

Witness: 'Yes.'

Barrister: 'He told you about the evidence of the others before you came in, didn't he?'

Witness: 'No he didn't.'

Barrister: 'He spoke to you before you came into court?'

Witness: 'Yes.'

Barrister: 'What did he say to you?'

Witness: 'He said you're a real prick.'

There's an exception to the rule about witnesses staying out of court. In criminal cases the police officer who laid the charge is officially a party to the proceedings and therefore present throughout, even though he or she will give evidence last. Having heard all the earlier prosecution evidence, such a witness is in the ideal position to plug a few holes in the case. And that's what they sometimes try to do.

Police are usually good witnesses, which is scarcely surprising, considering they're in fact trained professionals at it. Deliberate lying by the police is uncommon, though I've certainly seen it. But police are partial and inevitably want to win. Their evidence carries a lot of weight. For a magistrate to disbelieve a police witness was once an impossibility; now it's just a rarity.

One purpose of cross-examination is to weaken the other side's case, and for this, social media is an absolute gift. The stuff people post about themselves and others! There seem to be no inhibitions left.

The father of an assault victim told the court how his son's life had been ruined, how he never went out any more and was physically constrained by ongoing pain. Meanwhile the kid's social media posts included lurid accounts of raging and getting drunk, going dirt-bike riding and even sky-diving. I had a recent photo of him wearing a witty T-shirt that read 'Instant arsehole – Just add alcohol.' Thank you, Facebook.

Cross-examination can produce surprises, and sometimes disaster. Your aim is to extract concessions that help your side. While you want to maximise the benefit, there's a risk you'll ask one question too many and undo your good work. There's no way of knowing when to hold back. You rely on your intuition.

One classic story of a question too many came in a case over a brawl in which the victim's ear had been bitten off. A prosecution witness conceded he hadn't actually seen the accused bite off the ear. The barrister should have left it at that but asked, 'So how do you know he did?'

The answer came: 'Because I saw him spit it out.'

I've made similar mistakes myself from time to time, though never as spectacularly as that – nor as disatrously as in this old-time English case, which I can't resist quoting.

A young man was on trial for having sex with a girl under sixteen. He denied intercourse and said he and the girl had merely been lying in the long grass canoodling. The prosecution called an old farmer who'd seen the pair from a distance. Defence counsel asked him: 'When you were a young man did you never take a girl for a walk in the evening?'

The farmer: 'Aye, that I did.'

Counsel: 'And did you never sit and cuddle her on the grass in a field?'

The farmer: 'Aye, that I did.'

'And did you never lean over and kiss her while she was lying back?

'Aye, that I did.'

At this point the barrister should have stopped, but he didn't. 'And anybody in the next field, seeing that, might easily have thought you were having sexual intercourse with her?'

'Aye, and they'd have been right.'

18

Dressed the Part

Fashion tips for court

Appearances count; everyone knows this. It's why people choose to dress the way they do. But the question is: what do they want to convey? The answer's relevant to both lawyers and their clients. Take the lawyers first.

In the higher courts a barrister wears a wig and gown. Wigs are made of horsehair by craftsmen in London. They came in with King Charles II, whose father was beheaded and had more mistresses than you could poke a stick at. Before then lawyers wore velvet bonnets. A barrister's wig costs heaps. I bought mine in 1987 and it cost $800 even then. These days the going price has tripled – and that's for a normal-shaped head.

Critics complain that wigs make courts formal and intimidating but I'm in favour of them. Courts are serious places; I don't think they should be warm and fuzzy. Not everyone agrees, such as the students I once encountered attending court as part of their university course in social science. One of their criticisms was that courts were too judgmental! I bet they earned a Credit for that observation.

I lost my wig one day while walking back to chambers from the County Court. I'd taken it off and tucked it under my arm. That was officially against the Bar Rules, which stipulate that if you're 'robed' you have to wear the lot. Perhaps it served me right, but my motive was modesty. Personally, I don't care to parade in my finery out of court – unlike plenty of my colleagues who enjoy strutting along William Street like cockerels.

I must have dropped the wig in the street. It probably met its fate in a Melbourne City Council road-sweeping machine. Lying in the gutter, it must have looked like a run-over cat, an albino perhaps. Anyway, that was the end of my eight hundred bucks.

I didn't lose the rest of the clobber because I was wearing it: a black robe, a black bar jacket and bands. The jacket is like a waiter's vest and the robe is something like Zorro used to wear. Bands are the white tabs that cheapskate barristers wear round their necks instead of a jabot. Even bands aren't cheap. They cost about $90, though I got my mum to make mine out of an old bed-sheet.

The loss of the wig altered my career path. For the County or Supreme Courts I needed to borrow one. Sometimes my friends were wearing theirs so I had to run from pillar to post, trying to bot someone else's. It was such a hassle I ended up in jurisdictions where a wig isn't needed, the Magistrates' Court mostly. That's my excuse anyway.

For male barristers, all that's needed in the Magos' Court is a suit – one from Dimmey's will do, though I've also got fancier ones that I had tailor-made in Hanoi. I took ages to choose the fabric but they all turned out looking the same, something like a Sicilian undertaker might wear.

I have a choice of ties. I wear the dark, gloomy ones for serious cases and add a dash of colour for something more light-hearted – an amusing shop theft, say. My shirts are of two kinds. The best ones are from Hanoi again, where the people are the same size as me. They're famous brands you've never heard of like Valentino and Sadoga. I wear them for private clients who pay better. For Legal Aid customers I wear white shirts. They look like school shirts because they are school shirts. Size 16 if you must know.

I *have* to dress as I do; my clients don't. They have more choice and I sometimes wonder about the way they exercise it.

One lass turned up to court recently with two black eyes. I feared she'd been bashed by her boyfriend but her mouth was black as well, as if she'd spent the morning sucking a felt pen. She told me she was a Goth; it was her persona. I'd thought Goths were medieval Germans who built cathedrals but these days they're members of a teenage sub-culture. My young client was making a statement of resistance to mainstream notions of passive femininity. Good for her!

Incidentally, there's another group I run into called Emos, from the word 'emotional'. An expert tells me the two groups are opposites, insofar as Emos want to kill themselves, while Goths want to kill everyone *except* themselves. It was simpler when there were only bodgies and widgies.

My client another day was a young bloke whose spiky hair was so intricate it must have taken hours to arrange. He had two gold studs in each ear, a gold bracelet, so many gold rings they looked like knuckle-dusters and a gold necklace with a miniature ingot dangling outside his shirt. 'What's your occupation?' I asked.

'I'm on Centrelink,' he said.

I told him: 'Mate, you look like an advert for the Sovereign Hill Gold Museum. Let's get rid of the baubles.'

He did so reluctantly. 'I like to be well-dressed,' he murmured.

It reminded me of that quotation: 'Being well-dressed confers a sense of inward tranquillity that even religion is powerless to bestow.' I can't remember who said it. A tailor probably.

Now it's a free country and tastes differ. People's appearance is their own business; they're not national parks that the rest of us should have a say in how they look. But there are times when conforming to someone else's standards can be advantageous. Getting into a nightclub in King Street is one; staying out of jail is another. When a buttoned-up, middle-aged, middle-class magistrate wields the power to send you to jail, it might pay to defer, if not to their dress sense, at least to their sense of propriety.

Don't think I'm over-dramatising. Judges and magistrates notice everything, and people smarter than me act on the principle that it pays to dress appropriately. What about our famous gangster matriarchs? They flounce around in stiletto heels with fluffed-up hair like trollops. As soon as they get charged with murder they take to fronting the jury in a cardigan, looking like everyone's favourite auntie – and that's without the sympathy value of a motorised wheelchair (now back in the props department, I understand).

Some of my customers just don't get it. One lass turned up in a T-shirt with the caption: 'I don't give a stuff'. I told her the slogan might not impress the magistrate. She protested, 'But I always wear it when I come to court!'

Another bloke asked me what I recommended. I was about to suggest he dress as he would for a job interview, but thought better of it. Instead I told him to wear the sort of clothes you wear when you go to church. He said, 'The last time I went to church I wore a nappy.'

Then there's personal grooming. Young bucks turn up looking as if they're trying to grow a beard or haven't learnt to shave. Honestly! You can get a plastic razor for about 60 cents if you buy them six at a time in Coles. Not a bad investment if the way you look can save you a few hundred bucks in fines.

And what about the man who leaves two shirt buttons undone to flaunt his hairy chest? Sure, some teenage girl might be attracted enough to climb into bed with him. In my experience, though, a magistrate is unlikely to think, 'Wow, what a he-man! I'll let him keep his licence so he can continue to endanger the public by driving like a maniac.' Decorum before vanity; just a suggestion.

In advising clients how to dress, I've stopped being too emphatic. I had a young bloke who was on bail for shop theft. A week before his court date he got arrested again: the police caught him pinching a pair of strides in Myers and found a shirt and tie from K-Mart in his bag. Asked his reason for stealing, he said, 'My lawyer told me to get good clothes for court.'

What about tattoos? At one time only sailors or ex-convicts had them. These days even members of the royal family – females included – brave the needle to get themselves permanently disfigured. It's strange how aristocrats aspire to the fashions of the lower classes; it used to be the other way round. I usually get clients with tatts to roll their sleeves down. Hands with tattoos can be kept out of sight. You hardly notice 'TRUE LOVE' spelled out on someone's knuckles if they keep their hands unclasped.

Not everyone can hide his tatts so easily. One middle-aged client of mine had more tattoos than a Polynesian tribesman. He had a bluebird on each cheek and a dolphin on the back of his head. Something on his forehead proved to be the head of a snake, the rest of which curled around his skull and merged into his hair. He had children's faces on his legs, a panther and a dragon at his throat. The last two were so densely inked they were hard to make out. He told me they were there to obliterate the dotted line he'd once sported round his throat with the words 'CUT HERE'. He claimed to have a dog on his buttocks chasing a rabbit up his anus. I took his word for it.

I appeared for a young man charged with criminal damage. He'd gone into a used-car yard and stomped on the bonnet and roof of one of the cars. Then he'd used the roofs of seven other cars as stepping stones and put dents in the lot of them. On the last one he danced a fandango and caved the roof right in. He turned up to court with vivid red hair and a ring through his nose.

I said. 'You'd make a better impression without the ring. Does it come out?'

'No.'

'What about we cut it off. I've got some pliers in the car.'

'No way!' he protested. 'I've been on antibiotics for three weeks and the infection's only just gone down. I'm not going to take it out now.'

He gave his occupation as 'Going to demos' and told me he hated fat, capitalist pigs. I think he was just going through a phase. He probably runs his own computer software company these days.

Migrant Australians set a much better example than the natives in dressing for court. Where the Australian underclass dresses down, migrants dress up. They know they're going to be the centre of attention and they're eager to look their best. They sport fancy designer clothing to project an air of sophistication and high status. They're aware no-one can tell a Hugo Boss suit unless the label's showing, so they make sure the label does show.

The first time I saw the phenomenon I thought the wearer had a Post-it label dangling off his sleeve. In fact it was a temporary label. They're tacked on with a couple of stitches so customers can flick through the racks in shops and find their favourite brand without pulling the clothes off the hangers. The labels are intended to be removed, but fashion-conscious migrants, Indians especially, leave them attached. They also pull their sleeves back so their Rolex watches show.[9]

With one migrant client I made a useful discovery by chance. He was a shoplifter of Vietnamese background who'd been caught red-handed. Pleading guilty was in his best interests but my advice was falling on deaf ears. His extended family were at court, nice people, but not much help in getting the kid to see reason.

---

[9] I don't bother to flaunt my own Rolex. I got it in a street market in China, where it would have been made in some sweatshop for two dollars (just like the real ones).

While we were waiting for his case to start, I asked his family by way of small-talk what they thought of my suit. They were a bit taken aback. 'Your suit?' they asked.

'Yes. Do you like it?'

'Very nice.'

'Look where it's made.' I flicked open the coat to show a label in the lining which read 'Cong Ty May – Quoc Tuan' (plus a few accents and squiggles over the vowels). It was one of my $120 ones from Hanoi. I'd only mentioned it to demonstrate some multicultural empathy, but the effect was miraculous.

'Oooh!' they cooed with delight. 'Your suit from Vietnam!'

'Yes.'

'You go Vietnam?'

'Yes.'

'You like it?'

'Loved it! Terrific!'

It was like magic. They were all smiles now. The family whispered among themselves. 'Okay, we talk him. He plead guilty now.'

I'm toying with the idea of assembling a selection of tailors' labels.

I could put a patch of Velcro inside my jacket and attach the appropriate one to mollify clients of other backgrounds. One in Greek would be especially useful.

19

Bods in Blue

Dealing with the police

People in this world are of two kinds: those who feel safer when they see a policeman and those who feel less safe. I belong to the first group, my clients to the second.

A famous boss of London's Metropolitan Police once defined a good police force as one that catches more crooks than it employs. By that measure, Australian police forces aren't bad. Standards do wax and wane, though. Years ago wags used to say Victoria had 'the best police force money can buy'; these days it's hard to say which state takes the honours.

I have a lot of dealings with police, and friends ask me what they're like. I tell them the cops are just normal people like you and me, except they can beat the crap out of someone without getting into trouble. I'm kidding, of course; sometimes they do get into trouble.

Not long ago some police in a Victorian country town faced court for assaulting two hoons. It was all on video because the cops forgot the in-car camera was running. So there they were on Channel 7, punching and kicking the pair fairly savagely. Opinions about the incident varied. Callers on talk-back radio ran nine to one in the cops' favour. By contrast, two hard-bitten senior sergeants I know were quite shocked and thought the cops deserved jail. They didn't go to jail, of course; they got good behaviour bonds. Supposedly, we're all bound by the same laws, but I assure you the hoons wouldn't have got bonds if the punching and kicking had been the other way round.

It goes without saying the police aren't all perfect. A copper once confided to me: 'I was in the force for twelve months before I charged someone with an offence I hadn't committed myself.' Mostly, though, their deficiencies are ones of omission. Like anyone else, they have days when they're not at their best. Sometimes they're slack or tired or impatient. Sometimes they do favours, cut corners or turn a blind eye. They're clannish and stick together; in fact, they have the same kind of tribal loyalty to each other that criminals do. Otherwise they're exactly like ordinary people – neither more nor less virtuous. They just have more power.

To harmless senior citizens like myself, the police are polite and helpful. But younger people and ethnic minorities sometimes complain of the way the police treat them.[10] I'm sure they're often right: a job with power can attract bullies and people who enjoy throwing their weight around. Young, inexperienced coppers used to think they needed to act tough as a matter of course.

---

[10] This is called a Trust Deficit and it varies a lot. Among migrants from Afghanistan, for example, 90 per cent have 'a lot of trust' or 'some trust' in the police. For migrants from South Sudan the figure is 26 per cent. Source: 2015 Scanlon Foundation Survey.

In theory, police are answerable under the law like anyone else and their behaviour is supposedly subject to a high degree of accountability. I say in theory, because a police officer carries more clout than your ordinary citizen. A police member's word shouldn't be preferred over a civilian's just because he or she is in uniform, but that's exactly what happens. Without great effort and persistence, no ordinary citizen is ever likely to get redress for police misconduct.

The last time I looked at the figures, 85 per cent of complaints against police were 'unsubstantiated'. To succeed, a complainant needs almost irrefutable evidence. There's more chance of that in this age of CCTV and mobile phones, but it did occasionally happen in the old days. A colleague told me of one watertight case where his client was belted so hard the buckle left a 'Victoria Police' imprint on his bum!

Two years ago I ran a case in which a child witness had twice been spoken to by police. His second statement differed from what he'd said first. We wanted to get hold of the notes the police had taken of the first account. We served three separate subpoenas specifying exactly what notes we required from the police, but they were never produced. We argued the issue before the magistrate but my client couldn't afford the time or money to adjourn the case while the police complied. So we batted on without the notes and lost badly.

I lodged a formal complaint against the police on my client's behalf. It was a first for me. The complaint ran to four pages and was fully documented. I still consider it was entirely valid. The complaint went to the Ethical Standards section in the city. From there it was referred back to the very suburban police station we were complaining about!

The final determination was that no police had done anything wrong and it was all a misunderstanding. The complaint was shelved as unsubstantiated. The findings of the investigating officer were that only one police member had slipped up – and she'd now been counselled and retrained. So everything was fine.

In the course of the investigation, however, the police noticed my client had committed a minor infraction they hadn't bothered to charge him with earlier. So they laid a new charge. That was his punishment for daring to complain.

Being a police officer, though, is not an easy job. It carries definite risks and regularly calls for courage, both moral and physical. The police force is actually one of the most important and successful institutions to emerge from our way of life. Police in Australia are seen not as an oppressive force but as a community presence. Even so, they are probably the institution that's most taken for granted and, possibly, the least appreciated.

Police, incidentally, are pretty well paid. That's partly from their political sway, but also from the principle that they, like judges and magistrates, should be well paid to minimise the risk of corruption. The idea seems to work. In Australia no-one in their right mind would offer a bribe to a traffic cop; it's the last thing you'd do. Yet in many countries it's the first.

That's not to say our coppers are impervious to temptation. I've encountered a few cases where they've been on the take or where drugs or gambling money have disappeared. Nevertheless – though I can't speak for old-time bash-artists or drug squad detectives – the integrity and decency of your average police member on general duties commands respect.

Of course, like the rest of us, police officers do sometimes tell lies. Mostly, they do it to get themselves or colleagues out of trouble, or somebody else into trouble. The first motive is illustrated by the reaction of some police caught speeding on speed cameras. A number claim they were trying to catch up with a passing car in which they'd sighted a crook on the wanted list. Yes, even with their wives, kids and holiday gear on board they exceeded the speed limit to try and apprehend a dangerous felon. No arrests were ever made, though; it was always a case of mistaken identity. Give us a break!

As for getting someone else into trouble, I think it's rare for police to give false evidence against a person they believe to be innocent. But it's far from uncommon for a police officer who believes an accused to be guilty (as they generally do) to embroider and exaggerate the evidence to help secure a conviction. This kind of thing arouses the hatred of the criminal class. Such is their sense of fair play, they think it's fine to tell a pack of lies themselves, but not for the police to bend the truth.

The police I deal with most are the prosecutors, who in general are fair opponents. It's not them, but the investigating police, who occasionally get over-zealous and gild the lily. Mind you, prosecutors don't like to lose and a few occasionally turn sour when they do. On our side, we lose graciously because we get so much practice.

Sometimes I visit police stations to speak to prosecutors or get copies of documents. I push open the door and enter the lions' den.[11] This morning the

---

[11] Such casual encounters are less frequent these days. Prosecutors' offices are now fortified with locked doors and intercoms.

sergeant in charge of crosswords looks up from his desk and scowls. Having finished the cryptic crossword, he's on to the sudoku. He takes a sip from a mug of coffee and affects to resent my intrusion: 'What do *you* want?' he bellows. The inscription on his mug reads: 'If you're looking for sympathy, it's in the dictionary between shit and syphilis'.

I'm not looking for sympathy, though. I've actually come for copies of some witness statements, but I'm in a teasing mood and I say, 'I'm here to get justice.'

'Well, you're in the wrong place,' booms the sergeant. 'You know our motto: "Better an innocent man gets convicted than no-one gets convicted"!'

Apart from this banter I receive cooperation. In court I do my job, but out of court I'm not deliberately difficult with the police. If you give them a hard time, they make things hard back for you. No surprise in that; reciprocity is practised among all species of primates. Zoologists record it among mandrills and chimpanzees; I observe it among police prosecutors.

To cite another example of my cordial relations: I was invited one year to the local prosecutors' Christmas party. Besides myself, only one other barrister got an invitation. We felt quite flattered but wondered why it was just us. The sergeant explained, 'You were the only two not to win a contest against us this year'!

In court we cop a bit of ribbing too. One day I was waiting my turn while a fellow barrister addressed the court. I noticed the prosecutor taking notes, which was unusual for a prosecutor, especially this one. Leaning closer, I saw he was drawing four vertical strokes with a fifth slashed at an angle across them, the way prisoners in films scratch on walls to keep count of their captivity. It turned out the prosecutor was keeping a tally of the 'ums' and 'ers' uttered by my colleague. He lost interest and gave up when the count reached a hundred!

Some prosecutors, incidentally, study law part-time (partially at public expense) and do their assignments in working hours. Once they graduate some change sides and become defence counsel. It's interesting to see the transformation. As police prosecutors, backed by the full resources of the state, they're insouciant, confident, carefree. Once they swap sides they become as serious and harried as the rest of us.

I also have a bit to do with police jailers, the coppers in charge of prisoners held in suburban police cells.[12] When I arrive to see a client, I'm first made to wait in the police station foyer where an illuminated sign flashes: 'Your presence has been noted. Please wait', and where I know they're behind the one-way glass, chatting about their weekend. After a suitable delay they let me through to the watch-house counter where I sign in.

Nowadays lawyers confer with their clients in a proper interview booth. In days gone by you'd meet them in a corridor with the cops standing by, pretending not to listen. If you were really lucky in those days, you'd get ten minutes in private in an interview

---

12 In many places Protective Services Officers have now taken over these duties.

room. For my convenience the police once placed a client of mine in an interview room with me. After I'd left, my client remained there unattended and carved up the plaster walls with a twenty cent piece. He scratched 'Sergeant Glover is a cunt' and copped an extra charge of criminal damage for his trouble.

Now I knew Sergeant Glover, and he wasn't a bad bloke, but I challenged him. I said, 'How would you know it was my client? It could have been anyone. Most people hold that opinion of you.'

He said, 'We know it was your client because the room's only just been re-painted. The walls were perfect before you two went in. So if it wasn't him, it must have been *you!*'

This particular client was far from the only one harbouring animosity towards the police. Being sceptical of authority is a distinct trait in the Australian character, and in some ways it's a good thing. But there are those who take it to extremes and the police are inevitably the target for the disgruntled and anti-social.

I've just been watching a one-hour security video of one of my clients in a police cell. Granted he's a nutter, it still illustrates what the police have to deal with. For the first ten minutes my man pounds and kicks at the cell door. Next he soaks pieces of toilet paper in the toilet bowl and flicks them at the CCTV camera mounted in the ceiling. His aim's pretty good and soon the lens is spattered with droplets of water. He's gesticulating angrily at the camera all the time, of course.

At some point he loses his shirt (I don't see how; I'm skipping the boring bits). The only loose article in the cell is a cushion and he rips that into pieces. At this point an aerosol can of capsicum spray becomes visible at the bottom of the screen, held at arm's length by a rubber-gloved hand. A policeman comes into view, followed by three other gloved coppers who collect the pieces of the cushion while the first keeps my client at bay.

As soon as they're gone my man takes his pants off and points his backside at the camera. Then he sticks a finger up his arse, sniffs it and waves it belligerently. I just wish I'd watched the video before I shook hands with him!

Another time at the watch-house counter I could hear a couple of prisoners screaming and carrying on in the cells. I said to the jailer, 'I don't know how you put up with them.'

He replied, 'We don't know how you lawyers do.'

I said, 'But we only deal with them one at a time. You've got four cells full.'

The copper smiled. 'Yeah, but we don't have to be nice to them.'

Central to police power is the use of weapons. In my younger days police didn't carry firearms, but those days are long gone. Cops head out now in body armour, their belts dangling with baton and gun, and with other dangerous toys strapped to their thighs. Capsicum spray (they call it the 'party pack') is old hat. Their favourite gizmo now is the Taser, an electro-shock device which disables its target by 'neuro-muscular incapacitation'. It's meant to be reserved for absolute emergencies, but once a gadget is in the arsenal it's sure to be used. History is full of examples of weapons of last resort that are deployed the next day.

My client Marlo was one of the first in Victoria to be on the receiving end of a Taser. The local cops had been issued with it experimentally just days earlier and they must have been itching to try it out. Their opportunity came when Marlo had a barney with his girlfriend and she ordered him out of the house. She was a vindictive trouble-maker and he knew better than to argue. He started to pack his bag to spend the night at a mate's place. While he was gathering some belongings from another room, she slipped an old rifle barrel, a rusted length of metal tubing he'd found in the bush, into his bag.

Once he'd left, the girlfriend phoned the police and told them Marlo was at a certain address, armed with a gun. In spite of her history of making false complaints, the cops decided the situation called for immediate use of their new Taser. Four cars sped out to cordon off the house where Marlo and his mate were sitting in the lounge watching videos.

Partway through the evening Marlo went out to his car to grab another tape. As he walked towards it, he told me, a gang of masked strangers rushed at him. He turned and made a dash for the house and was promptly zapped with 50,000 volts. It felled him instantly in a spasm of involuntary twitching, which the police interpreted as resisting arrest. In the ensuing scrimmage (eight against one) Marlo was dragged along the ground and capsicum-sprayed into the bargain.

He was charged with umpteen offences and the Tasering wasn't even mentioned in the summary of facts. The prosecutor wasn't aware Tasers were in use and didn't believe me till he saw the pictures we had of Marlo's burns. Then it was all stops out for the coppers to cover their backs and justify themselves. Marlo got his picture in the local paper, complaining about police brutality. I don't know what happened to his formal complaint; found to be unsubstantiated, probably.

Don't think I'm unsympathetic to the police. I get to see some of the difficulties they labour under – and not just from the crims they're dealing with. They also battle a deskbound bureaucracy that smothers them with paperwork, idiocy and managerial jargon. There are mission statements, slogans and promises to provide 'service excellence to everyone'. Yes, the police force is now the 'police service', as if the coppers are ministers of religion or sex workers – who seem to be the only people these days who claim to actually perform a service.

I remember when POLICE in capital letters on police cars was changed to lower case to make it less confrontational! Now it's the opposite; they've got to look more authoritative. So in a $30 million exercise of waste and stupidity, Victoria changed the colour of its police uniforms. In a bonanza for the Bangladesh clothing industry, all current uniforms were junked and replaced by ones in a colour called 'Salute Blue' – which is virtually black.

It's laughable to think that somebody gets paid for these brainwaves, plus all the meetings, verbiage, networking, PR, handwringing and so-called community consultation! Why not let the coppers just get on with the job!

Until recently, Victoria Police were overwhelmingly Anglo-Celtic. There are now, finally, a smattering of Asian faces, though I fear some still have an uphill battle fitting in. The change is good for two reasons. First, on principle, I think the police force should reflect the mix of the Australian population. Secondly, in practical terms, police members from ethnic communities are now indispensable.

A policeman told me how he needed to interview some Sri Lankans, all with five- or six-syllable names. He phoned the house where the first one lived and arranged to speak to him. Since the fellow was busy doing a sixteen-hour shift at his local 7-Eleven, another of the twelve residents helpfully went down the police station and was interviewed in his place. Later, when the police needed to speak to that particular man, he'd already been interviewed, so a third one stood in and impersonated *him.* By the time the cops were up to the fourth witness it was almost impossible to unscramble who was who.

Another time I was waiting in a police station to see a client when the cops asked me hopefully if I spoke Chin Hakka. They had a Burmese suspect who couldn't speak English and they'd been waiting three hours for an interpreter. When the interpreter finally arrived, it transpired he belonged to some ethnic sub-group which had been feuding with the suspect's crowd for the past thousand years and they refused to speak to each other.

Strangely, even admirers of the police can create problems for them. My client Ronnie Cleghorn was one; he idolised coppers and aspired to be one himself. One evening at a nightclub he helped the crowd controllers detain a female suspected of stealing a patron's handbag. He flashed a police badge and took the girl away. Half an hour later the Fitzroy police turned up to collect the suspect, only to be told she'd already been handed over.

So the cops put out an all stations alert to catch the fellow impersonating a police officer (maximum sentence:

two years imprisonment). When they caught up with Ronnie he explained it was all a misunderstanding. He'd shown his ID on entering the nightclub and they'd jumped to the wrong conclusion. That police badge in his wallet came from an ornamental plaque he'd bought at the police museum; he'd sewn it into his wallet purely for decorative purposes.

When the police searched Ronnie's place they found the badge wasn't his only purchase from police sources. His wardrobe was full of caps, uniforms and paraphernalia only serving police are allowed to have. The copper who conducted the raid told me Ronnie had more badges than the Chief Commissioner! He was charged under the *Police Regulation Act* with possessing 'police accoutrements' and released on bail. You may not have known such a charge exists, so take care if you're tempted to buy one of those $60 police charity koalas with the blue and white ribbons. (Incidentally, the koalas are the only ones these days still wearing proper, traditional police blue.)[13]

Anyway, it turned out Ronnie hadn't even paid for his stuff. He'd bought it at the official police shop and booked it up in the name of a sergeant from the water police. The bills had gone out to a bogus address and the first the sergeant knew was when the shop manager reported him to be disciplined for unpaid bills. So the hunt was on again for Ronnie Cleghorn.

In the meantime Ronnie had donned his new purchases and flashed enough badges to get himself enrolled in the Police Savings Cooperative. Once he'd got his cheque book he went around town passing dud cheques and committing a heap of other frauds. He had a mania all right: when he fronted court he wanted to wear his uniform! He ended up going to jail, where his police accoutrements would have proved a distinct liability.

---

[13] Old stock only, I now notice. Sadly, the new ones are in black now, just like the humans.

I've acted for others on similar charges, though on a lesser scale. One pinched a police cap, intending to cut off the chequered band to make a chess board! I've also heard of a policewoman's cap turning up in a brothel. Apparently they had nurses' caps, school hats and so on, and the customers paid extra for the girls to wear a hat that matched the fantasy of their choice.

As for impersonating a policeman, another of my clients was accused of going to a house in the middle of the night, shouting 'Open up! Police!' He swore he'd actually shouted, 'Open up, please', but he couldn't explain why he was wearing a peaked cap at the time.

Yes, it's always easy for words to be misconstrued. I caught one prosecutor on a bad day as he was tackling a mountain of paperwork. Looking up, he muttered, 'Same shit; different bucket!'

I protested: 'Excuse me! That's my clients you're referring to.'

'Wrong again,' he said. 'I'm talking about you bloody lawyers!'

20

The Male Member

Sexual offences

'If you don't mind my saying so, men's dicks get them into a lot of trouble.' Thus spake my colleague Madeline one day, and she isn't wrong.

Sex, of course, is inescapable. People find it of absorbing interest and it intrudes into everything, the law included. Sexual offences form part of every legal code and have always been among the most serious of crimes. Magistrates' Courts, though, deal only with relatively minor sex offences. Even so, I'm sometimes disconcerted at what some of my clients get up to.

Some men, I've learned, enjoy waving their dicks around in public. They do it in parks, shopping centres, outside pubs and standing at the side of the road while the traffic drives by. My niece tells me weirdos used to turn up in the bushes at the back of her private girls' school. The girls used to rush over to have a laugh and call out ribald remarks – a good way of dealing with it.

One of my clients used to masturbate at home in full view of a bus stop outside his front window. I used to think flashers like that were abnormal, but it turns out I'm wrong. We got a psychological report on the bloke which explained that he had no intention of attracting attention and 'no deviant arousal needs'. Indeed, he possessed a very healthy psychological profile, with no evidence of psycho-sexual disorder. He simply had high emotional spontaneity and 'his masturbatory experiences' were part of this spontaneity. Great! That explained it! Everything was apples – except his wife was kind of pissed-off, not to mention the mago he faced further down the track.

Another bloke was a Peeping Tom with a taste for pinching women's undies off washing-lines. Arrested in someone's garden in the middle of the night, he told the cops he was only there to steal the bird-bath. Again, you might have thought he was something of a perve but no, it turned out he wasn't at all. He shelled out two grand for a psych report and got one saying that he, too, was pretty much normal, with a low risk of reoffending into the bargain.

The report was twelve pages long and I highlighted the helpful passages. Unfortunately, the magistrate read the report with more attention than I'd bargained for. Whereas I emphasised paragraph 31 – 'not a sexual deviant', he noticed paragraph 11 – 'scored high on the scale for voyeurism'. Asked how I reconciled the two, I stammered, 'It depends what you call a sexual deviant', which was the best I could think of at the time. From the mago's expression I could see things weren't going too well, but it still took me aback when my man copped six months jail on the spot.

I'm not suggesting the community should have to put up with this sort of thing, but standards change so quickly it's hard for your average pervert to know at any given time what's permissible and what isn't. In my youth we had to sneak a look at the National

Geographic magazine – preferably the issue about the Aztecs, with the drawings of bare-breasted maidens. Teenagers these days can see things at the click of a mouse which would have made our parents' hair stand on end.

One young client of mine was charged with waving his cock around at a supermarket checkout. He was drunk and had gone in with his mate late at night to buy some Nurofen for his impending hangover. The mate was at court with him, trying to be helpful. 'Couldn't we say the cashier made a mistake?' he asked. 'You know, like it wasn't his cock.'

'What was it then?' I asked. 'A salami ready to be scanned?'

'Something like that.'

'What, without a barcode on it?'

It's not just drunken hoons who indulge in this sort of activity. Some years ago another client was so well-dressed and respectable-looking I missed him in the foyer of the court. I was on the lookout for a sleazebag but this chap could have passed for the secretary of a Rotary Club.

He'd been on Platform 1 at Flemington Bridge Station, with a woman on Platform 2 facing him across the tracks. She was reading a magazine while she waited for her train, and every time she looked up there was my bloke with his cock out, playing with it. A train stopped on his side but he didn't board it. As it moved off he was still there so she phoned the police.

When they turned up they found my client standing on the platform: mid-forties, blue tie and a pin-stripe suit. He denied everything, though he was pretty pissed. 'Well,' said the coppers, 'you're the only person here who answers that description. Why would she make it up if it wasn't true?'[14]

'I wouldn't know,' he shrugged.

A surveillance camera was operating on the platform, though some of the

---

[14] Although it's the obvious question to ask, the High Court has ruled it impermissible in court. It subverts the burden of proof by suggesting that lack of evidence of a motive to lie means there is no motive to lie. Palmer v. R, (1998) 193 CLR 1, 9.

action was out of range. Before I went to the trouble of going into the city to view the footage (as you had to in those days), I thought I'd find out if there was anything worth seeing. I phoned the police informant and asked whether the man in the video looked like my client. He said, 'It's him all right.'

'And does it show him committing the offence?'

'Not exactly. What it shows is him walking over to a rubbish bin, pulling his pants down and having a crap in it!'

I asked my client whether that was what he'd done.

'Well, the toilets were locked,' he protested. 'I had to have a shit somewhere.'

'What about finding a secluded spot?'

'There weren't any.'

'Or behind a tree?'

'No trees.'

'Or catch a train to another station? A train stopped that you could have boarded.'

'Why should I put myself out? Anyway, what's the problem?'

'Well,' I said, 'a court might think it's a bit over the top to shit into a railway litter basket in broad daylight. It might think that if you did that you might have done the other.'

'Do you really think so?' he asked.

Here's another way a bloke can really get himself into trouble. He's a grey-haired Asian man in his sixties and two girls approach him in a shopping centre car park, asking for a lift to the city. He agrees to take them as far as Caulfield and on the way the younger one asks him to buy them alcohol. If he will, she promises, her friend will give him sex. He stops at a bottle shop and buys six cans of Jim Beam and Coke and the girls drink two each while he drives to a park.

By now he's telling them how beautiful they are and trying to touch them up. In fact he later admits to the police that he touched the breast of one of them. The police ask him if he touched the nipple. 'What's a nipple?' he asks back. He's only lived in Australia for sixteen years so his English isn't good enough to know words like that.

Once at the park the girls climb out while my man gets into the passenger seat and reclines it. The younger girl passes a knife to the older one. They disagree later whether they had the knife to rob the old bloke or only for protection.

Whichever it is, the older one opens the car door and stabs my man twice in the thigh and both girls run off. The wounds are deep and the bloke's losing a lot of blood. He calls for help but the street's deserted and no-one comes. He wraps the seat cover round his wounds and succeeds in driving home, where his wife and daughter ring triple zero.

An ambulance is on its way but the police arrive first to find the old bloke faint from loss of blood. They ask him what happened and, since his wife and daughter are listening in, he tells them he was attacked by two Indians in a car park. He spends three nights in hospital, with a further month off work.

Once he's back on his feet the police get him to come down to the station to give them extra details. Since he's already committed to a false version, he elaborates on it: terrified of Indians now, so much blood, thought he was going to die, etc. He signs the statement, acknowledging that a false declaration is perjury.

The police continue looking for Indian men but enquiries turn up two females involved in a separate knife robbery around the same time. The two are aged twelve and fourteen! They spill the beans and the police call my man back for another interview in which he admits to having told them a load of porkies. The cops have his son's phone number as a contact and the son gets to learn the truth. The fellow's wife isn't told, though, nor his daughters, nor his extended family, nor his boss. The man fears he'll lose his reputation and standing, his job, his marriage. Everything.

He manages to keep a lid on the incident. He's lucky not to be charged with abduction or attempted child sex. Instead he gets away with a fine for making a false statement. When it's all over he asks if he can claim crimes compensation. Talk about pushing his luck! He was hoping to have sex with a fourteen-year-old; if he'd succeeded he'd be doing about six years in jail.

Another bloke is done for offensive behaviour. All I'm told is the fellow's defence: 'My penis was out but I wasn't actually masturbating'. So what was it doing out? Taking a breath of fresh air? Getting a tan?

The young man comes from a religious family and brings his father to court. The father's in his sixties with a beard like an Old Testament prophet. He wears a sports coat of man-made fibres and forgets to turn his mobile phone off. It rings in court (ring-tone: 'The Hallelujah Chorus') and off he scuttles, not to be seen again until after his son's been convicted of wilful and obscene exposure.

The magistrate gives the bloke a dressing down and tells him his conduct was predatory. 'Predatory?' asks the bloke later. 'Isn't that something to do with crocodiles?'

Once the court adjourns the son disappears but the father hovers around because he's lost his Christadelphian magazine, which is running a serial of the Book of Job in verse. We check the seats in court but there's no sign of it; now he's got a gap in his collection. I promise I'll keep a look out for his lost property. That's me, so obliging.

Of course the main focus these days – and correctly so – is the protection of children. There's much hysteria about strangers and predators but most of it is misplaced. Statistically, children are at greatest risk from members of their own household. The most dangerous men are the successive partners of single mothers. But never mind that; these days any male can come into the firing line.

Here's one way it happens. An elderly man goes to a park. He's there every Wednesday evening when Little Athletics is on. He's not connected with any of the kids, so automatically the parents assume he's a pedophile. Nobody bothers to approach him and ask him why he's there every Wednesday, though it wouldn't have been hard. After all, he's not a Hell's Angel, he's an ordinary-looking old bloke.

In fact, Fred isn't there just on Wednesdays. He's down at the park every day, including the six days of the week when Little Athletics isn't held. On those other days he looks at the birds, watches people walking their dogs, sometimes reads the paper. He's there every afternoon because he lives round the corner and his wife won't let him smoke anywhere near the house.

But the parents complain to the police about Fred and report his rego number. The cops trawl through their records and discover that twenty-six years earlier he'd been fined for obscene exposure. So he's charged with being a sex offender 'loitering in a public place frequented by children' and, if convicted, risks being put on the Sex Offenders Register for eight years. In the event, that doesn't happen, but only thanks to the common sense of the magistrate hearing the case.

Every state now has Sex Offender Registration laws. Registered offenders have to make an annual report to the police, as well as notify them of numerous events immediately they happen: buying a new car, moving house, changing a phone number or email address, getting a tattoo. All offenders have to give the same information whether their offending was serious or minor. No individual assessment is made of how dangerous each of them is. Courts can't even order offenders of particular concern to be more closely monitored.

In Victoria at the present time there are 8286[15] names on the register, increasing daily. Instead of the police keeping close watch on a couple of hundred men who are a definite danger, they spend their time keeping track of thousands of low-level offenders who've been caught in the net. The system costs millions and no-one knows whether it's really any use.

Sex offenders are placed on the register for eight years, fifteen years or for life. It's unclear where Parliament plucked those reporting periods from;

---

15 Of these, 960 are in jail, 1200 are outside Victoria, while others have died or completed their reporting obligations. As at May 2019 those being actively monitored numbered 4436.

apparently Victoria got them from New South Wales, which took them from the United States. There's no evidence such lengthy periods do any good, but they produce spiralling workloads for the police.

Victoria's legislation is a disgrace. The wording of the *Sex Offenders Registration Act* is so sloppy and illiterate that a registered sex offender can spend successive nights with a child without being liable to report the contact, provided each night is at a separate location. This isn't just my opinion; I won a case in court on the point. Afterwards I wrote to the police, the Law Reform Commission and the Attorney-General, pointing out the loophole (and suggesting how to correct it). Each of them passed the buck. The authorities, it seems, are interested in the appearance of action, not action itself.

Men have killed themselves rather than face charges – or even the suspicion – of child sex offending. No crime, not even murder, is so vilified in the Western world, and to be accused of it, even wrongly, can ruin a man's life. Even criminals take the high moral ground. According to them, it makes their own bashings, thefts and burglaries pale into insignificance.

One offence that automatically puts you on the register is making or possessing child pornography. Before the internet, making images meant photographing, but 'making' now includes downloading. For saving an image of a naked child, you can face jail for five years. In some states the law doesn't distinguish between naughty teenagers exchanging rude photos with each other and the worst kind of stuff which is truly cruel and depraved.

Nor, for that matter, does it distinguish computer-generated images which have harmed no child in their creation. The justification for extending the ban to those images is to protect public morals and ensure 'a safe environment for children'. Yet in Japan pornographic 'manga' comics and 'anime' cartoons of schoolgirls are ubiquitous, while Japanese streets are probably the safest in the world for women. A paradox.

Penalties are heavy for child pornography offences because the consumer is part of the chain of crime in the same way as receivers of stolen goods are. Just as those who buy stolen goods encourage thieves, so those who buy child pornography encourage child rapists. While most children in commercial child pornography are not Australian, nevertheless a child somewhere has suffered in its creation.

Individuals who facilitate the dissemination of child pornography go to jail. But if the Westpac Bank facilitates payments for it – not once, but thousands of times – nobody goes to jail. 'Sorry,' says the bank, 'it was a "systems error".' So nothing happens except the chairman and CEO get golden handshakes and move on. No wonder people get cynical.

Adult pornography is now legal in a way unimaginable a generation ago and so is the provision of sexual services, where the interest of the law is no longer moral but regulatory. Brothels are required to be zoned and regulated and those who comply deserve to be protected from competition that flouts the town planning rules. Take Mrs Wang for example. The local council were chasing her for allegedly providing sexual services at her health massage salon.

I marvel at the time needed to investigate such goings-on. The council relies on private investigators who find it necessary to pay multiple visits. Their statements are amusingly coy: 'A sexual service was then commenced ... which I immediately terminated.' But of course!

One day a council officer paid Mrs Wang a visit. Naturally, she didn't know the identity of the girls working there – they were all independent contractors who'd given her dodgy names. Mrs Wang had told them no hanky-panky was allowed, but they just ignored her. When the man from the council said that wasn't good enough, she passed him an envelope containing $2000 in cash. She said, 'You very nice man. This present for you.'

I warned Mrs Wang she was at risk of a charge of attempted bribery, but she didn't know the meaning of the word. She'd brought an English-Chinese dictionary with her and studiously riffled through its pages. When I explained she was charged with letting her girls masturbate the customers, she didn't know 'masturbate' either. She started to look it up, then said she'd let me know her defence later.

'Fine,' I said, 'I'll leave it in your hands.'

21

Behind the Dunny Door

Perve in a public toilet

The term 'chambers' is a fancy word for a barrister's office. As a dentist has a surgery and a mechanic has a workshop, so a barrister has chambers. Mine at one time were in the Equity Chambers building in Bourke Street. Its facade is heritage-listed but not the rest of it, especially not my room. It was the cheapest in the building, a tiny cell formed by closing off one end of a corridor.

The room was so narrow it could only hold a student desk and one visitor at a time. My visitor today was Mr Dunbar, who sat squeezed against the wall facing my bookcase. The bookcase was filled with out-of-date textbooks and random volumes of law reports. As a reference library it was useless; its intended function was to impress the clients. It didn't seem to impress Mr Dunbar, though, but then he didn't impress me. He was middle-aged and overweight, with pale watery eyes and a wide salacious mouth. His handshake was moist and flabby. He was charged with offensive behaviour in a public toilet.

It was an effort getting him to the point, but his story began one Friday on his way home from work. He stopped off at a shopping centre and bought some batteries, a packet of Lifesavers and a Tattslotto coupon. He took the escalators to the lower level and headed for the men's toilets. He entered a cubicle, dropped his daks and sat down to pick his Tattslotto numbers. So far so good.

Now came the strange bit. It so happened there was a hole in the partition between Mr Dunbar's cubicle and the adjoining one. While he was sitting minding his own business, an erect penis emerged through the hole and pointed in his direction. He leant over and gave it a sharp smack with the Tattslotto coupon and it disappeared from sight.

The next bit, though, was even stranger. For some reason Mr Dunbar couldn't explain, he decided to return the compliment and poked his own cock through the now-vacant hole. Of course he immediately thought better of it, he told me, and promptly pulled it out again. The next thing he knew, the police were breaking down the door.

Unluckily for Mr Dunbar, the occupant of the next cubicle was an off-duty policeman. He was using the toilet, he said, when a penis appeared through a hole in the partition and a voice called out, 'Suck this!'

The copper shouted, 'Police here! Stay where you are!' and the penis vanished. (I bet it did!) The policeman stood guard outside the locked cubicle while a member of the public raised the alarm. Other police arrived and when the occupant failed to open up, they forced the dunny door.

Mr Dunbar was pleading guilty. Having admitted to being the owner of the relevant phallus, he didn't have much choice. My job was to keep his penalty low, but he didn't offer me anything by way of mitigating circumstances. He didn't seem to understand that narrow-minded people like police, magistrates and the general public might find his behaviour objectionable.

Mr Dunbar denied any psycho-sexual maladjustment. He refused to see a psychologist. He said he'd consulted his family doctor, who'd told him there was no risk of his reoffending. After all, he was just a normal married man with teenage daughters. Of course, he hadn't mentioned the incident to his wife; he didn't want to upset her.

On the day of the hearing Mr Dunbar was waiting for me outside the suburban court house, pacing nervously on a patch of threadbare grass. He had one thing going for him, that he'd never been in trouble with the police before. As we climbed the court house steps, he finally volunteered something he thought might help. In his spare time, he told me, he was an assistant scout-master.

I flinched at the news. 'Let's forget about that,' I whispered. 'It may not help.' He looked disappointed.

We waited half the morning and the crowd in court thinned out, just as we'd hoped. Luckily, too, the acoustics were lousy so only those in the front row or two could hear the proceedings properly. The mago could hear, though, and I watched his reaction closely as the prosecutor read the police summary. His bushy eyebrows stood out like an insect's antennas and bristled every time the word 'penis' was mentioned. They rose in surprise when the police announced Mr Dunbar had no criminal record.

The mago gave me the nod and my plea was one of the briefest on record. The gist of it was: 'My client is forty-six years old. He's married with two children. He can't explain why he behaved this way, but he's never done anything like it before and he promises he'll never do it again. Thank you.' I sat down.

His Honour looked perplexed and asked if Mr Dunbar had sought medical advice. I told him of the GP's reassuring words, but he didn't look convinced. He fired off a few stern words at Mr

Dunbar and fined him $800, a fair bit at the time.

After that, I dismissed the case from my mind. Once they're over, cases are like bandaids; you peel them off and forget about them. But twelve months later Mr Dunbar was back in my chambers. In fact, it was a year to the day: extraordinary timing – maybe something to do with the planets or the phases of the moon. The case concerned another Friday night, another shopping expedition, another public toilet. This time it was worse.

For one thing, Mr Dunbar hadn't been at home when the police came round to serve the summons on him. They could have been discreet and left a card for him to contact them, but they chose to leave the papers with one of his daughters to pass on. There were two charges this time: indecent exposure and offensive behaviour. They covered two incidents, each involving a youth of seventeen. There was one big difference, though. This time Mr Dunbar maintained he definitely wasn't guilty.

Over the previous year he'd changed his shopping centre but not his routine.

As normal, he'd gone to the public toilet one Friday to fill in his Tattslotto coupon. Sure enough, an erect penis made its usual appearance, this time below the partition separating the cubicles. Mr Dunbar was curious enough to investigate who owned the mystery genitals. He peered under the partition to see a youth wriggling on the floor.

As any scoutmaster would, Mr Dunbar thought the fellow needed a thorough ticking-off. He exited his own cubicle and banged on the adjacent door. When the door opened, Mr Dunbar noticed the young fellow was holding a lewd magazine – which he immediately confiscated. He demanded the lad's name and address with a view to contacting his parents, but the youth made off.

Alas, there's a Friday in every week and the following one found Mr Dunbar at the public dunnies once again. As chance would have it, the very same youth was standing at a wash basin. Here was a second opportunity to reprimand the lad, but again he fled. A few minutes later, as Mr Dunbar was drying his hands at the hot-air blower, the young man came back, pointed in his direction and said, 'That's him.' Two security guards stepped forward and asked Mr Dunbar to accompany them to their office.

Now, just because a case is one person's word against another's, it doesn't mean they cancel each other out. If a witness is credible, he or she is believed. And here it wasn't just a matter of 'word against word'. There was also corroboration in the form of an immediate complaint. I warned Mr Dunbar that if he subjected the victim to the court process and lost, he'd lose any claim to leniency. It would make a bad situation worse.

Mr Dunbar, though, insisted the youth's story was a complete invention. So the wheels turned and the hearing date approached. As a rule, evidence comes out more strongly from the witness box than it looks on paper, but I was hoping this case would be an exception. Clearly young Bradley was a Friday night regular at the dunnies himself. I hoped he'd present in court as a smart-aleck and a liar.

On the day of the hearing I got a nasty surprise. A young lad was sitting between his mum and dad at the back of the court. He had a slight facial tic and spoke over-loudly. I whispered to the prosecutor, 'Not your witness, is he?'

'Sure is.'

'Has he got an intellectual disability?'

'That's right. Mild.'

'Nobody told me.'

'Pity your client didn't.'

People like Bradley can make impressive witnesses. They seem too guileless to tell lies and courts make allowances for any misunderstandings or obvious mistakes. In the witness box Bradley came across as simple and unsophisticated and painfully truthful. He said he was washing his hands when he noticed a man in the mirror, The man's trousers were around his knees and he was holding his dick in his hand. The man was Mr Dunbar.

My cross-examination made little impact. Bradley stuck to his story and denied any contortions on the toilet floor. I asked him about the first incident. 'Isn't it true you had a book with you?'

He looked uncomfortable and turned away. 'Yes.'

'A book with pictures?'

A pause. 'Yes.'

'Rude pictures?'

Another pause. 'Yes.'

I pushed my luck. 'And you took that book there specially, didn't you?'

'No, I didn't!' he burst out, pointing at Mr Dunbar. 'It was his! He gave it to me!'

When my client gave evidence, he was the exact opposite of Bradley. He looked shifty, he prevaricated, he 'forgot', he denied things he later had to admit. He conceded his trousers had fallen down when Bradley saw him in the mirror. Loose elastic, he said.

Our mago this time was another old-timer who didn't hesitate to find the charges proven. The prior conviction was read out and I half-heartedly suggested the court order a pre-sentence psychological report. I drew a blank; His Honour's face was stony and expressionless.

I launched into my submissions on sentence and said everything favourable about Mr Dunbar I could think of. His was an unfortunate case. His married life seemed problematic. He was willing 'to seek professional help', as the cliché goes. I also pointed out that Bradley had done well in the witness box and hadn't suffered any great trauma by coming to court. Quite the opposite: he'd been vindicated.

It went against my better judgment, but Mr Dunbar insisted I mention his scouting activities. I passed up a reference he'd brought from the Scout Association. It stated they hadn't received any complaints about Mr Dunbar, but the way it was worded you got the idea they felt like adding 'as yet'.

The mago heard me out, swung his eyes towards Mr Dunbar and told him to stand. He said, 'You have committed two disgusting offences. I'd be failing in my duty if I didn't send you to jail. I sentence you to be imprisoned for one month on the first charge and three months on the second. I order the sentences be served concurrently. Remove the prisoner.'

Mr Dunbar looked shocked; probably I did too. Three months in the slammer, I hadn't expected anything quite that bad. His antics weren't the sort of thing you want to see in a public toilet, but at the same time I didn't see Bradley as a victim of adult exploitation. It seemed to me that no great harm had been done, not enough for jail anyway. Maybe I was too broad-minded. These days, of course, the sentence would be a damn sight heavier; he'd be looking at years almost, not months.

I don't minimise the consequences of sexual abuse to children: I've read enough of the report of the Royal Commission into Institutional Child Sexual Abuse. But there's a lot of difference between brutal sexual assaults on defenceless children and shenanigans behind the dunny door with a semi-willing adolescent.

I lodged an appeal against the severity of the sentence and Mr Dunbar was released on bail to appear at the County Court. I knocked back the brief to run the appeal; I felt I'd misjudged things. A colleague took over and told me the outcome later. Things had gone badly there too. The appeal judge made the sentences cumulative. It meant Mr Dunbar copped an extra month.

22

Palm Tree Justice

Eight years in Papua New Guinea

As a break from all this high-powered stuff, let me offer a flashback to when I started out in the law. I actually began my career as a solicitor in Brisbane. I hated it; the weather was too hot. I thought if I had to endure a tropical climate I'd prefer somewhere less primitive (joke). So I transferred to the firm's Papua New Guinea office.

It was a very small operation. There was just the resident partner, an Australian, and a local secretary who came in every day from a neighbouring village. Within two months the partner had decided to abandon the law and open a bar in Manila. That left me to run the show. In the end I spent almost eight years as a lawyer in Port Moresby. It's where I learnt my bad habits.

Much of the work was civil litigation for insurance companies. Reports would come in of dreadful traffic accidents in the Highlands, trucks loaded with passengers going over cliffs and so on. The claim forms would naively record, 'Six seriously injured and four seriously killed.' I became an expert on death claims, which entailed calculating the financial loss to the family from the death of their loved ones. In the case of children I was able to prove, what with the saving on food, housing and education, that a negligent driver had actually done the parents a favour by killing off their offspring!

The highest court was the National Court, where the judges at the time were still white. The first case I did there was about a motor-cyclist who'd been hit and injured. My opponent was also a novice but, unlike me, oblivious to his limitations. Half-way through the case the judge announced a sudden adjournment. He sent a message that he wanted to see us both in his chambers. We wondered what we'd done wrong.

It turned out to be Melbourne Cup Day and His Honour was sitting with his feet on the desk and his ear glued to a transistor radio. In conversation after the race, my opponent asked him what he thought of our performance in court. The judge thought hard, no doubt searching for a gentle way to express himself. Finally he answered, 'I've seen worse.'

After a couple of years my firm merged with another one and I did more work outside Port Moresby. To run cases in the provinces I had to fly, as the capital had no road links with the rest of the country. Conditions out of town were exotic, to say the least. In the Highlands, for instance, witnesses would turn up to court wearing 'arse grass', a belt with a clump of foliage front and back.

Sometimes I went to Kieta on Bougainville, where the big copper mine was and the heat and humidity were almost unbearable. In the weatherboard court house there was no such thing as air-conditioning, though the judge had a fan under his desk. Soaked in sweat in our black robes, we lawyers argued our cases in a miasma of heat and ignorance, gradually losing energy and interest like clockwork toys running out of puff.

I remember one case where an expat had lost an eye after a hunk of copper ore shot off a conveyor belt at high speed. Our defence was that he should have seen it coming and blinked in time.

In order to catch the next day's flight back to Moresby, we sat late into the night. I was making my final submissions when I noticed the judge had nodded off. Coughing and shuffling papers didn't wake him and my opponent was no help as he was unconscious too. I just kept talking till I got to the end and sat down. In the silence that followed the judge gave a start, then opened his eyes and said, 'Thank you, Mr Challinger. Much obliged.' I assumed he was obliged I hadn't woken him earlier.

In my early days we had stenographers in National Court cases. They took everything down in shorthand and produced a typed transcript. They divided their time between the National Court and Parliament, for which they recorded Hansard. I felt abashed these highly skilled people worked so hard on cases as mundane as mine, but one of them once assured me that taking down Parliamentary debates was a far greater waste of time.

Some years my parents visited me and, for lack of other entertainment, occasionally came to court to watch. They once sat in on a matrimonial case in which a deadhead husband was describing all the nappy-changing and fatherly attention he claimed to lavish on his newborn child. My mum, a forthright lady, didn't believe a word of it and made an aside to my father. The remark was overheard and appeared in the transcript as, 'A voice: "Rubbish!"'

The only criminal law I did in those days was for white expatriates or black politicians. They were the only classes of client who could afford to pay for a private lawyer. I had a few Members of Parliament as clients and the odd provincial politician. One of the MPs answered an accusation of rape by declaring in Parliament that he hadn't committed a rape to the best of his knowledge. Another had trousers which tended to fall down whenever he was drunk, which was much of the time.

One provincial bigwig was charged with forgery and we flew a handwriting expert up from Australia to give evidence. We were on an island a thousand kilometres north of Port Moresby when the expert noticed something he'd missed earlier. The angle at which the letter T was crossed in the disputed document was so distinctive it virtually pointed to our man as the forger. We had to smuggle the expert down to the airstrip and get him off the island before the prosecution twigged.

Getting competent local staff was very difficult. Davara, the clerk who did our title searches and lodged documents, was so irreplaceable we couldn't sack him in spite of his many misdeeds. One weekend, for example, he came into the office and drank all the beer in the office fridge. His key didn't give him access to the toilet in the stairwell so he pissed in the waste paper bin. He didn't exactly fill it, but two dozen stubbies contain eight litres of liquid and most of it passed through his micturatory system. He thought he'd been considerate; he barely splashed the office carpet.

After he promised to give up drinking we entrusted him with the new office car. On the very first Saturday he got boozed, hit a culvert and did a somersault in it. The car was totally wrecked and he was lucky to climb out unscathed. We didn't sack him for that either.

A year later we discovered he'd been fiddling the books. We had him charged and he went to jail for eight months, during which time the office conveyancing system barely functioned. On the day of his release we collected him in the replacement office car and brought him back to resume work.

Davara harboured no ill feeling and regaled us with outrageous yarns about his time in jail. The warders used to simply release any prisoner who was from their tribe. (I already knew this: a friend's houseboy was sentenced to a year and was back at work the next morning.) The day Davara was sentenced he was taken to jail in a Black Maria. About a dozen male prisoners shared the van with one female. Most of them had sex with her on the way, with the woman calling out 'Next, please!' Davara claimed he didn't take part because it was too hot and sweaty.

Over the years I used to visit Bomana Jail occasionally to see clients. The whites, housed in a section of their own, were allowed to sit under a mango tree to confer with their lawyers. I had a Lebanese-Australian there awaiting trial for smuggling hashish. He was said to be the king-pin of a Sydney drug syndicate. One day another Lebanese turned up at the office, claiming to be his brother, and asking me to arrange a professional visit.

I did so and we drove out together in my doorless Suzuki jeep. As we sat with Abdul in the shade of the mango tree, the 'brother' whipped out a dictaphone. He passed it to Abdul, who started dictating in Arabic. I was worried about getting into trouble but Abdul assured me he was only sending a loving message to his mother.

Abdul had been caught at the airport picking up four suitcases of hashish which had come in unaccompanied on a flight from the Solomons. When the case was heard the police insisted on bringing the hashish into court as an exhibit, all 62 kilograms of it. It made no sense to do this unless they'd intended some to disappear in transit. The shipment was piled on the floor near the witness box, and in the windowless courtroom the sickly smell was overpowering. I went to the front and inspected the stuff, trying to look expert. I whispered to Abdul in the dock, 'I'll try and nick you a bit.'

He said, 'I'm glad you haven't lost your sense of humour.' He ought to have been cheerful himself as he only copped eight months.

Sometimes I was drawn into helping our National staff and their relations. Poor old Uncle Rabia, for example, was regularly charged with practising sorcery, a crime that carried a year's jail. Having somehow acquired a reputation as a puri-puri man[16] he was often accused when someone in the

---

[16] In the Motu language, a sorcerer.

village died. It didn't matter whether there was a clear medical cause for the death – a heart attack, say – because it was taken for granted Uncle Rabia's sorcery had caused the heart attack.

His cases followed the same pattern. Somebody died and the relations laid a charge under the *Sorcery Act.* The first hearing date at Port Moresby Magistrates' Court would attract a couple of truckloads of the deceased's family. The trucks would park outside the court and there'd be much angry milling around, with tempers running high. The proceedings would then be adjourned for a few weeks.

On the next date only one truckload of angry relos would turn up. Another adjournment would be granted and the process continued for as long as necessary. Usually, by the fourth adjournment even the widow had lost interest and the case would be struck out. Besides, by then someone else had usually died.

Adultery was also a criminal offence in PNG, though the law was very unevenly enforced. In some provinces adultery was regarded with abhorrence, while in others it was considered as natural as sneezing – and of no more significance. The law, though, applied only to 'automatic citizens' of PNG, that is to say, those born there. Theoretically, any expatriates were immune from prosecution.

In practice it didn't work that way. Some PNG citizens seemed to resent white expats dallying with their wives. So a white defendant who wanted to contest jurisdiction risked the case being adjourned off into Court 1 for legal argument and unwelcome publicity. It was usually wiser not to take the legal point, but enter a tactful plea of guilty in the seclusion of Court 2. This, coupled with an offer of compensation, would dispose of the matter with the minimum of embarrassment. My delicacy of expression on these occasions was sometimes wasted, and I remember one magistrate being unduly blunt. He turned to a cuckolded husband and snapped: 'That white man fuck your missus. He can pay fifty Kina. That's enough for you.'

When shenanigans resulted in pregnancy the Children's Court would hear what were called affiliation proceedings. Every Tuesday a stream of cases came up for hearing in the fibro court house behind the cold store of the Steamships Trading Company. The court would rule on paternity and order the father to pay support. In the absence of blood tests and DNA, the decision depended greatly on the baby's appearance.

One morning a very alluring Melanesian lass approached me in the street and begged me to come down to court and help her with her paternity case. She'd been living with a white man, she told me, but also carrying on a liaison with a PNG National. He was a Tolai, a member of a distinctive ethnic group from the Rabaul area, and she was claiming maintenance from him. She carried a baby boy in her arms, a cute little infant who looked unmistakeably Tolai.

The putative father denied paternity and was represented by a PNG lawyer. The court had no time to hear a contested case that day and before setting a hearing date, the magistrate asked us how long it would take. I suggested two hours and was stunned to hear my opponent, who brandished a thick, red-bound book, give an estimate of three days. I was even more staggered to hear that according to his client, the girl had given birth, not to one baby, but to twins. Furthermore, one was black and one was white!

My opponent delved into his book, whose title was something like 'Encyclopaedia of Bizarre Medical Facts'. It recorded several such instances, the most recent being in Peru in 1924. My lass was even said to have admitted to her Tolai lover that she'd produced two babies, announcing 'I made one for him and one for you.'

When I quizzed her after court she was evasive in the extreme. Follow-up enquiries at Port Moresby General Hospital were no help, as their records didn't seem to run to such details as whether a birth had been single or multiple. I bowed out of the case when the girl's implied offer of payment presented ethical problems – and possibly an allegation of triplets next time round! I learned later she'd actually given birth to just one child, but not the Tolai baby she'd brought to court; she'd just borrowed him from a friend for the occasion!

In PNG even familiar offences acquired a Melanesian flavour. A Portuguese client, Gustavo, owned a gold mine at Edie Creek, site of the famous 1930s gold rush. His mine was on a rugged mountain top and his house there no better than a shack. He was a short, stocky man who'd lived there with a local woman for years and could speak pidgin, but not English. He was charged with assaulting a man of the Goilala tribe.

In PNG Goilalas have a frightening reputation for cunning and violence. They're a tribe dominated by bloodshed, squalor and pride, and that's not just my opinion. An anthropology textbook reads: 'Ordinary hamlets are clusters of dreary hovels, and despite their ample leisure the Goilala prefer to satisfy the bare necessities of life with the minimum of effort and thought for the future. In this drab wasteland of meanness and indifference are two founts of relentless energy – pigs and vengeance.'[17]

Gustavo's case was to be heard at Wau, which was a wild-west sort of place. The police there were careful not to fall out with the Goilalas, but for everyone else the law was rough and ready. Wau had a white population of 27, and I was told that every single one of them had spent at least one night in the calaboose on some pretext or other.

From Moresby, I flew by Cessna over the Owen Stanleys. I don't like small planes over mountain ranges so I took an air-sickness pill, which made me drowsy. When Gustavo failed to collect me at the airstrip, I curled up in the long grass and fell asleep. He turned up later in a battered Land Rover and drove me 30 kilometres up a rough, spectacular track to his mine. There, as agreed, he paid my fee in alluvial gold – not that I could tell if he

---

[17] C.R. Hallpike: Bloodshed and Vengeance in the Papuan Mountains; The Generation of Conflict in Tauade Society, Oxford University Press, 1977.

was short-changing me. It became irrelevant anyway as later, back in Moresby, my houseboy swept it up from the bottom of a drawer by mistake and threw it away.

The case started the next day before the local magistrate, a National. The Goilala was an evil-looking fellow, but very truthful. Indeed, there was no disagreement at all over what had happened. Gustavo and his workers had been down at the river emptying the sluices of gold when the cry went up, 'Goilalas are coming!' and his boys fled in panic.

The Goilala man admitted he attacked Gustavo (reason: 'He's got more gold than me'). Gustavo forced him to the ground, warned him off, then stepped back. The Goilala sprang up and went for him a second time. Again Gustavo subdued him then let him go. The third time the Goilala grabbed a piece of wood so Gustavo knocked him to the ground and disarmed him. The Goilala ran away and reported the incident at Wau. The police then came and arrested Gustavo.

We argued self-defence, a concept that seemed unknown in Wau.

His Worship: 'Your client had no right to touch this Goilala man.'

Me: 'But the Goilala attacked *him!*'

His Worship, with a baffled look: 'Of course! That's what Goilala do!'

Judgment was reserved till some future time and I took the Cessna back to Moresby. Three weeks later I was told the magistrate had gone on leave. Later still, I heard the court file had been misplaced. Presumably the Goilala's pride had been appeased. In true Melanesian style, the whole business fizzled out.

23

BSQ Esquire

When the customer isn't right

Beresford Shirley-Quirk's name wasn't the only grandiose thing about him. His business card was impressive too: it sported a shield with a family crest and a Latin motto. Tagged onto his name was the title 'Esq.', which denotes a rank in the English gentry a notch below a knight. The card described him as a nationally accredited 'Intermediator and Civic Senior Professional Exigency Support – Inter Alia', whatever that means.

I first encountered BSQ not long after I came to the bar. I'd see him strolling around the foyers of Magistrates' Courts: a tall, portly, distinguished-looking Englishman with silver hair and an ingratiating smile. He wore an expensive suit, an old school tie and a waistcoat dripping with watch chains and golden guinea coins. In winter he added a well-tailored overcoat and looked even more the man of substance. Before I saw his business card, I'd taken him to be a prosperous solicitor.

One day at court he approached me and complimented me on my advocacy. In a posh English accent he promised to send me a brief sometime. Before long, one duly turned up in the mail.

When my clerk noticed it, he positively erupted. 'You can't accept a brief from Shirley-Quirk!' he warned. 'He's not a solicitor at all. He's a charlatan! He latches on to some poor sod, makes out he's a lawyer and bleeds the sucker dry. He's even done time for impersonating a lawyer.' It was all news to me. I returned the brief.

BSQ didn't take offence. He remained his charming self and continued to chat amiably with me whenever we ran into each other. An amusing raconteur, he told me how he'd attended some English public school where the masters recommended he join the priesthood. He was thirteen at the time and replied – or so he claimed – 'If chastity's a requirement I'm afraid it's already too late.' Another time he explained how he'd come to migrate to Australia. 'I fell in love with an Ors-tralian girl and followed her to the colonies.'

As time passed I saw BSQ less and less. In fact he didn't cross my mind for years till one day I heard there was a brief coming in for me from Legal Aid. It duly arrived and I undid its pink ribbon and started to read. The client was charged with assaulting two Chinese women. To my surprise, the accused was Shirley-Quirk. He'd asked specially for me. Apparently he didn't want to represent himself.

His sad story was this. One day he goes to a computer swap meet. He tells the stallholders what equipment he has and they sell him a CD burner, which they assure him is compatible. When he gets home he finds it's not compatible at all. He can't make it work.

So BSQ does a business name search and fires off a few pompous faxes. They're addressed to Mrs Nancy Ho, who later claims she never received them. Even if she had – and even if her English was twice as good as it is

– she still wouldn't have deciphered them. The first one ends, 'Given these facts and expense, I invite your legitimate supply of the essential software gratis to resolve your neglect and disservice. I await your call. I reserve my rights and remedies.' Exactly his style.

Eventually BSQ gets to speak to Mrs Ho on the phone. He tells her he wants something to get the burner working but won't agree to pay anything extra. After all, the fellows at her stall – her 'servants and agents', he tells her – guaranteed the burner would work with his system.

Mrs Ho invites him round to her place, where she opens the door in baggy pants, 'dressed like a coolie', he tells me. BSQ brings the DVD unit with him but Mrs Ho won't give him a refund and they discuss other options in her hallway. First Mrs Ho recommends he download some software off the internet but BSQ rejects that idea. Next, she tries to talk him into buying another $80 unit, which of course he refuses out of hand. As a final option, she suggests he gets himself an installation disc. In fact, she pulls one out, a CD with a $10 price sticker on it, but also stamped 'Not for Resale'.

BSQ notices the stamp and assumes she is giving it to him free. He takes it and turns to leave. At that, Mrs Ho springs at him like a panther while he, with his DVD unit in one hand and the disc in the other, tries to fend her off. She calls for reinforcements and a second female, her niece Li-Li, bounds out of another room and joins the fray. Oriental limbs fly in all directions and BSQ deflects them as best he can as he wrestles his way through the front door.

The struggle continues on the porch where the three of them lose their footing and fall into the rose bushes. BSQ's Saville Row overcoat sheds a button and gets one sleeve ripped off. Finally, our bruised Intermediator and Senior Professional makes it to his car, leaving his Blackberry and silk tie (never found) on the front lawn.

Now begins the race to the police station. BSQ is at a disadvantage here because he has to bypass Cheltenham due to a past misunderstanding. That previous incident blew up when the cops there wouldn't accept his purported seatbelt exemption and he refused to give them his name and address. He ended up spending a night in the cells, and paid the cops back by lodging a formal complaint and writing lots of long letters to the Ombudsman. After that saga, the Cheltenham police didn't like BSQ very much.

Instead he heads for Prahran and tells his story there. The Prahran police offer to go and arrest Mrs Ho, but BSQ has a pang of conscience about putting her through the wringer over a lousy $10. In fact, he's so gallant, he doesn't make a written statement at all and says he'd think about it overnight. So events turn in favour of Mrs Ho, who's made it to Moorabbin and now has the police there eating out of her hand. BSQ ends up the one facing charges.

When the cops arrest him the next day he stands on his dignity. They read him his rights: he may inform a friend or relative of his whereabouts; he may contact a legal practitioner; he may contact the consular officer of the country of which he is a citizen. Then the transcript of the interview reads like this:

> Q. Do you understand these rights?
> A. (No audible reply.)
> Q. Do you wish to exercise any of these rights before the interview proceeds?
> A. (No audible reply.)
> Q. What is your age and date of birth?
> A. (No audible reply.)
> Q. Are you an Australian citizen?
> A. (No audible reply.)
> Q. Are you a permanent resident of Australia?
> A (No audible reply.)
> Q. Do you intend to refuse to answer our questions?
> A. (No audible reply)

The cops try to coax him into saying something but BSQ stands mute. They suspend the interview and bring in a senior sergeant, who explains that they're required to record the conversation. The sergeant says, 'If you object to this procedure your reasons for such objection must be recorded.

Could you please state your reasons for objecting.'

Again, no audible reply.

The cops try a different tack. They tell him they plan to go to his address and search for Mrs Ho's CD. If he won't consent, they'll apply for a search warrant and he'll stay locked up for a few hours while they get one. This threat seems to have some effect. When they ask him if he consents to the search the transcript records, 'The suspect nods.'

The police take BSQ back to his place where they find and seize the CD, the earpiece to his Blackberry and the one-armed overcoat, to which they've already recovered the matching button from Mrs Ho's rose garden. They return to the station, and by now BSQ is talking at last. He disputes Mrs Ho's version indignantly. He declares: 'I deny each and every allegation! I accuse my accusers of unlawful assault, reckless assault, assault by kicking but not limited to the things I mention here. I reserve all of my rights and remedies. I vigorously oppose and defend! I am falsely accused!'

On the day of the hearing BSQ reminds me how he was dressed at the time: in a suit and overcoat, with a Bluetooth device pinned to his lapel and an ear-piece in his ear. He hadn't gone dressed for a fracas, he points out, and I entirely agree. I know he'd much sooner shoot off a couple of prolix faxes than get his knuckles bruised. 'Beresford,' I tell him, 'you're a loveable rogue.'

He gives half a smile. 'I ah-gree with the loveable, but I take issue with the rest of your epithet.'

The case begins and Mrs Ho steps into the witness box. She's small, feisty and formidable, and looks like Chairman Mao's second wife, the one who headed the Gang of Four. Her mouth snaps open and shut like the jaws of a Siamese fighting fish. 'This person say he purchase DVD burner not work I say come my place we change for you. I open door he come in, pass me DVD unit.'

She doesn't agree she offered BSQ the disc for nothing. 'I say what you want me to do. He say take back or give me free, I say take back goods only if faulty, software cost money, not for free I can't do that.'

As for her account of the fight: 'He just use his left hand grab software run to door. I say excuse me you can't do that he turn round use his hand punch my nose.

'After that I try to get my software back. Even I jumping cannot reach his hand. I feel how can this happen! I just let him punch I don't revenge.

'He kick me many times, he open door I shout help, call police. Li-Li come out. She say no, no, no. I follow man to Mercedes car, I say you cannot do this, that's all I say. After that I shocked and go Moorabbin police very quick.'

The second witness, the niece Li-Li, speaks good English, worse luck for us, and says she was doing her accountancy homework Module 3 in another room when the melee broke out. She adds more details of the incident: how she saw the man try to punch Aunty's face, and how they all fell off the porch (something Aunty forgot to mention at all). I cross-examine both women but don't make much headway with either.

When it's our turn, BSQ draws himself to his full height and strides purposefully into the witness box. He intones the oath in a plummy, ecclesiastical voice. '*I swe-aah* by *Awl -might-tee Gawd...*' No wonder his school recommended he join the church.

BSQ's version is that Mrs Ho 'lured' him to her home. He went expecting redress and when she offered him the disc he took it, thinking she'd seen reason. Instead, she pounced on him, clinging so tightly he had to apply his open hand to her face to free himself. The niece joined in and he fell down the steps with the two attached to him like a pair of limpets. He managed to dislodge the niece but Mrs Ho clung to him till he got to his car and made his escape.

The prosecutor cross-examines BSQ and scores a few points.

'What caused you to think you could just take the disc?'

'It said on it "Not for Re-sale". Seeing she'd refused a refund, I took the CD as of right.'

'But once she tried to stop you leaving, didn't you know then she didn't want you to take it?'

'I had no chance to think. I was under attack.'

'But if you gave it back the attack would stop?'

'I didn't know that. I didn't know what might happen next.'

'What else could happen next?'

'I thought a door might open and a gang of Chinamen might appear with knives and daggers.' (That bit doesn't help us much!)

Unsurprisingly, we lose. It's two against one, and they're females into the bargain.

Before imposing a sentence, the mago gets to read BSQ's criminal record. He does have prior convictions, but they're unusual ones. He beat a perjury charge and one of perverting the course of justice, but went down for engaging as a private enquiry agent without a licence. He's also got convictions for fraudulently using a franked postage stamp, falsely representing himself as a migration agent and impersonating a

Commonwealth officer. His biggest black mark is for holding himself out to be a solicitor. The Law Institute gave him a hard time over it and got an injunction against him, which he apparently breached. He spent 58 days in maximum security for contempt of the Supreme Court. He tells me his prior convictions are honourable scars from his various battles for justice.

Anyway, there are no priors for violence, so the mago goes easy on him. He takes into account that it was a minor dispute which blew out of all proportion. BSQ cops a fine of $750, which I think is pretty fair in the circumstances.

BSQ doesn't agree, though. He's a litigious fellow and thinks he's had a raw deal. He asks me about an appeal but I advise him to forget it and go home and lick his wounds instead. I can't see him doing any better on appeal; indeed, he could do much worse. Legal Aid ask me for an opinion and I put it in writing that an appeal's not warranted.

Four months later I got a letter out of the blue on fancy crested letterhead with heraldic motifs. BSQ ran his own appeal at the County Court and he's writing to tell me he won.

24

Liberty of the Subject

Applying for bail

A person accused of a crime is simply that: accused. His guilt or innocence hasn't been determined, and until that happens he's presumed innocent. Unless there are reasons in law against it, he's also entitled to bail until his case is decided.

The entitlement doesn't apply if the accused is charged with new offences when he's already on bail or subject to some form of corrections order. Or where he has prior convictions for certain drug or sex offences or crimes of violence. In the event of any of these, the onus reverses and the accused remains in custody unless he persuades a court it's unfair to keep him locked up. The legal test is to show 'compelling reason' why his detention isn't justified.

Bail is also refused where the risks of granting it are unacceptably high – where the accused might abscond, for instance, or interfere with witnesses or keep committing crimes. Sometimes these risks can be minimised by specific conditions of bail: to surrender a passport, to observe a curfew, to sign in daily at a police station. These days cash bail or a surety is unusual in the lower courts. Money isn't the issue. A person's liberty shouldn't – and generally doesn't – depend on whether he's got ready cash or wealthy friends.

Ideally, courts decide applications for bail promptly; the liberty of the subject should take priority. In the city they usually get called on early in the day, but in suburban courts, where there are fewer magistrates, there's often a delay. If my bail app hasn't started by late morning I try to hold it off. Rather than be hurried on just before lunch I prefer to wait till the afternoon. It's something I've always done from instinct but science, I learn, has proved my intuition sound.

Research[18] has turned up some intriguing facts about judicial decision-making. A study of over a thousand Parole Board decisions in Israel showed a curious phenomenon. At the start of the day most applications for parole were granted, but as the morning wore on the success rate fell, until just before lunch it reached zero. After the break the success rate jumped abruptly to 65 per cent, then began to fall again. The pattern was clear even after taking into account the serious cases you'd expect to be turned down.

At first glance, then, it looks as if it all depends on the judge's blood sugar levels. It seems to vindicate the cynics who say justice is what the judge had for breakfast. That view, incidentally, has been held for centuries – or at least since 1712 when Alexander Pope wrote:

---

[18] Shai Danziger and others, 'Extraneous factors in judicial decisions' in the Proceedings of the National Academy of Sciences of the USA, reported in the Economist, 16–22 April 2011.

The hungry judges soon the sentence sign,
And wretches hang that jurymen may dine.

It turns out, though, the variation isn't so much to do with the length of time since the last meal, as the number of cases since the last break. The explanation is that decision-making is mentally taxing. Judges get tired and start to look for easy answers. In the parole scenario the easy answer is to maintain the status quo and refuse the application. In the bail scenario the default position is to leave the applicant locked up.

So I wait till the afternoon. This is sometimes tough on the client, who's on tenterhooks, sweating it out in the cells. It's hard on family members too, who have to wait around all day to give evidence or simply be present. Family and friends are well-meaning but often ill-informed. Sometimes they don't even know what their loved one has been charged with. And just as my client tells me whatever he thinks will enhance his chances of getting out, so do his supporters.

One client's girlfriend was eager to get him released. She'd dragged her father to court to vouch for him. The father smiled and nodded half-heartedly. I asked him, 'How many times have you met Theo?'

He said, 'Actually, I've never met him.'

'So how do you know what he's like?'

'We've spoken on the phone.'

'How often?'

'Once.'

'When was that?'

'Yesterday.'

On other occasions the parents *don't* want their drug-using child released. They want him to stay on remand and dry out. They think their kid is better off out of temptation's way. Often I agree with them, but that's not the point. My client is their son and it's his instructions I'm duty-bound to follow, not theirs. Mostly, the parents understand.

A client gets one shot at bail. If it fails, he can't try again unless circumstances change or new facts come to light. It's therefore important not to go off half-cocked. Clients have trouble accepting this and curbing their impatience. Often they insist we go on, even when it's against their best interests. Being in custody, they can't do their own legwork – things like organising witnesses, obtaining reports, getting proof there's a job available, arranging accommodation or a place in rehab. Clients think it all happens automatically whereas the work falls on the solicitor – or on me.

Accommodation is usually the biggest obstacle. A lot of clients have nowhere to live; they've been kicked out of home and are sleeping rough. Often the only bail address on offer is with shady associates to whom the police will object. Just this week a client in custody told me he had permission to stay in an unoccupied house. I asked when the owner would return and was told, 'When he gets out of jail.'

Anton, another client, tells me he has a bail address with a female friend. I recognise her name as a regular client of a colleague, Tim. I chase Tim up and ask if the woman is facing any charges herself at present. He gives a wry smile and says, 'I'd be surprised if she isn't.' So much for that possibility.

There are services to help people with housing but their resources are limited. I latch onto a court support worker for help with Anton. She works her way down the list, trying to arrange somewhere for him to stay. Odyssey won't do assessments in the cells, Moreland Hall won't accept anybody on bail, St Vincent de Paul's aren't taking anyone this month, Harrison Youth Services have a seven-day waiting list. OAT, whoever they are, won't touch him.

It's in a situation like this that you sometimes go beyond the call of duty. In TV shows some lawyers go undercover and do their own investigations, but that's not what happens in real life. Running around for bail apps is the closest I ever come to that sort of thing, and it seldom turns out very well.

Johnno, for example, assured me he was boarding with his mate Spider and that Spider's mum was happy to have him back. He gave me an address but no phone number. It wasn't far, so I headed out over lunch. The house was a well-kept brick veneer with ornamental rocks and a wishing-well in the front garden. The place itself looked respectable but there was techno-rock blaring from inside and a hotted-up car in the driveway. I had to hammer at the door before it finally opened an inch and a face glared through the crack. Spider.

I asked if his mum was there and explained Johnno's predicament. But Spider's mum was at work, earning a living while Spider occupied himself playing video games. Still, he did confirm Johnno had lived there for two weeks before his arrest. I asked if he was welcome back and Spider said, 'Only if he starts paying some fucking rent' and slammed the door.

Another time I was briefed by Legal Aid in a bail application on the other side of town. They warned me the client was 'difficult'. His application certainly didn't look promising; he had a long criminal history that included a dozen convictions for failing to answer bail in the past. This time he was being held for shop theft; he'd gone shopping with a pair of scissors and cut the bar codes off a stack of DVDs. According to him it was all the Public Trustee's fault because they had control over his pension and wouldn't give him enough spending money.

On my way to see him in the police cells I ran into the psychiatric nurse, who was just leaving. He told me my client had no psychiatric illness but was only brain-damaged. That was good to know. He also mentioned the client was 'very difficult', which was less good.

The brain injury was from a car accident years before and it hadn't mellowed his manner, which was demanding and belligerent. He scowled at me through the glass of the interview booth as I tried to explain his situation. His only chance of getting bail was if his sister Debbie would offer him a bed and promise to get him to court on the next date. But Debbie lived miles away and wasn't answering her mobile. The client told me I'd find her at the learning centre at Magda Grove where she did a computer course every

Wednesday. No-one at the Legal Aid office was keen to track Debbie down, so I went looking myself.

Magda Grove was a down-at-heel shopping strip. I parked outside a Turkish video store and walked down to the Community Learning Centre. Two large women lounged on a bench in the open, puffing on cigarettes. Computer course? They nodded towards a former school building on the other side of the road.

I walked across and went in. Community Learning was in full swing in several rooms. An educational video was showing in one. At least, I think it was educational, something to do with rabbits. In the next room a clutch of women sat around a table loaded with cakes. They looked positively hostile as they noticed me peeping in; either it was the man-haters' support group or the cake-decorating class. I must have been the first male in a suit to venture inside this century. 'So, who are *you,* mate?' they demanded.

They'd heard of Debbie, but the computer course had finished the week before. The woman in charge indifferently checked a list of names but drew a blank. Nobody could suggest any other leads. I drove back to the police cells and broke the bad news. I told the client he'd have to adjourn his bail application for a few days while Legal Aid made contact with his sister.

He said, 'You're a fucking drone, pal. Tell them to send me a decent lawyer next time.' So nice to be appreciated.

I tried for bail once for Viseth, a Cambodian bloke, though he had Buckley's chance. His prior convictions filled 27 pages. The typing was double-spaced so it really only amounted to twenty, but it was still a lot. He couldn't remember how many times he'd been to jail. I flicked through his record and counted eight or nine times at least.

His was a tragic story, even if you took it with a grain of salt. He'd been born near the Vietnamese-Cambodian border, where his father was blown up by a land mine when he was four. An uncle who was a border guard removed him from his mother – virtually abducted him, he said – and took him into the jungle. There, he was starved and ill-treated and made to run messages across the border. He witnessed war at first hand and saw people maimed and shot. For a time he was pressed into service carrying weapons for the Khmer Rouge.

At some stage Viseth was taken in by Buddhist monks and placed in a school. He ran away and spent years looking for his mother. When he was fifteen the Red Cross Tracing Service located her in Melbourne, and a year later he succeeded in joining her. She'd remarried in the meantime and had four new children, one of whom had even been given his name. The new husband refused to acknowledge him in any way, and relations with his mum alternated between rejection and reconciliation. Having lived on his wits as a child, he was an indiscriminate thief. Soon he started using drugs; he had more excuse than most.

This time he'd burgled a house in broad daylight and been caught red-handed. His face was bruised; he'd been roughed up by the drug dealers to whom he owed money and who'd pressured him into doing the burg.

The mago had no choice but to refuse bail. He was sympathetic, though, and said he'd consider a renewed application if we could line up someone to help from the Cambodian Buddhist community. Support from a source like that seemed his only chance of any long-term future. Viseth smiled all the time, by the way, a cultural thing. My Cambodian clients always smile, no matter what.

Just before Christmas one year, I did a bail app for a bag-snatcher. The police opposed bail; they said he was a serious risk of reoffending. He was targeting elderly women, pushing them over and making off with their handbags. Despicable crimes really, though I did my best for him. When we got a knock-back I had a debrief with the cops and told them how unfair they were. I said, 'Christmas is the peak bag-snatching season and you've deprived my client of his livelihood!' It was the sort of joke you shouldn't make, but sometimes a jest is the only way to ease the tension.

Another applicant for bail was a female drug user, who'd recently given birth. She was so addicted that at eight and a half months pregnant she was still climbing through windows committing burglaries. Immediately after the birth, her baby was taken into care from her bedside. We were in the County Court and I hoped to argue that she should get bail to be with her baby; it would have been a very strong argument if she'd cooperated.

The solicitor had arranged counselling appointments and a course for her to learn some mothering skills, but she was recalcitrant. I tried to talk her into saying the right thing, so I could quote her to the court. I asked, 'Can I tell the judge you're desperate to keep your appointments?'

'I'm not keeping any fucking appointments!'

'Well, can I tell him your number one priority is to reunite with your baby?'

She said, 'You can tell him I'll suck his cock if he'll give me bail!'

Another difficult client. Bail refused.

Don't think all contested bail applications are losers, though. In fact they succeed at least half the time.

They're proceedings where good advocacy and preparation can make a difference. In part, that's because the court has to reach a decision on incomplete and untested information. Common sense and pragmatism help. Certain facts can be decisive: a client will lose his job without bail, he'll jeopardise his accommodation, he's the sole carer for children, he has serious health problems.

Offering sensible conditions sometimes carries the day, ones that minimise the risk of further offending. Drug-users can agree to testing and treatment and have their compliance taken into account if they're found guilty. Problem drinkers can be released on condition they abstain from drinking.

One of my clients was a habitual drunkard. The police said they wouldn't oppose bail if he would stay off the grog. The mago considered releasing him with the condition, 'Not to drink alcohol'. Expressed in such absolute terms, it was about as realistic as ordering a dog not to bark, so I suggested adding the phrase 'to excess'. The words were inserted and left conveniently undefined. 'Shit, I never drink to excess anyway,' said the bloke, who could easily put away a slab a day.

When they do get bail, clients are very relieved – yes, and grateful. You occasionally get some heartfelt thanks from the client and his loved ones. Sometimes, though, there are no loved ones. Some blokes get bail and have to make their own way to the boarding-house we've arranged for them. The Salvos can help with a travel card, but I generally slip the client twenty bucks or so. It means they can buy a pie or a packet of smokes on the way. Other colleagues do the same, even though it's not tax deductible.

It means that if you lose a bail application you save yourself $20. Even so, you still feel the disappointment if you lose one you'd hoped to win. You report back to the solicitor and put it behind you.

I failed one day where I'd been briefed by my mate Coxy. I phoned his office to let him know how it went. He seemed to have taken a day off, as I got a recorded message saying, 'Due to unforeseen circumstances this office will be closed next Tuesday.'

I wondered how he'd known in advance, if it was unforeseen. I left my own message: 'Due to unforeseen circumstances our client is still in custody.'

25

Mystery Man

Hard yakka pays off

Police records list aliases as well as real names. Sometimes people have half a dozen they don't even know about, mostly permutations on initials or middle names, or spelling errors the police themselves have made. So a Jamie Payne's details might include the aliases Jamie M. Payne, Jamie Murray Paine, James M. Payne and so on.

According to the police my client this morning, Frank Boyce, has 26 aliases, which seems rather a lot. They include such names as Simon McIntyre, Herbert Green, John Arthur Armstrong and David Gallagher, which don't look like transcription errors to me.

Frank is being held in the cells and I wait in the foyer of the police station till they call me in. I'm ushered through a couple of heavy doors and sign in at the watch-house counter. Then they lead me down the corridor to the interview booths. There's a tape measure on one wall and footprints painted on the floor where prisoners stand to have their mug-shots taken. There's a pile of soiled linen in one corner and a whiff of carbolic in the air.

I take a seat in the interview cubicle and the police jailer clicks the door shut behind me. Through the glass I see a grey-haired gent with a pleasant, innocuous face. He's in his late sixties and gazes at me with the wide, perplexed eyes of a friendly Labrador. The police have told me he's only answering to David Gallagher this morning, but they've got it wrong. My client tells me he's definitely Frank Boyce, with a date of birth he can't remember.

'Could it be the 26th of February 1952?' I ask, glancing at his record.

'I don't think so,' he mumbles. 'Isn't it 1953? June or July?' He gives me a cagey look. 'What year is it now?'

Frank was picked up yesterday, pinching groceries from Coles. He couldn't give an address because the vacant house where he used to squat has been demolished. In recent weeks he's been camping out in a bark humpy on the banks of the Merri Creek. He tells me he's not on Centrelink and his health is poor. He's hardly had a hot meal in weeks.

Of course, his diet's improved now he's locked up and the cops tell me he's eating like a horse. He's also had a hot shower and some clean clothes from the Salvos. It strikes me that he's better off where he is, with a roof over his head and three square meals a day. But Frank doesn't feel that way; he's itching to get out on bail.

Normally, it wouldn't be a problem. On a minor shop theft, most people wouldn't be in custody at all; they'd just receive a summons. But there's something of a mystery about Frank Boyce. When the cops checked his fingerprints, a match came up with five other names, including a Herbert Green. Two years ago this Green had been charged with an unprovoked assault at a shopping centre in Glenroy: punching and injuring an elderly woman. Green was arrested, fingerprinted and bailed to appear at court. When he failed to turn up a warrant was issued to arrest him. Frank Boyce is being held now on that warrant.

This time round the police oppose him getting bail. They say Frank Boyce is one and the same as Herbert Green. They say he has no proper address and that if he gets bail he'll disappear again. Through the glass I explain all this to Frank.

'I don't know anything about it,' he says.

'Glenroy?' I ask. 'Ring a bell?'

'I've never been to Glenroy. I don't even know where it is.'

'Ever heard of Herbert Green?'

His brow creases in thought and he shakes his head. 'Never.'

'Ever used that name yourself?'

He frowns and looks mildly offended. 'Of course not.'

He's well-spoken with a gentle manner but tends not to hear when he doesn't want to. He also seems canny about the legal system and an expert at changing the subject. He goes off on a tangent about the shop theft: 'I'm not guilty, you know. I went into the shop intending to use a food voucher and then I couldn't find it.'

I say, 'Frank, we're not talking about the groceries. We're talking about an attack on an old lady. The police think Herbert Green is you. They think you assaulted a lady at a shopping centre.'

'Do they?' He stares at me with a look of worried surprise.

'Yes, an old lady. For no reason. Did you ever do that?'

'I've never done anything like that in my life!' he protests. 'Please, I just want to get out of here. I'm a sick man. I've got a terrible cough, you know, and my legs are all swollen up. Oedema, the doctors call it. I can hardly walk.'

I steer him back to Herbert Green. I say. 'Okay, it's not your name and it's not your date of birth. The trouble is, this Herbert Green's got your fingerprints.'

'Has he? Goodness! How did he get them?'

'Well, I was hoping you might tell *me.*'

I've already checked with the police about the prints. The computer made the match and the police have double-checked, then triple-checked.

There's no doubt, they say. They've even faxed Boyce's photo to one of the police who investigated the assault. His reply reads: 'That is the man I interviewed; he gave the name Herbert Green; he failed to appear on his court date.'

So Frank Boyce faces multiple problems getting bail: a nasty assault, a previous failure to answer bail and the new shop theft. The cops also question his mental capacity and, apart from all that, he's got nowhere to live. Without a fixed address he isn't going anywhere.

The more I explain it, the worse Frank's hearing gets. 'You'll have to speak up. I'm deaf in one ear.' He leans forward and puts his good ear to the grille below the glass, but he doesn't want to hear what I'm telling him. Which is that it's going to take a few days for us to come up with somewhere for him to live.

In court I adjourn his application for four days. He interjects a few times from the dock to tell the magistrate about his dizzy spells, his hearing, his malnutrition and – especially – his legs.

I hope four days is enough. As it turns out, I'm being wildly over-ambitious.

Frank's solicitor is Miriam from Legal Aid and she arranges for the police to take Frank to hospital for a check-up. The report comes back, saying his blood pressure's fine, his ECG and chest X-ray are normal, his urine's clear. There's no mention of deafness in one ear, nor oedema for that matter. The report concludes, 'We believe this gentleman's cognitive function is at his normal baseline. Whilst his short-term memory is reduced, he is not acutely confused. We are discharging him back into police care.'

It's Miriam's job to try and arrange some housing and she's a paragon of persistence. In the state of Victoria there aren't too many beds available at short notice for old codgers in doubtful health with mild dementia. The four days turns into ten days, then into a month.

Miriam represents Frank in court on successive remands but receives no thanks for it. He gets stroppy and sacks her, then reinstates her. He argues that by the next remand date he'll have effectively served a six-week sentence anyway. He wants to plead guilty on the spot but since he denies being Herbert Green, the magistrate won't accept the plea. This, I'm told, makes him go right off.

'You're from the ACTU,' he shouts at the mago. 'You're controlled by the unions! This is is imprisonment without trial! I'm being incarcerated and tortured and I'm a sick man!' As Miriam recounts the outburst, I wonder how much is fair dinkum and how much an act.

After Frank calms down Miriam goes to speak to him in the cells. Like me, she finds it hard to make herself heard. Whenever she asks Frank an inconvenient question, he can't hear her. She resorts to writing things down and passing notes to him, but now his eyesight goes bad too and he can't read them. Dizziness overcomes him and he has to lie down.

As well as telling me all this, Miriam mentions something else rather curious. In the police station foyer she's noticed a Missing Persons poster on the wall. Among the faces, she tells me, is one that looks just like Frank. Missing from Central Queensland, says the caption.

I don't inspect the poster myself. I'm not good with faces and I don't want any more complications. Anyway, the name on the poster is Loveridge.

'Is that one of his aliases?' I ask Miriam.

'Not according to his police records.'

'Good,' I say. 'Let's assume it's not him, unless the poster mentions swollen legs.'

As the days turn into weeks, Frank gets transferred to the Metropolitan Remand Centre. Our one big problem is to find him somewhere to live. Miriam puts his name onto every possible housing list and has him assessed by social workers, support agencies and Mental Health. We amass a whole sheaf of reports. In summary they say:

Report No.1. Not acutely confused.

Report No.2. Very confused; unfit to be tried.

Report No.3. Can't say; need more information.

Report No.4. Needs a supported placement.

Report No.5. Can't help with housing.
Report No.6. Qualifies for funding; eligible for permanent residential care.
Then with Number 7 we strike gold: Bed available!

The bed is at Charles Hammond House, a hostel for elderly men. It offers private rooms and all meals. It provides all necessary supports, with doctors, psychs and social workers visiting daily. There are recreation facilities, supervised outings and the place is near shops and a community house. A nurse is in attendance at all times. It's perfect.

By now the cops suspect Frank Boyce isn't so much ill as cunning, and they dig their heels in. 'It took us two years to catch up with him and we don't want him slipping through our fingers again. What of it if he's got somewhere to live?' they argue. 'What's to stop him doing a runner once he gets bail?' But we've got that covered: Charles Hammond House has excellent security.

In court I call the support worker to give evidence. The hostel, she explains from the witness box, houses 45 men, mostly in their sixties or over. Each resident has his own room and en suite. There's a billiard room, a TV room, a library and supervised outings.

'Would Mr Boyce go on outings?' I ask.

'Yes. We're very concerned to have him socialising. At the Remand Centre he's been very isolated. He keeps to himself and sometimes refuses to leave his cell. His eyesight's poor and when he sees movement and shadows he fears for his safety.'

'So how's he been coping generally?'

'He's finding it very difficult.'

The mago's lapping it up and I keep up a flow of Dorothy Dixers. 'At the hostel, would he have his own key?'

'To his own room, yes.'

'To leave the hostel?'

'No, not for that. Some residents do have a personal code to go out the front door and down to the shops. Not everyone, though. Some residents have disabilities and can't find their way back. Mr Boyce would be in that category.'

'And the codes?'

'They're like an electronic key. They let the staff know who's outside at any particular time.'

'And Mr Boyce won't have a code?'

'No.' (Frank pays attention to this bit. Maybe his hearing's coming good.)

'What's to stop him following someone else out?'

'The outside door is through the main foyer and there's a staff member at the desk to prevent that sort of thing.'

'Is the desk always attended?'

'Twenty-four hours a day.'

The magistrate asks, 'And how would he reach the hostel, if I granted bail today?'

'My colleague and I would drive him directly from court,' says the worker. Her colleague's sitting in the back of the court: also female but the burly type and tough-looking. She'd be more than a match for old Frank Boyce.

So we have a win at last; bail is granted. After two months and two days, Frank regains his liberty. Stooping slightly, he steps from the dock and they lead him downstairs to the registry to sign his bail papers.

I remind him he's not out of trouble yet. He's due back at court in a month to contest the assault charges. 'I understand that,' he nods, 'but all that time on remand, it's a long sentence even if I was this Herbert Green and had committed that horrible crime.' He's got a point, I think to myself, as he trots off under close escort.

Next day Miriam phones me with news from Charles Hammond House. Once Frank arrived they showed him to his room and left him to settle in. Twenty minutes later they went to check on him. His room was empty and he was nowhere to be found. He'd let himself out the emergency fire exit and hasn't been seen since.

26

Trade Secrets

How the system works

Like plumbers and brothel keepers, barristers have to be licensed. Plumbers go to trade school and do an apprenticeship; barristers go to university for four or five years, do another year of practical training, then have to pass the Bar exam. Brothel keepers just fill in a form.

We have this in common too: our services are valued more highly before they've been performed than afterwards. A plumber's charges look reasonable when the toilet's blocked and overflowing. A barrister's fee looks fair when the client's facing six months in the slammer. (I make no comment on the urgency of a brothel's services.) My point is that in each case the customer is apt to forget how pressing the need was once it's passed. For all three occupations, payment up-front is highly advised.

I mention money because, after all, barristers go to court to earn their living. When a solicitor briefs us on behalf of a client, the solicitor becomes liable for our fees. When we're engaged directly by a client, it's up to us to ensure we're in funds.

Popular wisdom has it that when newly-qualified barristers start out they're interested only in the law and not in the money. In time that changes till they're interested only in the money and not the law. Near the end of their careers, it's said, they're not interested in either. I sometimes wonder which stage I've reached; it seems to vary day by day.

Much of my work is for Legal Aid so I know I'll get paid, if slowly. Legal Aid rates are fixed but with private clients we negotiate our own fees. Strangely, some of us don't charge enough. Many clients seem eager to pay more than they need to and flock to my pricey colleagues, thinking that because the latter charge more, they must be better. This erroneous belief creates a curious phenomenon: busy barristers with too much work double their fees to deter custom and find they've got more work than ever.[19]

Appearances and marketing seem to count. My colleague Royce told me how he did a job in the country and had to offer his Legal Aid client a lift back to the city. As they walked to the car park, the client's face fell at the sight of Royce's car and he said, 'I'd have thought a barrister would have a better car than that.' Yet Royce's car is a Mercedes! An old model certainly, but still a Mercedes.

When even Legal Aid clients are that snobbish, what chance do I stand with my second-hand Toyota Corolla? In fact, at one time I had a twenty-year-old Renault with doors of three different colours as a result of minor bingles. A solicitor who knew the car once stipulated on my brief that I was to

---

[19] Economists call this a Veblen good, after the man who first noticed demand for certain goods increased even as their price increased. The higher cost only raises their exclusiveness and appeal as a status symbol. T.B. Veblen, The Theory of the Leisure Class, 1899, Macmillan, London.

park at least 200 metres from the court house to ensure the client wouldn't spot me in it!

Barristers are subject to the same economic laws as everyone else: we respond to incentives. At one time the Legal Aid fee for running a contested hearing in the Magos' Court was $420. If the case resolved into a plea of guilty, the fee was $380. But a plea of guilty could be polished off inside an hour whereas for the extra 40 bucks you might spend the whole day in gruelling disputation. So barristers often sold their clients on the wisdom of pleading guilty. Indeed, I overheard one ask a colleague once, 'You're not just telling me to plead guilty so you can go home early, are you?' I thought: mmm, she's hit the nail on the head there.

Recently, Legal Aid increased the fee for running a contest to $700. That means the extra work yields not $40 but $300. Strangely, lots of unpromising cases now suddenly seem worth running.

Here's another example. One day I got a gig as duty barrister to assist people who'd turned up to court that day without a lawyer. I'd be needed only until all the unrepresented cases were dealt with. My fee was at an hourly rate up to a maximum of six hours, and I thought to myself: I bet this is going to take *exactly* six hours. And I was right, it did!

There's yet another occupation barristers resemble: taxi-drivers. Like cabbies, we're not allowed to refuse a fare. We're governed by what's called the 'cab rank rule' which means that if we're offered work in our field at a proper fee, we can't knock it back. The rule's designed to ensure that even unpopular litigants can find a barrister. Without it, Nazis or racists or pedophiles might find it hard to get representation at any price.

It's this rule, incidentally, that does our image a bit of harm. The public misunderstands and thinks, 'If barristers are willing to represent a Nazi swine like that, they must be willing to do anything for money.' In fact, by accepting the brief, the barrister is motivated by ethics, not avarice. It should reflect to the profession's credit, not discredit.

Of course, a person doesn't have to be a Nazi to be unpleasant. Plenty of non-Nazis can be obnoxious; they're the clients you'd prefer to avoid and you develop a sixth sense about them. One morning I went to a police station to see a new client in the cells. I found a colleague already in the foyer, waiting to see the same man. Apparently the fellow had spoken to two separate solicitors over the phone and they'd each briefed a barrister. My colleague had got there first but offered to relinquish the job to me. Smelling a rat, I insisted the client was his. It was a wise decision, as I heard on the grapevine later the fellow was an absolute fruitcake.

While I'm divulging trade secrets, let me mention one respect in which the profession of barrister is unique. While you can sue a plumber for an incompetent job and a surgeon for botching your operation, you cannot sue a barrister for negligence in presenting your case in court.[20] In part, this immunity is founded not so much on justice as on the need to make the system work. Without the rule an unsuccessful litigant could blame – and sue – his barrister. If he appealed the first case and lost he could sue the barrister who conducted the appeal, and if he failed again he could blame that barrister, and so on indefinitely. A barrister is immune because of the law's need for certainty and finality. What a relief; I'm glad I'm not a plumber.

Most of a barrister's work comes through solicitors. In Victoria we have a system where every barrister is a member of a 'list' run by a barristers' clerk. Having a stable of barristers means that if one becomes unavailable another can step in. The clerk organises the bookings and provides accounting and other back-up services. For this, he or she takes 5 per cent of the

[20] For the full reasoning see D'Orta-Ekenaike v. Victoria Legal Aid, (2005) 223 CLR 1, where the collective judgements of the High Court run to half the length of this book.

barrister's fees. Some lists have two hundred members, so a clerk can do quite well financially, certainly better than some of the struggling juniors on the list.

The story is told of a clerk sitting in a fancy restaurant enjoying a lunch of lobster with a glass of dry white. Through the window he notices a shabbily-dressed barrister on his list shuffle past, nibbling a sandwich he's brought from home. The clerk remarks, 'There goes one of those bastards who takes 95 per cent of my earnings.' I remind my own clerk that if barristers are parasites on society, then the clerk is a person who lives off parasites!

But are we really parasites? Or do we perform a useful function in society? After all, people can always represent themselves in court if they wish. In that respect, barristers are different from plumbers because, apart from changing your own tap washer or shower head,[21] you aren't allowed to do your own plumbing. You've *got* to engage a

---

[21] These are permitted under the Building Act 1993, Section 221D (2)(a).

licensed plumber to replace a downpipe, whereas if you want to, you're free to represent yourself even on a charge of murder.

But is it a good idea to represent yourself in any court proceeding? The answer is no. Every day I see clueless citizens floundering through the system without the faintest idea of what's important or even relevant to their case. A trained advocate is a necessity for the administration of justice – and not just for the litigants. Without lawyers the court system would grind to a halt. A case where an accused represents himself takes twice as long as it otherwise would, if not three times.

Our years of study mean we possess knowledge that non-lawyers don't. In the lower courts that esoteric learning isn't often needed because most cases turn on the facts, not on abstruse points of law. But we do possess a capacity for analytical thought, as well as practical skills about procedure and presentation. We know what decisions courts are likely to make on a given set of facts. A lawyer can't predict every outcome with certainty, but we can be pretty close to the mark most of the time. In short, we offer experience.

The law is one field where experience counts for quite a lot. Some clients actually value it, which makes for a heavier burden of work as the years go by. Whereas solicitors and plumbers can employ more staff to share the load, barristers can't. We're on our own. Ours is one of the few occupations where as you advance, you have to personally perform more work, not less.

There's a camaraderie among members of the Bar which clients sometimes mistake for collusion. The collegiate spirit can also extend to police prosecutors and comes from dealing with each other frequently. It creates trust; we know we can negotiate with one another in good faith. But it doesn't mean we're not fair dinkum when we oppose each other in court.

Some barristers have big egos. They're star performers in a script written by themselves. I've even heard the word psychopath applied. In its correct sense it means someone with a propensity for impulsive risk-taking, combined with a lack of guilt and shame. It's not just prisons that are full of psychopaths; company boardrooms are too and, yes, sometimes barristers' chambers.

Some barristers play it tough all the time; others vary the approach depending on what's at stake and how strong their case is. Bluster, bravado, condescension, filibustering and gamesmanship are all common techniques. One barrister never uses the toilet when he's at court because he cross-examines best on a full bladder.[22]Another sports eyebrows that make those of Bob Menzies look like a crew-cut. They're like antlers on a stag and serve the same purpose: threat-display in mortal combat.

---

22 There may be something in this. Researchers at the University of Twente in the Netherlands concluded that people exercise better judgment when they have a full bladder. Apparently the brain's self-control mechanism provides restraint in several behavioural domains at once. See Mirjam Tuk, in Psychological Science, May 2011.

Years ago when I did civil work, I used to carry leather-bound law reports into the courtroom and arrange them conspicuously on the bar table. I put little slips of paper in them as bookmarks; the idea was to unnerve my opponents by hinting I had some legal authority they didn't know about. These days my opponents bring in laptops and iPads and unnerve me.

I was once opposed to a Brisbane barrister much senior to myself. If I thought he'd go easy on me I was wrong. After I'd made my final address, he leaned across to me and whispered, 'Challinger, if I'd eaten alphabet soup for lunch I could have shitted a better address than that!' He laughed it off later as 'constructive criticism'. That's how they do it in Queensland.

A day in court creates anxiety; any decision you take could be the wrong one. You also face pressures of time, the adversarial process and the ever-present fear that you've overlooked something. Deciding what questions to ask, and when to press on and when to back off, all calls for judgment. It's a worry.

Unremitting conflict is stressful. Some barristers find it hard to stand the tension, and when there's an adjournment they can't resist being amicable and showing what good types they are. This is the thing which clients sometimes misunderstand. It also carries the danger that a jocular remark can be badly misinterpreted three months later.

Conflict draws on adrenalin – and testosterone too, it turns out. According to the latest research, males in a competitive situation experience a rise in testosterone levels if they win, and a fall if they lose. These hormonal ups and downs are found too in male wrestlers and chess players – not to mention lizards and rhesus monkeys. The explanation is that if a losing male continues to be aggressive, the chances are (in the case of a rhesus monkey) that he'll be seriously hurt, or (in the case of a male barrister) further clobbered. Natural selection lowers the testosterone of the losers, who back off and survive. It all makes sense in evolutionary terms, but sometimes by the end of the day I just feel weary.

I was looking a bit harried the other day and my client said, 'Mate, I couldn't do your job.' I thought to myself: I'm not sure I can either. The pressure isn't just from the conflict. It's from making decisions and exercising judgment. Judgment, incidentally, is something that comes with the passage of time. It can be learned, though I don't know if it can be taught. At the beginning of my career, I was advised to acquire a sense of judgment – but not told how. So helpful! Something like telling a king to rule wisely.

A barrister expends nervous energy in taking on the client's worries and assuming responsibility for his case. I remember an instance from my Port Moresby days where our firm were the lawyers for the University of PNG. One year the place erupted in rebellion and the students took over the campus. The vice-chancellor rang and begged me to apply for an urgent injunction to get the most dangerous radicals excluded. (He got the names wrong and we excluded the moderates, but that's another story.) A stenographer and I headed out to the uni and, having run the gauntlet of the rebel students, we made it into the office of the besieged vice-chancellor. The minute we arrived and I began dictating affidavits, the VC and his band of academics sprawled out and relaxed as if their worries were over. I was being paid, not just to do the work, but to take over the worrying.

What makes a barrister's job interesting is that our clients are actual people. While I don't become their bosom buddy, I do forge a rapport with them and try to treat them with respect and consideration. I did a case in the country for a burglar and was heading for home at the end of the day. The client was also returning to Melbourne and asked if I could give him a lift to the station. I did, but when he checked the timetable it turned out there was no train till dawn. Maybe I'm too humane, but I put up with him all the way back to Melbourne and shouted him a Chiko Roll and a Coke into the bargain.

There are other occasions when one helps out clients who are down on their luck. Sometimes at lunchtime, I sling them a few bucks or arrange a $12

Salvos voucher for them. The clients go to an eatery and enjoy a slice of quiche and a cappuccino while I sit in my car and eat a peanut butter roll from home and a No Name muesli bar.

One poor bloke received $465 a fortnight in benefits, from which he had to pay $435 for his supported accommodation, plus another $20 a month towards his accumulated fines. It left him $5 a week for everything else, barely enough for a bar of chocolate, much less a cask of wine, which he much preferred. I'm not Mother Theresa but I helped him out.

You try to be considerate in other ways, too. Part of a criminal barrister's job is imparting bad news: telling clients they have a lousy case, that they're going to lose their driving licence or go to jail. You try and break it to them firmly but gently.

Though we make light of it, there's high drama when someone is sentenced to jail – for the first time, anyway. You have to prepare the client for the worst, and even the stoical can find the prospect daunting. Even where jail is well-deserved, you have some human feelings about it. Personally, I try to be reassuring, though some colleagues are more blunt. When one client asked his barrister whether he should bring his ten-year-old son to court with him, my colleague replied, 'Only if he knows his own way home.'

Recidivists, of course, don't care so much. Mainly they want to make sure they go to the prison where their mates or relations are already doing time. I remember one who wasn't bothered about serving another sentence but wanted to be released at the same time as his son. 'What's your son in for?' I asked.

'Nothing much. Just stabbing a pedophile.'

Another time I appeared for a respectable businessman on some minor charge. He was terrified of going to jail, though there was no chance whatever of that, as I repeatedly told him. In the event he got a fine. Either he was hard of hearing or was so nervous he didn't take it in. I led him out of the courtroom and into an interview room. Anxiously, he asked me what had happened.

'Didn't you hear?'

'No. Am I going to jail?'

It was naughty of me but I couldn't help myself. I nodded. 'Afraid so.'

'Oh no! For how long?'

'Er ... a long time.'

'When do I go?'

'They're coming for you now!'

He looked so panic-stricken, I put him out of his misery immediately. He was relieved enough to forgive me my little joke. I don't know what I would have said if he'd lodged a complaint about me with the Bar Ethics Committee.

Another cleanskin client did cop a jail sentence. His family were all in court: mother and father, wife, sister and friends. It was beyond me why'd all turned up, as their presence was no help whatever. They shuffled out of the courtroom, distraught and sobbing; it was like mass hysteria. I excused myself to visit the fellow in the cells and cheer him up.

When I reached the cells I found him distraught and sobbing too; perhaps it was a family trait. Through his tears, he asked after his family and I stretched the truth a little. 'They're fine,' I fibbed. 'They're pretty composed. Yeah, they're handling it okay.' Then I went back and assured the family he was handling it well, too. White lies, to be sure, but what else was I going to tell them?

27

Parental Guidance Recommended

Children's care and protection cases

The Children's Court is a sad place. It's stressful, it's demoralising, it's alienating. You wonder what the world's coming to. There's a group of lawyers who specialise in the Children's Court and are there day after day. I don't know how they do it. Most of us can't stand the place.

The court has two sections: the Criminal Division and the Family Division. Both are depressing but in a different way.

The Family Division deals with children in need of care and protection. Where parents aren't looking after their kids properly, the welfare authority, the Department of Health and Human Services (DHHS), steps in and brings their cases before the court. Various degrees of supervision can be imposed, with the ultimate sanction being to remove the kids permanently from their parents' care.

Now, most mothers and fathers, even neglectful and incompetent ones, tend to love their children. Believe it or not, they actually resent their kids being taken off them by government officials. They want to have their say in court. But the Family Division is under-resourced and the Department staff over-worked. The system runs like a creaking, badly-oiled steamroller. Many parents find themselves in its path and some of them get flattened.

The parents come to court all psyched up to have their say and stick up for their kids. They expect something to happen – to get justice, even. But in every child protection case there are umpteen procedural hearings, and no matter how many reports have already been written, more are always needed. So the parents wait all day till they're utterly drained, then go home without understanding why nothing happened.

The lack of resources has always been dire. There have never been anywhere near enough magistrates. I remember years ago, jostling among a scrum of lawyers at the registry counter where a deputy registrar was trying to allocate seven cases between two courts. All of us were clamouring to get a start and avoid our cases being adjourned for three or four weeks – not to mention getting paid less for the day.

'Mine's only a two-dayer,' one of us insisted.

'Well, ours is only one,' shouted a second.

A third: 'I've got priority from April.'

A fourth: 'My client's with IDS' (Intellectual Disability Services).

The third: 'We're IDS too.'

A voice from the back: 'We're all IDS!'

'Mine's a self-mutilator!'

'I've got a bed-wetter!'

It might sound humorous, but these were people's families and children we were talking about.

Of course, it's hard for the court, too. The calibre of the parents is usually pretty low. Court officially starts at ten but absolutely no lawyer expects their client to get there before 10.30. One day I was waiting for an applicant mother. I called her at ten to be told she was still in Kilmore, 80 kilometres away, and on her way to the Salvos to ask for the train fare.

A fundamental problem in the jurisdiction is that DHHS combines two functions. It's both a welfare body and a regulatory one, so the protective workers are performing a double, and incompatible, role. Parents don't know where they stand with the Department and whom to trust. If they accept help and confide their problems – drug use, say, or family violence – then their admissions are used against them later. If they're guarded in what they say, the Department accuse them of lacking candour and failing to cooperate.

And, of course, the disparity in power is enormous. Ill-educated parents battle on alone while the Department has the entire resources of the state at its disposal. Protective workers can and do play favourites. Once the kids are out of the parents' care, the Department holds the whip hand. It can starve the parents of information, place their children with carers living miles away, disrupt their access, ignore their wishes on the ground the Department knows best, and undermine their resolve with vague promises they have no intention of keeping ('We'll consider more access soon'). On more than one occasion I've seen a protective worker actively trying to split a husband and wife up and destroy their marriage in pursuit of her own ideas of social engineering. I hate the underhandedness of the system and the unfairness of it.

Department workers compile reports and submit them to the court. In no time the reports, and the statements, notes and memos on which they're based, grow into massive, unmanageable files. Some wag thought up this riddle. Question: How can you tell if a baby is neglected? Answer: First weigh the baby, then the baby's file. If the file weighs more than the baby, then the baby is neglected.

The reports are repetitive, tendentious and riddled with second-and third-hand information. In most courts the Hearsay Rule prohibits evidence of what another person has said, but in the Children's Court the rule doesn't apply. Theoretically, it's to allow the comments and wishes of young children to be communicated through adult witnesses to the court. But when the Department's workers have an axe to grind, it turns into a game of Chinese whispers.

I once represented a father who'd taken his son on access. At changeover, when he returned the boy, the kid's shirt had red stains on it. The mother suspected (or claimed to suspect) the stains were blood. She took the kid to the Children's Hospital. On the mother's say-so the clinical notes recorded the stains *were* blood and speculated the child may have vomited it.

The Department wanted to squeeze the father out of the picture. So the next DHHS report recorded that the child *had* vomited blood while in the father's custody. The report after that went a step further, noting that the father had failed to act protectively and take the child to hospital himself. In fact, the stains were beetroot, but it took a medical witness and an hour of court time to follow the trail and work it out. As I said, Chinese whispers.

A minor, but irritating feature of the Department's reports is their ghastly circumlocution. You expect them to be self-serving, condescending and, in this age of word processors and cut and paste, repetitious. But quite as verbose, surely not. Nobody mentioned in a family report ever 'says' anything; the verb 'to say' is unknown. So are the verbs to state, assert and tell. In Welfare reports people always 'indicate'. ('The grandmother indicated she could help at changeovers and the mother indicated that would be acceptable. I indicated this to the father, who indicated...')

I once counted the word 'indicated' twenty-seven times on a single page! I highlighted them with a pink marker pen to illustrate to my son, then aged eight, the standard of prose produced by university graduates. Later, during the course of the proceedings, I had to hand up my highlighted copy to the magistrate. He made no comment, though he must have noticed. Still, I don't know what he might have said about it – sorry, I mean indicated.

Also, as you might expect, the reports are riddled with jargon. They overflow with phrases about 'taking stock', 'reaching developmental milestones', 'addressing issues' and 'putting strategies in place'. I read it all and cringe inwardly.

Just as the English language takes a pounding, so do the subjects of the reports. I know the Department's lawyers are run off their feet, but sometimes the parents suffer abominably. When one troubled young woman gave birth, an emergency order was made at her bedside granting custody of the newborn child to the Secretary of the Department. The next hearing was scheduled at the Children's Court the very next day and the girl dragged herself from her hospital bed and waited all morning at court. Her barrister explained the situation to the officials and asked for her case to be called on early. But the lawyer for the Department had six other cases to deal with and the welfare worker was waiting on a report to be faxed from the hospital. By four o'clock, nothing had happened and the mother was told to go away and come back another day. Absolutely disgraceful!

The process of negotiating with the Department can drive you to distraction. Even if you reach agreement, there's endless haggling over the precise wording of the orders. I represented a fourteen-year-old Aboriginal girl. Her grandmother was with her, a dignified lady whom I liked a lot. The Department quibbled over every minor point, so what should have taken an hour to sort out took five. At 3.30 we got the resolution we'd offered at ten. I still don't understand why they were so obstructive. As we left the court, the grandmother finally snapped and started shouting about the Stolen Generation. The security officers exercised some discretion and let her get a few things off her chest. So they should.

The Family Division is so emotionally charged that many people reach breaking point. Once I was sitting in an interview room when I heard an outburst, then an announcement over the PA system asking everyone in the court foyer to leave by the front door.

I stayed put. I'd never known the place so quiet. Such tranquillity!

After a while security came in and said, 'You were asked to leave.'

I said, 'I'm not in the foyer.'

So they let me stay for a while till the whole building was evacuated. Someone had been sprayed with capsicum foam and the stuff had got into the air-conditioning. The staff, I'm told, were delighted and went off for a few hours' shopping.

In the Family Division, expert witnesses abound: psychologists, psychiatrists, experts in early childhood development, exponents of Attachment Theory, psychotherapists, medicos, teachers, access supervisors, mothercraft nurses. There's a school of opinion that all expert witnesses should be treated as worthless on the grounds that whatever one says, another expert can always be found to say the opposite. After spending a few weeks in the Children's Court you tend to agree.

Consider this example. A program on sexual abuse was being conducted in a school. It ran for one hour a day for two weeks. That's right, not just a one-off session, but every day for ten whole school days in a row. They must have squeezed it into the curriculum by cutting out unimportant subjects like reading and arithmetic.

A cardboard box was provided in the classroom. Students could write questions anonymously and post them in the box; answers would be provided during the sessions. One girl wrote asking what to do if she 'thought' her father had previously abused her but didn't any more. Exactly what she was referring to was never made clear.

Of course, the experts conducting the course soon worked out who'd written the anonymous question and zeroed in on her. She came from a migrant family and her mother was summoned urgently to the school the following morning. The mother, whose English was basic, arrived expecting to discuss her daughter's schoolwork. Instead, she was confronted by the principal, two police, an interpreter and two sexual abuse workers who informed her that her husband was a dangerous child molester.

Over the next days the zealots applied pressure to the girl. One of them collected her from school on the pretext of driving her home. She took the girl to an office and quizzed her till the girl broke down in tears and agreed to whatever was put to her. Once she'd acquiesced, she was taken to McDonald's for a treat and given a teddy bear as a reward.

Expert witnesses from each side assessed the father, who was a respectable, educated businessman. The Department's expert reported that the father constituted an extreme danger to all young girls and especially to his daughter. The equally expert psychologist on the family's side reported that the father in no way fitted the profile of a sex offender!

The girl had been removed from home 'for her own safety' and boarded out with a white Australian foster family where the food was unfamiliar and some of the kids had serious behavioural problems. When the girl's father moved out of the family home, the Department reluctantly allowed the girl to return to her mum and siblings. The case progressed slowly until, after months of separation and anguish, the Department's case unravelled and the family were reunited. What an achievement for the community!

Harmless but struggling families who fall into the clutches of DHHS have the devil's own job extricating themselves. By contrast, parents who are unpleasant, recalcitrant and physically intimidating get away with it by bluffing the officials into closing their files after a brief intervention. During my time practising in the Family Division, the Department confiscated plenty of kids from clueless but innocuous battlers, while returning several children to violent bullies to be maltreated and, in one case, bashed to death. Still, the Department always know best.

I appeared for clients with an extremely rebellious and uncontrollable child. The parents had been preached at by Department experts and gone to all their parenting courses, but were still at their wits' end. One weekend the kid climbed onto the roof of the house and sat hurling tiles onto the driveway and refusing to come down. The parents phoned the Department's emergency number and eventually a couple of experts turned up. They did absolutely nothing, apart from waiting till the tantrum abated and the kid came down of his own accord. In spite of having been powerless themselves, the Department still condemned the parents for their failure to 'negotiate a solution' with the child.

To me, the idea of negotiating with children is fatuous. 'Behave or I'll reason with you!' Kids are invincible as negotiators because they're unremitting in getting what they want, and have no sense of responsibility or remorse. Responsible parents, on the other hand, are full of doubts and remorse and give in to their children, and to each other. Even well-behaved kids win most of the time, so negotiating with cunning, manipulative children who've learned how to get their own way is doomed to failure.

The Department functionaries thought otherwise, and in court I cross-examined them on what the parents should have done. Despite my best efforts I couldn't get a straight answer out of them.

'The parents should have reasoned with Aaron,' they insisted.

Me: 'As you saw yourself, he was impervious to reason.'

'Well, they should have tried different strategies.'

'What strategies?'

'The ones they've been taught.'

'Which of those should they have tried?'

'That's not for us to say. We teach the parents; they're the ones who should put them into practice.'

It went on like that for twenty minutes. What a cop-out!

Running a case like this just brings out the worst in everyone. On the first day you feel irritated by the Department, by Day Four you loathe them. The conceited know-all psychologist, the charlatan counsellor with her 'working through' and 'taking on board'. It shouldn't be like that – you shouldn't get so involved as to lose all detachment. In the case I mentioned we had a partial win and the parents were pleased with the job I'd done.

They said they thought God had sent me to them. Not God, I told them, just Legal Aid.

Sometimes parents represent themselves. It's a major disaster. Never mind the lack of any knowledge of law or procedure, the problem is that they have no hope of being objective. It makes a bad situation worse. I heard of one father who represented himself in the days before there were security checks at court entrances. He went to the bar table and put a box on it. Inside the box were dead rabbits. He opened the box, implying that something similar would happen to the social workers unless they gave him his access to his children!

Magistrate X was the phlegmatic type. He looked up with a bored expression and drawled, 'Yes, thank you. That will be Exhibit 1: box of dead rabbits.'

When the father tried the same stunt in the Family Court, the judge pressed the duress button and the SWAT team rushed in and dragged the bloke out. The judge made an order he not see his children for the next century!

There's a tale about the laid-back magistrate. A barrister friend recounts how she was part-way through a criminal case before a different magistrate. Some court staff came in and the proceedings were interrupted with urgent whispering to the police prosecutor, who was the only policeman in the building at the time. He excused himself, explaining that a man had been reported slumped dead in a car parked nearby. The prosecutor went down to investigate and gingerly approached the car containing the suspected corpse. It proved to be Magistrate X meditating!

Sometimes barristers are briefed to represent the child him- or herself. In the Family Court, a child's representative has to act in the best interests of the child, but in the Children's Court it's different. Here, you have to argue for what the child wants, which may not be at all the same thing as what's in their best interests. Even if the child's instructions are confused or inconsistent, we're obliged to put them to the court in that form; we mustn't try to impose a structure or consistency which doesn't exist. Adults are often perplexed by what goes on in court so it's no surprise children can be completely bewildered. Kids sometimes express strong opinions, but it often strikes me that their thinking is more muddled than we generally assume.

I represented one fifteen-year-old lad who did know what he wanted. Having run away from home, he just wanted his parents to accept he was his own person. There'd been conflict with his mother and she'd taken out an intervention order against him. It was sad; nobody wanted to be on bad terms, but somehow it had just happened.

I spoke with the mother and she accepted that the kid had voted with his feet, but she wanted him to come home for Christmas dinner. I told the kid; he wanted it too and we worked out a compromise. We had to go into court to have it confirmed. The boy wasn't allowed to speak to his mum till the magistrate gave the okay.

Sometimes I have to say to kids, 'Give your mum a hug.' They want to, mostly, but a gentle nudge can help them break the ice. This time I didn't need to say it; the boy and his mum stood up and embraced. Both were in tears. It was quite emotional. I had a tear in my eye too.

As we left the courtroom the clerk followed us out with a message from the magistrate. How touched he was. Seeing the family reconcile had brought a tear to his eye too. That made four of us who needed the Kleenex.

For once I felt I'd achieved something. Later I mentioned the outcome to one of the barristers for the Department. I told him the magistrate had also shed a tear. 'Oh him!' scoffed the Department rep. 'He's always shedding tears.'

28

Romper Room

Children's Court crime

The second section of the Children's Court is its Criminal Division. This is where juvenile law-breakers are dealt with. I say 'dealt with', as opposed to punished, because in this court the interests of the child are paramount, so punishment takes a back seat.

A nervous kid once asked, 'What's going to happen to me?'

I reassured him. 'This is the Children's Court, son. Nothing will happen to you.'

In Victoria the relevant Act provides for ten levels of sentencing. The least severe (other than the charge simply being dismissed) is an 'unaccountable undertaking'. This means the child makes a promise to behave himself, having been told that if he breaks the promise there will be no consequences whatsoever. An unaccountable undertaking is to the law what a placebo is to medicine.

The theory is that the child has already been punished by being put through the court process. Personally, I wonder. The process goes right over the heads of some of them. Anyway, children are resilient and for most, the court process is a good deal less traumatic than being raised by their parents. In my opinion, the proceedings should be more formal than they are. They should signal to the kids that the community treats what they did seriously, and that it's not just a trivial matter to be sorted out by a cosy chat.

The next level up in the sentencing scale is an accountable undertaking. Breaking this promise has consequences. The kid can be called back to court and either let off the promise or asked to make a new promise (but with no extra time). In an extreme case he can be fined up to $100, which he's almost certain not to pay. Draconian, eh!

The most severe sentence is to be detained in a Youth Justice Centre. The facilities there include a swimming pool, table tennis, basketball courts, billiard tables, trade school workshops, excursions, trips to the cinema, day release, phone calls, computers and the internet. The place is air-conditioned in the summer and the food is good. Some question the deterrent value of this regime.

I also wonder how strict the discipline is. I once phoned a client there at 9.30 in the morning and was told to ring back later as he was still in bed. I'm told the place is actually run by the inmates – the biggest and toughest of them, at any rate. So the most unpleasant thing about YJC for the smaller and younger of the kids is that they're at the mercy of bullies and thugs.

I appeared once for a boy on a charge of escaping from YJC. He was among a group taken to the cinema as part of their rehabilitation. The warders (the correct term may be 'Youth Workers') had chosen some repugnant American film, full of gangs and violence. I couldn't have imagined anything less suitable, but the staff wanted to see it, and that's the main thing.

Instead of sitting one at each end of their charges, the warders sat together so they could chat to each other. When the lights went down two delinquents in the middle of the row decided to abscond. They were the toughest of the kids and, finding it hard to squeeze past the others, ordered them to join the escape. In the darkness nine youths cleared off and made for the railway station. The train on the outbound platform was late arriving and four, including the ringleaders, were recaptured. My client and four others had been city-bound and got away.

My lad went straight home to his mum where he was arrested two days later. He explained that the ringleaders were violent bullies and had threatened the rest of them. He said he'd only absconded under duress and had actually wanted to stay and see how the film ended. I forget what penalty he copped for the spree. Hopefully, an unaccountable undertaking.

I had another escape case years ago where my client raised the defence of necessity. There'd been an outbreak of scabies at the Centre and he'd been issued with some cream to rub into his scrotum. When he applied it, the pain was so excruciating he jumped the fence to seek emergency medical treatment. The case got written up in a humorous way in *Truth.* Sadly *Truth* ceased publication last century so my cases never make it into the papers at all these days.

Some of them do deserve a bit of publicity (though the Act prohibits the young person being named or identified). A kid robs a parked car while waiting for his mate's girlfriend to have an abortion – after all, he has to pass the time somehow! His twelve-year-old brother accompanies him for something to do; he's playing truant because school's too educational. Another client doesn't make it to court because he's in the burns ward at the Alfred Hospital. While unconscious from drugs at a party, his friends sprayed him with aerosol and set his hair alight so they could film it for YouTube! Maybe I'm old-fashioned but I find these sorts of things shocking.

From a barrister's point of view, there are two advantages to the Children's Court. First, there's always work if you're willing to take it. Secondly, you can run a case from a seated posture. That's because in the Kiddies' Court nobody has to stand to address the magistrate. No, you don't want the court procedure to be too intimidating for young Cody, who's sitting there in the front row with his grandmother. His body language says it all. Insolence. Indifference. Incomprehension. Dumb hostility to the unfairness of the grown-ups' world.

What about insight, you ask, or remorse. Are you kidding?

Today the magistrate is a recent appointment who hasn't been around long enough yet to become completely disillusioned. Cody's counsel addresses the court while his yobbo mates lounge, smirking, in the back row. Cody himself sprawls across the front seat, arms extended, a look of boredom and resentment on his face. The magistrate tries to coax something out of him other than monosyllabic defiance.

'Now, Cody, I've heard all the good things your barrister has said about you. Is there anything you'd like to add?'

'Nuh.'

'Is there anything you'd like to tell me about yourself?'

'Nuh.'

'Do you like school?'

'Nuh.'

'What *do* you like?'

Looks at the ceiling. 'Nothin'.'

'Well, what about sport? Do you follow the football?'

'Dunno.' A pause. 'S'pose so.'

'Well that's wonderful!' enthuses the mago. 'Interested in sport! That's very positive! Sport's marvellous for young people.'

No wonder the cops call it Romper Room. And they're not alone in holding the place in low esteem. In private, a former magistrate once advocated burning the Children's Court down. He declared: 'It serves no useful purpose.'

Now, don't let me appear too jaded. The court is full of anxious, well-meaning parents and normal kids who've done the wrong thing. Many mums and dads are good people who take it seriously. The kid gets a fright. He's supervised for a time by Youth Justice and pulls his socks up. Some of their workers are good; they do succeed in turning some kids around.

Of course, a lot of the kids are struggling with problems that would send anyone off the rails. Rosa, for one, who sits there looking sleepy as if nothing that's happening has any bearing on her. Mum's in rehab, Dad's in prison and she's in a place called the Children's Court. Why wouldn't she be sleepy? She's faced it all: parents with drug and alcohol problems, family violence, sexual abuse, family breakdown, poverty. For boys, the absence of a father – or any decent male role model – is a yawning gap in their lives.

Teachers tell me it's not uncommon for kids to report they've got a new dad after every holiday, as mum swaps one disastrous boyfriend for the next. On being spoken to about his father, one kid asked, 'Do you mean my father at the moment?' A mother confided that her boy got unsettled every time he visited his biological father. The man was in jail serving a sentence for murder. What chance does that kid have of normality?

Some children have trouble at school; they find it hard to learn and easy to forget. That's where the community needs to invest resources and find ways to engage and educate them out of the mainstream system. Of course, funding for schemes of this kind is a low priority for any government.

I had one lad in an indigenous education program. Four of his subjects were: 'What's Doin' 1A', 'What's Doin' 1B', 'What's Doin' 1C' and 'What's Doin' 1D.' It sounded a bit bizarre but I'm in favour of it if it works. I asked him what he actually studied in those subjects and he said, 'Stuff about relationships.' At court he was accompanied by his grandfather, who was trying to mentor him and give him a bit of adult guidance. The kid seemed to treat the old man a bit offhandedly, and I told him he should respect his granddad. He said, 'I do. I really respect the old cunt.' They were his exact words! Yes, all that education was paying dividends after all.

There are other kids who make you despair. You can't help thinking they need a bloody good smack. Anti-social, recalcitrant, violent. They're fourteen years old and already streetwise. In the old days kids that age would be have been pinching Mars bars from Coles; these days they're robbing people at knife-point. You wonder why they've turned out so badly till you meet their parents. Then you change your mind about who needs the smack.

Growing up is all about accepting responsibility, and you live in hope the parents will actually grasp this. Some have no idea. Some even give their younger kids a day off school and bring them to court to 'support' their brother on his big day. Inevitably, the youngsters adopt the anti-authority, anti-police attitudes which their older brother and parents already share. Of course, some parents don't even bother to turn up to court for their kids. Those are the ones you're probably better off without.

Parents who ought to put their foot down pander to their deceitful children and swallow their obvious lies. Some migrant parents seem particularly feeble and ineffectual, in fact downright useless. They offer excuses: 'It's all the fault of that Robson boy', while Robson's parents are saying the very same thing about 'that Islander boy'.

This kind of parent always finds someone else to blame: the police, the school, 'the system', their kid's lawyer. Yes, even I'm blamed for suggesting their darlings are in the wrong for kicking someone's head in at a bus-stop and then telling a pack of lies about it. But it's the extreme cases that stick in your memory and all you can do is try and keep your dismay in check. At times it's like observing the customs of a different planet.

Fetu, for instance, was already on bail for a very serious assault. He broke his curfew, gate-crashed a party and committed an even worse assault. Why? Fetu thought someone else there was going to attack him, so he struck first.

As the victim fell to the ground, he hit his head on a metal ledge. He was in a really bad way. His parents were notified and raced to the hospital. When they got there, their son was on a trolley with drips and wires dangling off him. A team of nurses and medicos were rushing him into surgery. Nobody would tell the parents anything; they had to sit and wait. When the police arrived, they were carrying clipboards marked 'Homicide Squad'. The parents thought their boy was dead. They must have gone through hell.

The victim survived, but at court Fetu's parents didn't give the boy or his parents a thought. 'Fetu told us that boy was going to hit him,' they said. And it was all the magistrate's fault anyway, placing him on bail in the first place. The parents had wanted to send him back to Samoa to live with his uncle. None of it would have happened if he'd been free to leave the state.

Some of the assaults are horrifying, and not just those committed by males. Ashlee was at the Plaza Shopping Centre when she noticed one of her friends being reprimanded by a middle-aged woman. Naturally, she sprang to her friend's defence and punched the woman five times. In the fracas, Ashlee had her hair pulled so she dashed into the nearest shop, emerged with a hoe from the garden tools department and with one swing half-scalped the victim.

About mid-morning on the day of court, Ashlee phoned me, saying she'd gone to Werribee by mistake and was now on her way to Melbourne. That was going to take an hour and a half, assuming the trains were running. I waited till the afternoon but she never turned up. I was glad to be out of the case.

Another lass, Laura, was in company with a gang of female pals as she wheeled a pram carrying her baby, Cherokee. As they were crossing a railway pedestrian bridge they spotted Megan coming towards them. There was a rumour that Megan had been playing up with Cherokee's father, so Laura and the rest of them decided to teach her a lesson. The group overpowered Megan and held her down while Laura burned her with a lighted cigarette till she handed over her money, jacket and mobile phone.

At court Laura was pleading not guilty. She brought a statement from another of the girls, which read, 'I was there when Laura and Megan had that misunderstanding. All that happened was that Laura said, "You slut. How does it feel to be a slut?" Then there was this scuffle and that's all.' The author didn't make a statement to the police because she was worried she might get into trouble herself; she was the one who ended up with Megan's jacket.

The kids, by the way, are usually suffering from a variety of psychological conditions. Even if they're not too clever with their schoolwork they soon twig that a medical diagnosis absolves them of any responsibility and gives them a licence to do whatever they please. Curing them now becomes the job of their counsellors or doctors.

Asperger's goes without saying; everyone's on the spectrum these days. But there are plenty of others. Take your pick! There's Oppositional Defiance Disorder, which means they don't like doing what they're told. There's Explosive Personality Disorder (losing their temper). There's Adjustment Disorder, a catch-all that comes in six varieties. There's Attention Deficit Hyperactivity Disorder (fidgeting). Nobody knows what causes ADHD but it's an absolute epidemic. It's sheer coincidence that it develops in kids with backyards too small to play in, who gorge themselves on junk food and spend their lives in front of flashing video screens. And of course, there's no cure except Ritalin. Turning off the Nintendo and conversing with them is the last thing you'd try.

Recently I was in the Children's Court for a kid named Jaydon. His family kept referring to him as LP. When I queried the mother, she said, 'We never call him Jaydon at home. LP's his nickname.'

'Where does it come from?' I asked innocently.

'It stands for Little Psychopath.'

It may have been a joke, but I fear not. They thought it gave him something to live up to. I looked on the bright side: at least they knew how to spell it.

29

Off Their Face

Drugs

Drugs are a fact of life, I don't need to tell my readers that. They're a huge problem, and not just in Australia. They afflict even the most orderly and wholesome of countries. I learnt this in Switzerland some years ago when I came across dozens of discarded needles and blood-stained tissues on the steps of the Swiss Parliament. In rich and poor countries alike drugs cause mental illness, degradation and death. They make criminals of otherwise law-abiding people. And nobody knows quite what to do about them.

I venture a bit of philosophy here. In principle, I subscribe to the libertarianism of John Stuart Mill, which maintains that people should be free to do as they wish, provided they don't harm others. It might seem to follow, then, that if they choose to spend their lives spaced out on drugs, we should let them do so.

The catch is that almost all human activities have effects on others, mostly harmful in the case of drugs. The principle is therefore less useful than first appears. Using drugs affects the user's spouse, children, parents and employers. Collectively, the community bears the burden of supporting and medicating a legion of unproductive addicts, and dealing with the violence and mental health problems drugs cause.

Some people argue for legalising drugs. They say that most of the harm they do comes from trying to prohibit them. If drugs were legally available, they contend, users wouldn't need to turn to crime, jails would be empty and drug mafias out of business. In any case, they argue, attempts to suppress drugs are doomed. The war on drugs is unwinnable: just look at Prohibition in the US in the 1920s.

Personally, I'm not convinced. Nor am I sure the analogy with Prohibition is sound. There's a big difference between trying to prohibit alcohol, a drug in common use for centuries and regularly consumed by three quarters of the population, and trying to prevent the introduction and spread of substances used by a small minority. Just because we can't successfully prohibit one dangerous drug is no argument for allowing new ones to take hold. As for the 'War on Drugs' being lost, so are the wars on shop theft and speeding and double parking.

The community should aim at two things: first, to prevent drug-taking at all and second, to minimise the harm where prevention fails. Pursuing both aims at the same time leads to some untidy compromises. For example, there are sharps bins for discarded syringes in the toilets of every Magistrates' Court in Victoria. They're not there for diabetics; they're an acknowledgement of the limits of the law's power to prevent intravenous drug use.

Again, every day in courts, defendants attribute their criminal activity to drug use. They tender expert reports which detail their use of drugs daily or weekly or whatever. Possession and use of those drugs is against the law, but these open admissions never lead to charges being laid. I don't say they should, only that they're another illustration of the letter of the law bending to expediency.

In considering the legalisation of drugs, the question to ask is whether the benefit would outweigh the harm. In some countries it might: of the world's eight most murderous countries, seven lie on the cocaine-trafficking route between the Andes and the US. In Australia the balance of risk is different. I think prohibition here plays an important role in reducing consumption.

On the other hand, paradoxically, the very illegality of drugs is an attraction to some foolish young people. Quite apart from their 'highs' and pleasurable feelings, they enjoy the glamour and self-importance that comes with taking drugs. They love messaging each other, cruising round late at night, acting tough and splashing their money around to score. But some of these cool, wannabe gangsters can quickly get out of their depth.

A client of mine starts selling drugs for profit. His excuse is the usual one, that he's selling to support his own habit. He receives an SMS from strangers wanting to buy some ecstasy and arranges a rendezvous behind a Macca's car park. Two cars turn up and block him in. A gang of toughs then help themselves to his supplies, relieve him of the night's takings and steal his car.

They hoon around in it for two days, knowing my man can't risk reporting its loss. Finally they crash it and, as he's the registered owner, the police pay him a call. He spills the beans and ends up being charged with drug trafficking, with his car a write-off and a dangerous gang after him for dobbing them in. Glamorous, all right.

Another case. A young woman is infatuated with a swaggering drug dealer. She lets him move in with her but has 'no idea' what he's up to. Soon her garage is full of stolen goods and the house stashed with eight grand in cash. She doesn't know what he keeps in his bum bag, nor why they're parked in a quiet industrial area at midnight, waiting for a friend of a friend. When a car drives up and a blue light starts flashing, her boyfriend thrusts his bag at her and she hides it under her top. When the cops open it they find ecstasy, amphetamines, heroin, a bit of everything.

She claims she knew nothing of what was going on, even after a video is found on her mobile phone showing her weighing out powder on electronic scales. 'That was just a joke,' she protests. When I tell her she's facing a conviction for drug trafficking, she doesn't take the news well. She suddenly remembers she wants to visit the US where a drug conviction will debar her. Not such a joke after all. She sacked me, incidentally, and went to another barrister who gave her the same advice for double the price.

Dealing with drug-using clients presents all the problems of dealing with your average criminal, but in a more acute form. First of all, they commit serious crimes; very few burglaries are committed these days except by druggies. And it's desperate junkies who carry out despicable spur-of-the-moment street robberies or bag snatches, where old ladies are pushed – or sometimes punched – to the ground and injured, and are never the same again.

Secondly, drug users are the least truthful of all clients. Many are skilled and manipulative liars who have an answer for everything. Addicts frantic for their next fix will tell you anything to attain that end – absolutely anything, true or untrue. Their promises are worth nothing, a fact sadly not grasped by many loving parents desperate to help their drug-dependent offspring.

Another striking feature of some is their self-absorption and misplaced sense of victimhood. They see themselves as victims, and insist you do too. Their sense of self-importance is astonishing. Some consider themselves not just important but even admirable – yet at the same time powerless. The greater their addiction, the greater the sympathy they claim. Recently I was given a report on a drug user stating that he'd reduced his consumption to 129 bongs a week. What precision! How would he even keep count? He's conjured up a figure in his head, the higher the better.

Another client detailed his past to a counsellor who set out this history: 'Tony started using alcohol and cannabis at fourteen and cocaine at seventeen; he tried LSD at nineteen, magic mushrooms at twenty, heroin and ecstasy at twenty-two and methamphetamine at twenty-five.' At least his memory was still intact! Or imagination, more likely, for the worse his addiction, the more important it made him in his own eyes.

Some think that being drug-affected absolves them of all responsibility. A client of mine sneaked a diner's mobile phone off a table at KFC. It was all recorded on CCTV but he claimed not to remember. I reminded him the footage showed him walking past the table twice, checking it out.

'I wouldn't know. I was off my face.'

'And then you moved your bike closer to the door for a quick getaway. The court's going to think there was some planning involved,' I warned him.

He merely shrugged. 'Like I said, I was off my face.' He didn't think any further comment was called for.

Some are so far gone their entire sense of normality is awry. The Department of Health and Human Services intervenes to protect the children of an addicted mother. At the Children's Court a statement by a little girl of six recounts: 'Mummy stuck a needle in her arm. Then she died. Then she woke up again and her friends said the police were coming and we all jumped out the window and ran away.' To the mother and her friends, the used needles scattered under the TV unit are as matter-of-fact as ballpoint pens to the rest of us. When the welfare workers found used syringes on the front seat of the mother's car, she said, 'So what? The kids sit in the back.'

Parents of drug users find themselves in a quandary. I feel sympathy for many of them. Often they've been lied to, threatened, manipulated and blackmailed. They've had their houses smashed up, they've been robbed and deceived. Finally they reach the stage where they go to court and get intervention orders to exclude their kids from the house. Often they feel terrible about it, but I don't think they should reproach themselves.

Some are desperate for their kids not to go to jail. They want them sent for treatment in a drug-free environment. 'Jail won't help him,' they say, even though some jails actually are drug-free environments. Yet ordering drug users into rehabilitation doesn't work unless the will is there. You can lead a horse to water but you can't make it drink. In my experience, nothing can help unless the drug-user is motivated to help him- or herself. Often they have to reach rock bottom before that happens, and with some, it doesn't ever happen.

Courts have drug and alcohol counsellors to take offenders under their wing, to supervise them on bail and report back to the court. Their usefulness depends on their personal qualities. If they can create a rapport with their subjects, there's at least a chance of success.

Another method for getting someone off illegal drugs is to replace them with legal ones. Using chemicals to get off chemicals, a brilliant idea. To wean addicts off heroin, doctors can put them on methadone, a substance which reduces their cravings. Yet in the past, doctors put people on heroin to wean them off methadone!

Methadone (invented in Germany under the Nazis, by the way) was originally intended as a brief treatment to help addicts get through the first week or so of withdrawal. But I meet addicts who've been on it for ten years or more. Methadone's become an industry in its own right, with an army of medicos, pharmacists and counsellors dependent on it themselves.

Sometimes users do succeed in kicking their addiction and becoming drug-free. Sometimes with chemicals and doctors, sometimes alone, sometimes with religion, sometimes in residential programs. I'm in favour of whatever works. It doesn't matter whether cats are black or white so long as they catch mice.[23]

One of my clients had been in a residential facility and showed me the

23 Deng Xiaoping's maxim on the opening up of the Chinese economy in the 1980s.

timetable for Phase 1 there. The first activity of the day was called 'Huddle'. All the residents gathered to hold hands and hug each other. Apparently it worked for some people, but possibly too well for my client. He didn't reach Phase 2 because he formed a sexual liaison with one of the female huggers and got kicked out.

There used to be an accepted hierarchy of illicit drugs, with cannabis at the bottom and heroin, as the most dangerous, at the top. I can't say I agree with it. Opiates have a tranquilising effect and some addicts are able to lead normal lives, provided they have access to the stuff. In fact, heroin seems positively benign compared to the current scourge of stimulants such as amphetamines and crack cocaine, which can temporarily transform people into dangerous lunatics.

Crystal methamphetamine, commonly called ice, is the worst of the lot. It turns its users into violent, paranoid maniacs. It's also extraordinarily addictive. Users of it can serve six months in jail, then relapse within a week of their release. I've seen several instances where established family men in their thirties have tried ice and immediately become hooked. Their addiction was so destructive that within a year each had lost his job, his savings, his home, his marriage and his family.

Cannabis is by far the most widely used illegal drug. It became popular in the 1960s and '70s when smoking it was a Bohemian thing to do. It relaxed you and made you laugh. I thought it was harmless fifty years ago when my pals and I puffed it in the Monash Uni cafeteria.[24] How wrong I was!

True, many people tolerate it well, but if you smoke it for long enough or if you're especially susceptible, it too sends you round the bend. And cannabis is getting stronger all the time; nowadays the concentration of THC (tetra-hydrocannabinol, the active ingredient) in hydroponic cannabis has gone through the roof. According to a recent study, a potency of greater than 10 per cent increases the risk of

24 Like President Clinton, I didn't inhale!

psychosis five-fold.[25] Yet high-potency strains are available with THC of 25 per cent or more.

In the course of my work, I can't remember seeing a single diagnosis of psychosis which didn't implicate cannabis. I say implicate because cause and effect isn't entirely clear. Do the mentally ill self-medicate on cannabis or does cannabis cause the mental illness? Perhaps we'll find out shortly. Cannabis laws in the US and Canada have recently been relaxed, and the consequences to public health may soon start to show up. European researchers are delighted: laboratory animals are an expensive way to research cannabis but, as they point out, 'North Americans now come free.'

Clients often grow their own cannabis. It seems reasonable, even preferable, because it spares them the need to mix with shady drug dealers.

---

[25] Di Forti & others: 'The contribution of cannabis use to variation in the incidence of psychotic disorder across Europe (EU-GEI): a multicentre case-control study', Lancet, 19 March 2019.

But like growing tomatoes, you can inadvertently raise a bumper crop. Word gets out and soon people are queueing at your door asking for favours. Before you know it, you're selling the stuff. It's a slippery slope to becoming a drug trafficker.

Not long ago I acted for a middle-aged client charged with cultivating cannabis. At first glance he seemed to have a plausible excuse. His dog suffered epilepsy and a friend had given him some butter infused with cannabis to treat it. The stuff did Fido the world of good: the seizures became less frequent and less severe. So the fellow started growing his own cannabis; he even had a letter of support from a vet.

My sceptical eye spotted a flaw in his story. I asked, 'How many dogs do you own?'

'Just the one.'

'So why did you need 73 plants up to a metre tall?'

He didn't have a ready answer.

In all states there are diversion programs and cautions for cannabis, and good behaviour bonds without conviction for first offenders. Police turn a blind eye to local users who are otherwise law-abiding. Hillbilly types with a few cannabis plants in the backyard are generally left alone unless they start making trouble or selling on a big scale. When they're raided they admit they smoke for pleasure – though I had one who claimed to be growing a low-resin, high-fibre variety to supply rope for the macramé industry!

Drug courts for serious offenders operate on the principle of the carrot and the stick. Counselling, testing and other supports are provided, including accommodation. If the offenders come good, they can avoid jail. If they slip up they go inside for a week, then get a second chance. Apparently the courts are pretty successful, but I still find it bizarre to be asked in a courtroom to join a round of applause for a recidivist burglar who's gone a month without relapsing.

Drug use has no easy answers. Nor too many happy stories – or funny ones. The closest to the latter is the story my colleague Miriam told me about a couple of her clients. The two were doped up on amphetamines (it comes as a white powder) when they broke into a house and ransacked it for stuff to steal. In a drawer they came across a small box of whitish powder. Eager for a top-up, they inhaled some of the contents – though without much effect, apparently. There was plenty left so they took the box with them.

Further down the road they decided to have another snort and pulled out the box. This time they noticed some dates on the side and an inscription reading, 'Darling Betty, Rest in Peace'.

Besides feeling queasy at what they'd just ingested, they felt a pang of conscience. They returned to the house and, not daring to go back in, left the box on the nature strip. They pinched some flowers from the next door garden and arranged them artistically around the box. Alas, it was collection time for indestructible rubbish and the garbos assumed the floral tribute was junk and scooped the lot away.

The two were identified from their fingerprints and interviewed later by the police. The copper was impressed by their embarrassment and remorse – and he knew one fact they didn't. The birth and death dates for Betty were rather close together for a human being, but exactly right for the life span of your average pet goat! The *Age* reported the case under the delightful headline, 'Snuffed Goat gets up Burglars' Noses'.

30

Old Lags

Classic old-time offenders

The life of a down-and-out has ups as well as downs. There's the excitement of being chased by police and waking up in strange places. There's the pleasure of shouting obscenities at passers-by and stepping in front of cars to make them skid to a halt. There are handouts from kindly do-gooders and the fun of getting pissed with your mates. On top of it all is the sense of freedom which comes from having no responsibility of any kind, not even for yourself.

Men of this sort get restless without excitement and their escapades help keep me employed. Some even enjoy exchanging repartee with learned legal counsel such as myself; they certainly relish being the centre of attention in a Magistrates' Court.

Danny was one: scruffy and unshaven, with a bung eye that made him look crafty. Facing charges over a pram-load of scrap metal from a building site, he was more interested in telling me his life story. 'Back in 1955,' he recounted, 'I used to wag school and have it off with this sheila in the long grass behind the Ratsak factory.'

'Sounds romantic,' I nodded.

'We used to take a Tontine pillow to lie on.'

'Good planning.'

He was a cheerful dero in his early seventies with eighteen pages of prior convictions. In the 1960s, I noticed, he'd appeared at Moonee Ponds Court for seven weeks running, surely a record.

Danny even had a prior conviction for sacrilege, the only example I've ever seen. Sacrilege is the crime of breaking into a place of divine worship with intent to commit a felony. At common law it once carried the death penalty. Danny couldn't quite remember, but he thought it was the time he'd busted into a synagogue and urinated in the corner.

'What made you do that?' I asked.

'It was an accident. I was boozed up. I thought I was in a Catholic church.'

Danny had graduated from alcohol to other intoxicants and was now Melbourne's oldest practising glue-sniffer. This got him into strife too, even though glue-sniffing itself isn't against the law. He liked to carry a hatchet so he could cut the ends off tubes of glue to extract the last of the vapours. I admired his thrift; I cut the ends off tubes of toothpaste myself, though not with a hatchet.

One day Danny ran into an old acquaintance and, after sharing half a tube of Tarzan's Grip, they started arguing. Danny happened to be thrown through the front fence of someone's house, and when they spotted the hatchet they called the cops.

Danny was a witty and likeable man and it was a shame to see a wasted life like his, but a moralising pep-talk from me wasn't going to make him repent. I can't remember the outcome at court but he must have learned his lesson. I ran into him in the city a few weeks later with a coil of copper cable slung over his shoulder. He told me he always asked permission now before taking anything from a building site. It's nice to think there are still generous people around because his find looked quite valuable.

The last time I saw Danny was in Little Bourke Street near my chambers, where he spotted me inspecting the contents of a demolition skip. I was after a few off-cuts for a shelf at home and he told me he knew where there was stash of three-by-two. He offered to take me there but I started feeling nervous. Call me a piker, but I turned him down and ended up going to Bunnings.

Kenneth was another colourful old-timer whose company was entertaining in medium doses. Legal Aid warned me he was a classic old-time vagrant, so I expected the type who carries a plastic shopping bag of possessions in each hand. In fact, Kenneth had just one bag, a big overstuffed duffel bag, which he dragged along with his left hand. His right hand was free – at the ready to clutch any bottle within reach.

Kenneth was seventy-two and looked eighty-two; he must have had a liver like a wrung-out sponge. He too had prior convictions that made fascinating reading. His very first appearance was in the Children's Court in 1948. He was given a bond with a condition not to play truant from school and not to frequent billiard halls. It didn't seem to have reformed him.

His first conviction for being drunk and disorderly was in 1954 at Melbourne Petty Sessions where he was fined ten shillings. I read all this because the police had rather unsportingly raided their archives and raked out his entire criminal history. Usually they don't bother with stuff from the days before computers, but for some reason they'd attached all his priors, including pages of typewritten entries from decades ago. The litany of drunkenness, brawling and petty crime was a study in social history. I noted, though, he'd beaten a heavy charge in 1960: wounding with intent to murder – acquitted at the Supreme Court. I hoped he wasn't expecting to get off today.

Not that he faced anything heavy this time round. Quite the opposite: he was charged – yet again – with being drunk and disorderly, absolutely the very bottom of the criminal scale. Kenneth had already spent four hours in the cells, so all that could possibly happen was to be convicted and discharged. I couldn't work out why Legal Aid had granted him funding. I think they just liked him.

They'd let him loose with a dictaphone and told him to explain what brought him to court. His dentures fitted badly so the tape was interspersed with various clicks and whistling noises, as well as lengthy pauses. His story was long and involved, starting with a house of his in the bush which burnt down. Somebody then lent him a caravan but that caught fire too, as did a replacement from the Salvos.

The story then jumped to his recent trip to Melbourne to celebrate his birthday. He'd arrived by train from the country and, after a few drinks at a pub, he dropped in at the Vic Market for a free pie from a charity van. As usual on his city visits, he spent the night under the Swan Street Bridge, where he kept three blankets hidden among the girders. His tape contained tantalising passages such as, 'Now, about the amount of alcohol what I drank...' Then he'd go off at a tangent.

Anyway, early the next morning Kenneth was woken in his cosy spot by the first tram of the day rumbling overhead. He got up, but a passing blowfly buzzed into his mouth and caused him to vomit. Some busybody called the police on him, and when they turned up they threw him into the divvy van so roughly he banged his head and lost consciousness. Next thing he knew, he was lying across the tram tracks where the police had placed him so he'd be run over.

The prosecution version was otherwise. The tram driver's statement detailed how a shabby, unshaven male had boarded his tram and fallen asleep. After a while there was a thud and the driver noticed the male lying on the floor. He stopped the tram, shook the bloke gently and asked him if he was all right. The male replied: 'Get fucked.'

The driver reported to Fleet Control and when the tram passed the depot, a supervisor and some waiting police boarded to remove the man. The coppers said, 'Wake up, mate! It's the police. You can't stay here.'

The male said, 'Fuck off, I wanna sleep.'

The police said they then arrested him, took him to the police station and lodged him in the cells for four hours for being drunk in a public place.

Kenneth was shaking his head. 'Wasn't nothing like that.'

I tried a different tack: 'After they let you out off the cells, did you get medical attention?'

'What for?'

'Concussion.'

'Course I did.'

'Who treated you?'

'I treated me-self.' He rummaged in his bag and pulled out his medical kit, a square tin labelled 'Ballantyne's Chocolate'. He opened the lid and the compressed contents burst out like a jack-in-the-box. There was a tube of ointment, 'For Animal Treatment Only'. ('That's for me back,' he said.) There were foils and blister packs of pills and even a couple of condoms. He saw me notice the condoms and gave a lewd wink, 'I'm only seventy-two, mate. You never know when you might strike lucky.'

Kenneth had spent time in the cells and the court let him off without further penalty. He told me he'd only disputed the charge because he didn't want the Salvos to think he'd been drinking. Also, having lost three dwellings to fire, he professed to be worried about his insurance rating! I think he just wanted a yarn and a bit of attention.

Others of this kind aren't always as innocuous. Take Mick who, at first glance, is another battler. He left school at thirteen to work in Bryant & May's match factory, and over the years he's cut cane, dug ditches, picked fruit, done everything. Working as a die setter, he got his right hand caught in a machine and lost one finger and part of another. To find him at court the solicitor recommends I look for a bloke with only three and a half fingers on one hand.

Actually, Mick's easy to find. He wears a pair of baggy strides and a chequered sports coat like Happy Hammond used to wear on the 'Tarax Happy Show' in 1961. It may even be that very coat because it looks as though it hasn't been cleaned or pressed since at least then.

I'm meant to help Mick with an intervention order application he's defending. He's buggered his lungs smoking and the way he coughs and splutters he sounds like an out-patient from a TB ward. I feel guilty to be as healthy as I am and cough a bit myself from time to time to demonstrate some empathy. He's friendly enough but a bit intense, so I try and put him at ease and develop some rapport. I say: 'Mick, at your age, you would have done Nasho.'

'Yeah. 1957.'

'Good,' I say. 'That'll help. You're a war hero.'

'I never left Puckapunyal.'

'Doesn't matter, you served your country.'

'Only in the cook-house. The bastards wouldn't let me have a gun.' His expression darkens as he mentions firearms and I start to have second thoughts about him.

Mick's in strife over an elderly couple he met at a soup kitchen. I assume the oldies help serve the food, but no, they're on the take as well. Apparently there's a regular circuit – hot meals at the Morton Road Uniting Church every Monday, sandwiches and coffee at Centre 31 on Tuesdays and so on. The same clientele does the rounds and Mick runs into Tom and Doris every time he has a free feed. When he tells them he's getting evicted from his boarding house Tom and Doris, who've got a house of their own, offer to put him up.

So Mick parks his derelict ute on their nature strip and moves in. For a while things go well but Mick likes to collect indestructible rubbish from the side of the road. He grabs whatever's going and takes it home to sort out later. Before long he's amassed enough to fill a 32-foot container and Tom and Doris give him his marching orders.

With nowhere else to go, Mick keeps putting off his departure till one day a row flares up. What with his accommodation worries, Mick's calmed his nerves with half a bottle of whisky and a handful of Rohypnol. It blunts his self-control and in an angry moment he gives old Tom a smack in the teeth. Of course, he regrets it immediately and helps the old man to his feet. To make amends, he offers to let Tom even the score and hit him back. Tom asks, 'How many free hits you gonna give me?'

Well, Tom's old and decrepit so Mick offers him six free hits. Tom agrees and Mick stands there while Tom wallops him six times as hard as he can, which isn't all that hard. At this point Doris gets in on the act and demands a turn.

'But I never hit *you!*' protests Mick and argues the point. Finally, though, he agrees to give Doris three free hits and she lays into him. 'Shit, those punches hurt,' he tells me. 'I mean really hurt. She's a bloody tough old hag, that Doris.'

So Mick thinks he's expiated his misdeed and that everything's back to normal. He even assumes he'll stay on living there, so he's dismayed when the cops turn up and tell him to clear off. He's even more upset when they serve him with an application for an intervention order to keep him away. He doesn't want an order against him because he'll lose his guns.

'What guns?' I ask.

'Couple of rifles. The cops have taken them.'

I make enquiries and the police tell me they seized the guns months ago after Mick's brother reported him as a safety risk for his mental health and alcoholism. The appeal period's long expired, but Mick's obsessed now. He launches into a diatribe that the magistrate's a Freemason and the police and his brother are part of a Masonic plot. By now, to be honest, I'm starting to see Mick in a different light. I can't help noticing his trigger finger is one that's still intact.

The police also tip me off about a suicide attempt and I ask Mick about it. He says, 'I shot me-self all right, but nothing to do with suicide!' He clarifies his motive: a lady friend was goading him to be a man. 'Yeah, she kept on at me to shoot me-self ... you know, nagging me that much I thought I'd better do it just to shut her up.'

'Fair enough,' I nod.

'So I held me gun like this.' Through his shirt, he grabs a fold of his belly and motions a muzzle against it. 'Yeah, and I pulled the trigger.'

'What happened?' I ask. 'Flesh wound?'

'Flesh wound be buggered!' he shouts. 'Shot one of me kidneys out!' He lifts his shirt to show a whopping, semi-healed gunshot wound on his fat, fleshy stomach.

The sight's so grisly and unexpected I recoil as if I've copped an upper cut from Doris myself. For a moment I don't know what to say, but Mick stares at me with such a crazy, sinister, expectant look that I don't want to disappoint him. 'Don't you worry, Mick,' I promise. 'We'll get you those guns back. Just not today.'

31

The Armenian Connection

Daylight robbery

One day I get a brief from solicitors called Kortis & Co. They've never briefed me before and I've never heard of them. It looks like an ethnic name and I wonder what it is. Estonian? Czech? Could even be Greek. Whatever it is, though, I won't argue because the brief fee is $1100, which is quite juicy by my standards.

The papers are couriered over, together with the DVD of the client's interview with the police. The client, Teddy Azarian, is of Armenian descent. I don't like the sound of that: I've only done work once for Armenians and they ended up not paying.

The client's phone number is a landline, which is unusual in this day and age. I suspect it means the police have seized his mobile, and it turns out

I'm right. The number I've got actually belongs to Teddy's mum, who answers when I ring. Her English isn't the best, but her meaning is clear. 'Teddy no take you. Too much of money. I can't-a pay, very embarrassed, I'm on the pension. So sorry.'

'No problem if you don't want me,' I say.

'No, no, Teddy want you but too much of money. Very sorry.'

I phone Jim Kortis and tell him I've been sacked. 'No,' he says, 'she's just angling to get your fee down. I'll speak to her.' That suits me because I hate haggling over money, especially with Armenians. I tell Jim I'll do it for $880, nothing less.

'That should be fine,' he says and sure enough, within twenty minutes he calls back to say it's a goer after all.

Teddy's been charged with robbery, which means theft with violence: maximum penalty 25 years, in theory. The police say he and two others lured an Afghan refugee to a park and robbed him of $2900 dollars and a mobile phone. I wonder who the lawyer is for the other two, but it transpires they haven't got a lawyer because they haven't been charged. Strange.

I watch the DVD and Teddy's interview with the police makes painful viewing. His performance is one of the least convincing I've ever seen. There are lengthy pauses after every difficult question. Even with the easy ones Teddy's eyes dart back and forth as he tries to work out whether it's a trick question or not.

His version is that his mate Melek phoned him one day and asked to be picked up and taken to the train station. Melek's lost his driving licence and doesn't like walking. So Teddy collects him and his girlfriend (name unknown, but with mental health problems, he says). No sooner has he dropped them off at the station than Melek rings again and asks for a lift to Federation Park instead.

Teddy turns back, picks them up again and heads for the park. They're driving down the access road toward the netball courts when Melek tells him to stop at a Ford that's parked on the verge. Teddy pulls up in front of it. A

Middle Eastern type charges over to his window and yells, 'Show me the laptop!'

Teddy doesn't know what he's talking about, and when the bloke reaches through the window and tries to take his keys, Teddy grabs his wrist and twists it. He adds in passing that yes, Melek and the girl were out of the car by this stage. And, yes, there was a bit of argy bargy, but no, he didn't see any of it because he was looking straight ahead the whole time.

Next thing Melek and the girl jump back in and tell Teddy to drive off. He makes for the Adeney Street exit but finds the boom gate down. So he does a U-turn and drives back. As he passes the Ford, the Afghan takes a picture of his car.

At court on the day Teddy and his mum are punctual, which is a nice surprise. Mum's all in black, glancing at her son with a mixture of pride and anxiety. Teddy is tall and thin, and radiates untrustworthiness.

What's really strange is that Melek and the girl still haven't been charged. Teddy can't explain why. 'Anyway, I hardly know the bloke. I've only met him a couple of times in my life. And I don't know the girl at all. He never introduced me.'

I accept that at face value till the prosecutor lets drop that Melek is actually Teddy's cousin, and that the two of them stood trial together for deceptions a couple of years ago. When I ask Teddy about it, he says, 'Oh, I'd forgotten about that. I suppose I do know him but I don't see him very often. Like, we mix in different circles.'

The case is called on and we head for Court 4. Our mago today is Mr Fenby, who's a new appointment. He's at pains to be pleasant and beams like a cuddly toy.

The victim, Mr Samim, is a young Afghan who gives his occupation as slaughterman. He's built like an Olympic wrestler with muscles bulging through his dark T-shirt. Through an interpreter he tells his story in a halting, disjointed way. He tells of once buying a mobile phone from a man and girl he met in the Plaza. Two months later, he says, he bumped into them again and they told him they had a laptop to sell. So he gave them his mobile number.

'That same day they rang me and said to bring the money and meet them at the station. I went to the bank and took some money out. At the station the man and woman said to go to the park. I drove there and waited for them.

'They came in a car with a third man driving. They got out and said to show them the money. I pulled it out: I had $2900 in my hand. Then the man punched me and grabbed the money. I dropped my mobile phone and they grabbed that too and kicked me in the stomach.

'They went to their car so I ran to the driver's window and tried to take the car keys. The driver squeezed my arm, then he drove off. After a while the car came back going very quick and I took a picture on my phone as it drove past. Then I asked an Australian lady to help me and she phoned the police.'

The whole things sounds dodgy. It's a strange way to go about buying a laptop – unless you're in the market for stolen goods. And Mr Samim's bank transaction is strange too. There's a copy of his bank statement on the police brief which shows he withdrew almost his entire balance. It suggests a drug deal gone wrong. There are lots of things to ask Mr Samim when it's my turn.

'How much money did you take out?'

'I don't know.'

'It was $4748, wasn't it?'

'I don't know.'

'You cleaned your account out. You only left 28 cents in it.'

'I don't remember.'

'Well, look at your bank statement.' (The clerk passes it to him in the witness box.) 'Look at the balance. Twenty-eight cents, isn't it?'

'I can't read.'

'A laptop doesn't cost $4748, does it?'

'No.'

'Why did you withdraw so much?'

'I wanted to send money to my family in Afghanistan.'

'Wouldn't you send it through the bank?'

'I send it through my friend.'

'If you wanted a laptop there are plenty of shops to go to, aren't there?'

'Mmm.'

'You can buy laptops at Myers, can't you? At JB Hi-Fi? At Harvey Norman? You can inspect them and choose which one you want to buy?'

'Yes.'

'If you wanted a laptop why didn't you go to a shop?'

'It's cheaper on Gumtree.'

'Gumtree? But you can't read.'

'My friend helps me.'

'But this wasn't Gumtree. These were people you met in the Plaza.'

'I didn't know there were bad people in Australia.'

During all of this there's a lot of cross-talk between Mr Samim and the interpreter. Mr Samim queries something, the interpreter responds and the two get into a private discussion. A five-word question from me produces a minute-long exchange. The rest of us haven't got a clue what they're saying.

'You say you took a photo of my client's car?'

'Yes.'

'But these people had stolen your mobile phone!'

'They only stole one phone. The Department of Immigration gave me another one when I arrived in Australia.'

I haven't finished with Mr Samim when we break for lunch. And when I get back after eating my cheese roll, the prosecutor comes over and says the hearing can't continue.

'Why not?' I ask.

'The interpreter's just told me he's got a problem. He knows Farsi but the witness speaks Dari. Different language, apparently.'

'Well, they seem to understand each other,' I say.

'There's words in common, but he was having trouble, you could see that.'

So it's over for the day. The police pull the plug and we adjourn part-heard. The police will arrange to book the right interpreter next time and the case will continue from where we left off. The good part is that the public coffers will have to pay my bill. It's what happens when a case gets adjourned through no fault of the accused. It's especially nice because I feel justified in charging the marked fee of $1100 rather than Mrs Azarian's discount price.

Two months later we're back in court. A Dari interpreter's been lined up ☐ or so we're told. He looks young and a bit lost, but he's got a lanyard round his neck with an ID card dangling off it, so he looks official. First of all he has to take the interpreter's oath.

'Step into the witness box,' says the bench clerk. The interpreter and Mr Samim look at each other then squeeze in together as in a slapstick comedy.

'Just you, Mr Interpreter,' says the mago and there's another clumsy sequence as the two get in each other's way as Mr Samim steps out of the box.

'Raise the Koran in your uplifted hand,' instructs the bench clerk.

The interpreter understands the word 'hand', but 'raise' and 'uplifted' seem beyond him. He doesn't touch the holy book, which rests on the ledge, wrapped in a tea towel. Instead he holds up his hand as if he's half-heartedly stopping traffic. He looks flustered and I feel a bit sorry for him.

'Lift the Koran. Lift it up.'

He finally does so.

'Repeat after me: I swear by almighty God...'

'I see a mighty God.'

'That I will well and truly interpret...'

'That I will fully interpret.'

'All matters and things...'

He hesitates. 'All man's things.'

The mago interrupts. 'What level interpreter are you?'

'I am para-professional.'

Mr Fenby blinks. 'Para-professional? I've never heard of that level before.' He looks perturbed and asks the interpreter and witness to leave the court. Even that seems beyond their ken, and they hesitate till the police informant takes the initiative and ushers them both out the door. At least the informant has a good command of English, which isn't surprising as his name is Brian Jackson.

Once they're out of the way, the mago asks, 'How can I be satisfied with this interpreter? He didn't even understand being sworn in! How can I possibly rely on his accuracy?'

Naturally, I'm in full agreement; anything to put a spanner in the works.

I throw in my own two bobs' worth: 'Definitely ... no question of it ... completely inadequate ... a travesty...'

The magistrate asks: 'Can we get another interpreter today?'

Good question, and I happen to know the answer – which is next to no chance. I looked them up on the internet yesterday. There are nine accredited Dari interpreters in all of Australia. Only three are in Victoria and one of them is 200 kilometres away in Shepparton.

In fact, I did some other scholarly research on Wikipedia too, just in case something might turn on the accuracy of the translation. I've printed off pages of stuff and was all set to ask the police informant many profound questions, such as: 'Are you aware, Sergeant Jackson, that Dari derives from the Middle Persian court language of the Sassanid Empire and comes in seven dialects?' But the occasion won't arise now to show off my newly-acquired knowledge. A pity.

Instead, the case is adjourned again, with Mr Fenby deciding to abort the hearing entirely. Next time round we'll start the whole case from scratch. This is a pity too, because our next magistrate may not be as agreeable as Mr Fenby. On the other hand, it's only eleven o'clock and I can go home with an order for my fees to be paid again. This time the court orders the Chief Commissioner of Police to shell out. That'll teach him not to check out Dari dialects and the Sassanid Empire!

We're given a new hearing date of the fifth of August, but Teddy leans forward to me and whispers that the date's not good for him. 'It's the same day my sister tragically passed away.'

I look back and see that his mum's eyes are welling with tears. 'When was that?' I ask.

'Last year.'

'I'm sorry,' I say. No wonder Mum's emotional. I explain to the court and we get another date instead.

A little later I'm speaking to Teddy in the foyer when the clerk approaches and says there's some snag with the second date. We're given a third, the sixth of September, but Teddy says, 'Can we make it later? That's the day my sister tragically passed away.'

For a moment I think I'm hearing echoes. I say, 'You told me it was the fifth of August. How many sisters have you got?'

'No, I got it wrong before. The fifth of August was the day she ran away from home.'

'Ran away from home?' I ask. 'How old was she?'

'Thirty-six.'

It all sounds sus. I tell the prosecutor I was misinformed about the sister's date of death; I don't want to be accused later of pulling a swiftie. Teddy explains, 'My sister had a seizure or a heart attack or choked or something, the doctors never explained it. It was very tragic. My mum was really upset.'

So another two months pass before we front up yet again. It's another mago this time, one with a tough reputation. He used to be a crown prosecutor, they say; not the best draw for Teddy.

We get down to business. The Afghan tells his story again, more coherently this time, and I ask him the same questions. Why would he buy a laptop from a couple of shonks in a park? Why would he take $4748 out of his bank? And if he had $2900 in the park where did the rest of the money go? As I said, it sounds like a drug deal gone wrong.

At the end of his evidence, the prosecutor asks Mr Samim if there's anything else he'd like add. 'Yes,' he says. 'Thank you for listening to me, Judge. You are very wise and I know you will believe me and I thank you from the bottom of my heart. That is all.' Must be the way they do it in Afghanistan.

With Mr Samim finally out of the way, the police informant gives his evidence. Part of it is bad for us, because the cops have got Teddy's mobile phone and his call records. The records show calls from his phone to Mr Samim's *before* he arrived at the park. That suggests Teddy was in on the plan to get the Afghan to an isolated spot. They also show calls to Melek after the incident. That's bad too because Teddy's told the police he had no contact with Melek afterwards.

I ask the informant about Melek and the girl.

'On the evidence, they look like they're the instigators, don't they?'

'Possibly.'

'Well Mr Samim says they were the ones who punched and kicked him and took his money. He says Mr Azarian didn't get out of the car.'

'Mr Azarian was the getaway man.'

'So why haven't the other two been charged?'

'We haven't located them yet.'

'Not yet? It's been over a year!'

'They seem to be evading us.'

'Are you still looking for them?'

'Definitely.'

That's how the prosecution case closes.

Now it's our turn. An accused doesn't have to give evidence, but he can if he wishes. Sometimes it's best not to. Sometimes an accused's defence is at its strongest at the close of the police case – before he gets into the witness box and makes a mess of things! But there's a bit much here that calls for an explanation. So Teddy gives evidence.

He explains the calls from his phone to the Afghan. Melek made them; he'd asked to borrow Teddy's phone while they were driving to the park. And why was that? He said his own phone was out of credit. Sounds reasonable.

Then there are the subsequent calls to Melek. In his recorded interview Teddy denied he spoke to Melek after the incident, but his phone records show twelve separate calls that evening. The printouts give the duration in seconds. The longest is 1257 seconds long, which is about twenty minutes (lucky I'm good at sums).

So what did Teddy say to Melek? 'I was asking him, like, mate what's the go? What happened? Why did you involve me?'

And why did Teddy tell the police he *hadn't* spoken to Melek? 'I must have misunderstood that question,' he mumbles. Hmm. A bit feeble but it's the best he can come up with.

The prosecutor then cross-examines Teddy and ends with this:

Police prosecutor: 'According to you, this was all Melek's doing?'

Teddy: 'That's right.'

'If he came to court he could tell us what happened and get you out of trouble?'

'That's right.'

'Did you ask him to come?'

'Sure did.'

'What did he say?'

'He said he thought he'd get himself into trouble.'

'So he isn't much of a friend, is he?'

'Say that again!'

Now it's time for some submissions from me. Certainly Teddy was at the scene, but the prosecution have to prove more than that. They've got to prove he was acting in concert with the other two, that he knew what was going to happen and that he agreed with it or encouraged it in some way. Teddy says he didn't, and in the absence of Melek or the girlfriend there's no witness to contradict him. I actually think the point is valid, but that doesn't mean the mago will.

Call me a pessimist but I'm thinking Teddy's a goner. So does he, from the sweating he's doing, and with his mum all keyed up and ready to start crying. But the mago says he finds the evidence conflicting. He's impressed Teddy gave evidence and he's not impressed with Mr Samim. I don't know if he's impressed with my brilliant submissions because he doesn't mention them.

'I can't make any findings on what happened,' he says. 'Charge dismissed.' I ask for costs against the police and they're granted.

Mum can't quite follow what's happening. She doesn't know whether to burst into tears or start sobbing for joy. But when I pack up my papers and head for the door, she twigs it's gone our way. She and Teddy are all smiles – and so am I. I'm walking away with three orders for costs, a hat trick. I'll have to wait a couple of months for the Police and the Appeals Costs Fund to cough up, but I know I'll get paid in the end.

You little ripper! Give me an Armenian client any day!

32

Unhinged

Mental health cases

In Victoria there's a tribunal called the Mental Health Review Board. It consists of three members: a chairperson who presides; a community member who's there to protect the interests of the community; and a psychiatrist who's there to protect the interests of psychiatrists. I'm there to protect the interests of the patient. Fat chance.

Whenever I get a brief in this area, I feel duty-bound to warn the solicitor of my track record. I say, 'Do you know my success rate in this jurisdiction? It's zero. I've never won a case there yet.'

'Don't worry about it,' they reply. 'None of us ever have.'

The tribunal convenes at the hospital where the client is detained as an involuntary patient. That's a headache in itself because these days it's murder finding anywhere to park near a hospital. By the time you've circled the joint three times without spotting a vacant car space you already feel at one with your manic clients.

You get to see them an hour before the hearing. If they're considered dangerous you meet them under the eye of a psychiatric nurse. My client Jean wasn't in the dangerous category, so we met in the canteen of the psych ward. At the next table some gentle soul was drawing with a set of Derwent pencils. Another fellow stood hunched nearby, slowly raising and lowering one arm as though he was a boom gate. A third was dressed in shorts, wide-brimmed hat and bandoliers, with a water bottle strapped to his belt. Apparently he was an explorer. Jean told me she was desperate to get away from him and the rest of the loonies.

She'd completed her own application to the tribunal and it read: 'I am completely normal. I have occasional anxiety attacks and I feel my heart is broken. I am not insane, therefore I don't belong here. I do not believe Gerald has any intention of harming me again. He will pick me up from hospital as soon as he is released from prison.' Her handwriting was neat and legible – much better than that of her treating doctors, that's for sure.

The doctors' scribbled notes were harder to read. They were full of notations like: 'Confused and irritable ... feelings of hopelessness ... bashed by her boyfriend ... no insight ... perplexed, misinterpreting things, bizarre delusions ... disorganised and psychotic. Admits to increasing marijuana use over the past few months.'

Jean seemed pretty sane to me till she confided she was actually an angel and her thoughts were being controlled by the explorer. Usually it's television sets controlling their thoughts and telling them to kill themselves – or other people. Scary stuff.

When I front the tribunal, I get to put my client's case. My clients always want to be discharged. They deny any illness and never admit they might be a danger to themselves or others. They refuse to take medication except under compulsion.

The treating psychiatrist then gets a turn to ask the client a question. It's always the same question and it always sets them off: 'If you aren't ill, why do you think you're in hospital?' The client gives either of two answers. One: it's a conspiracy, or two: everyone else is mad. The answer, whichever it is, plays into the medico's hands.

One client, a young lass who did look on the slim side, was said to be suffering from anorexia nervosa. Her body mass index was half what it should have been but she wanted to be discharged and go home. She said she'd be living with her parents who would supervise her nutritional intake. It sounded reasonable, though the parents weren't there to confirm their willingness to help.

The psych asked, 'Are your parents still on their water diet?'

'Yes,' she said. 'They're up to day eleven.'

'And how long have they got to go?'

'Another three days till they're fully cleansed.'

'I see, and what are they eating?'

'Oh, they aren't eating anything! They just drink water or orange juice.'

The absence of the parents started to seem like a plus for us.

Another female client was preoccupied with a single issue. At her insistence I went to great lengths to correct an error that appeared on her file, namely that she believed her house had been painted with blood. What she'd actually said, I had to explain, was that the electric wire into her house had a tube attached to it. The tube contained blood and unknown powers drew energy out of her and stored it in the blood. That set the record straight.

'How do the unknown powers do it?' she was asked.

'I don't know.'

As I say, in this jurisdiction you always lose.

One time I had to go to the hospital where my mother had done voluntary work for many years. In fact, I'd occasionally helped serve cups of tea in the kiosk myself, which had earned me a sticker for a reserved parking place. Worse luck, the sticker was out of date and I had to find my own parking spot like everybody else.

Incidentally, Mum never much relished going to the Waratah Wing where, as she put it, 'the nut-cases are locked up'. She was there once, re-stocking the Coke machine, when an inmate informed her he was the Prime Minister. 'In that case,' she snapped back, 'why don't you do something about interest rates?' At this, the PM backed off and disappeared. A flicker of sanity? Who knows? Mum thought she was being therapeutic.

Anyway, this time I went through the heavy entrance doors to meet my client, Lorraine. The staff showed me to a room and suggested I keep the door locked because, as they put it, 'David's rather rowdy today.' Whoever David was, his cries echoed along the corridors. 'Eh, EHHH Wha-a-at? Eh, Ahhh! AHHH!!' Also audible were occasional shouts of, 'Go away, David!'

In the end I did get to see him, an elderly fellow wearing underpants for a hat and a half-torn shirt over his jumper. His face was old and sad and atavistic. Apart from his shouting, though, he didn't seem to be too much trouble – especially not to the doctors and nurses, who were safely locked inside a central, glass-enclosed control room. Patients who wanted attention had to tap on the glass and wait till a window slid open an inch or two. The doctors all looked to be Indian. Like taxi-driving, psychiatry seems to be a job only Indians are willing to do.

Lorraine was middle-aged with a bad complexion and a truculent manner. She didn't look that crazy to me, but they never do. Mind you, I changed my mind once I read her medical records. According to her file she made a habit of smearing her own faeces on walls and passers-by and, indeed, eating it! I didn't know whether to keep the interview room locked to shut David out, or unlocked for a quick escape in case Lorraine got the urge to smear me with shit. Luckily she'd taken her medication that day.

At first she told me she ate her own faeces because the food in the hospital wasn't very good. Also, she explained, she had no teeth and could only eat soft food! She didn't know why she did it and said she was ashamed. What could I say? I felt sorry for her yet revolted at the same time.

A few days earlier, she'd somehow got out of the hospital and made her way to a motel. The manager noticed her prowling round the motel forecourt naked, and called the police. Her clothes had 'fallen off', she told me, though she couldn't remember how. Lorraine didn't get discharged either. So much for the Mental Health Review Board.

Another administrative tribunal, the Guardianship Board, is somewhat similar. One day I went to represent a client before it at a hearing in offices in Carlton. Belinda had an intellectual disability and her finances were in the hands of the Public Trustee. Dissatisfied with this, she was applying to regain control of her own money. Two support workers were waiting in the foyer but there was no sign of the client. The workers were beginning to worry because it was unlike Belinda to be late.

Ten minutes later she sailed jubilantly in. A big, jolly, blowsy lass, she explained she was late because she'd called in at a hotel on the way and played the poker machines.

Apparently, it was her first time ever and the worst possible thing had happened – she'd won! Ninety bucks she picked up.

'That's very nice, Belinda,' the workers said, 'but you can't win every time.'

'Yes I can!'

'Nobody can, Belinda.'

'*I* can! I *always* win! I'm gonna go back and win more.'

'Maybe you should be happy with what you've won already.'

'No! I want more!'

We were about to be called in for the hearing so I got up from my seat. As I stood, Belinda lunged my way. A dollar coin had slipped from my pocket onto the chair and she pounced on it triumphantly. 'See! See! I always win!'

'Belinda, that's Michael's money.'

'No it's not. It's mine! I found it.'

The workers tried coaxing her to give me the dollar back, but without success. Then they started to apply the heavies and Belinda flared up. I didn't want to be mercenary but I didn't think we should just give in either. To break the impasse, I suggested we toss for the dollar.

After more argument, Belinda agreed. I let her call and she chose heads. I tossed: heads it was! She was giddy with glee. 'I *told* you! I *told* you! I *always* win!'

People like Belinda may have their foibles but they're often cheerful and good-natured, with a sense of humour. You can have a lot of laughs with people with an intellectual disability. Later on I got on famously with Belinda, even though I was a dollar down.

Mental illness, of course, is different. It's a huge problem and so much of it seems self-inflicted. It's rare to find a paranoid schizophrenic who hasn't been smoking cannabis. Again, I pose the question: does the cannabis trigger the mental illness or follow it as an attempt at self-medication? Cause or effect? I know what I think.

Mental illness plays havoc with the patient, the community, the public health system and the legal system. But it's the patients' families who bear the brunt of it. I had a young client whose mother was a schizophrenic. She drove him to distraction and he started misbehaving himself: getting drunk, doing graffiti, stealing from shops.

At least he received a bit of support. His mother occasionally got respite care so he could have a break from her. He also took part in a program for young people living in households where a family member had a mental illness. The participants produced a CD, to which my client contributed an original song. He offered to give me a disc but I doubted it would be my cup of tea. Besides, I wondered if he could spare a copy for me.

In fact there was no shortage; the participants had each received eighty CDs, and so far my kid had only managed to give away seven. Next time we met he brought me one and I played his track later at home. It was far from soothing and, at the risk of breaching copyright, I set out the refrain:

Then she schizes out
Lots of screaming and shouting
Makes me wanna yell
From a goddam building
From a goddam building

From a goddam building building
building building building

Intriguing stuff and, believe me, the words were better than the music.

Simon, another of my clients, was a diagnosed paranoid schizophrenic. He'd had a meltdown and spent five months as an inpatient in the Waratah Ward, which set a new record. Soon after being discharged, he was picked up drunk and drug-affected in possession of a 30-centimetre knife. He told me he wanted to plead not guilty on the grounds of mental impairment.

For a mental impairment defence, he needed to establish that he hadn't known 'the nature and quality' of his conduct, or that his conduct was wrong. In other words, he'd have a defence if he thought the knife was, say, a banana. But when the police had asked him why he'd been carrying the knife, he told them he had a lot of enemies and it was for self-defence. I explained that this wasn't the answer he'd give if he thought he was carrying a banana. He applied his remaining powers of reasoning and agreed to plead guilty.

Mention of knives reminds me of the automatism defence to a charge of murder. It's a bit of a digression, but I'm talking about those killings where the accused claims he was unconscious of what he was doing and had no control of it. He went into the kitchen, picked something up and – before he knew it – the knife had gone in and the victim was dead. The funny thing is that these offenders always pick up a knife, never a teaspoon or a spatula. They never grab a tea towel and start drying the dishes in an autonomic state. Why should that be?

The answer might throw some light on a case I did recently. A woman with paranoid schizophrenia had incurred $30,000 worth of parking fines. She said she couldn't help it by reason of mental illness. We made an application under the *Infringements Act,* which gives the court power to reduce or waive the fines. Personally, I couldn't see the nexus but the court let her off.

Now, psychiatric illnesses are slippery things. They're not like whooping cough or measles or tetanus, which are separate and identifiable. The symptoms of schizophrenia, bipolar disorder, major depression and others overlap, so that diagnoses by different medicos can and do differ. And of course, with mental illness symptoms can be faked.

It got me wondering whether my client can keep to the left when she's driving and stop when the traffic lights turn red. Because if she can't, she'll lose her driving licence, mental illness or not. I rather suspect she takes care to obey the road rules. She grasps that only with parking and toll-road infringements does schizophrenia give her a licence to do as she wants.

I've got a case coming up shortly for a bloke who suffers from a psychiatric syndrome with a strange, hyphenated German name. They've given me thirty pages of information about it. The behavioural features include lying and blame-shifting – of which I've already seen plenty. On page 4 there's a warning list of things that are likely to set him off. Triggers include talking to him too much – as well as not talking to him enough. Being overly sympathetic is wrong – and so is being indifferent. Using the word 'don't' is out: it gets him offside.

I hope I can strike the right balance; I'd better keep reading the other 26 pages.

33

Troubled Souls

The underclass

The sad, the bad and the mad: which is which? Often it's hard to tell.

The sad are the easiest to pick. Some started off as wards of the state because their parents couldn't look after them. They weren't delinquents themselves but they were sent to reform schools with the naughty kids because there was nowhere else for them to go.

Here's a police statement that somehow survived fifty years to turn up on one of my briefs.

VICTORIA POLICE STATEMENT
17 June 1968
Name of witness: Sandra Delaney
Address: Women Police Division, Russell Street
Occupation: Policewoman
STATES: Re Stephen Gregory Barnes.

Approximately 10.15p.m. on 29th September 1968, Miss Judy Barnes, mother of the baby came to the policewomen's office.

I said, 'Are you the girl who rang from Williamstown stating that you were unable to keep the baby and had nowhere to live?'

She said, 'Yes.'

I said, 'How old is the baby?'

She said, 'Almost four weeks now.'

I said, 'When did you take him from the hospital?'

She said, 'Last Friday week. I signed the adoption papers then I changed my mind.'

I said, 'Why can't you keep him now?'

She said, 'I didn't realise it would be so hard. I have nowhere to live and I can't get a job with him. I haven't anywhere to go tonight.'

I said, 'Have you any money?'

She said, 'About $2.'

I said, 'Have you any relations or friends who could take you?'

She said, 'The night I took my baby from hospital I rang my father and he said I could come home with him. Shortly afterwards my mother rang and she was drunk and said I couldn't come back there and bring disgrace on the family. She is an alcoholic.'

I said, 'Where do your parents live?'

She said, 'Mount Gambier in South Australia.'

Application was then made for the baby's care and protection and he was conveyed to Allambie. The mother was taken to Swinburne Lodge.

Stephen Gregory Barnes, now middle-aged, sat in front of me, a sad, unloved, demoralised man. He'd spent his childhood in an orphanage and his youth in jail. His early years had set the pattern and he'd never come good. He was simply an unsuccessful human being. He couldn't trade on a lousy childhood for ever, though, and he was going back to jail again no matter how eloquent I was.

As a kid he'd been bullied and brutalised – and sexually abused of course, that goes without saying. His experiences had produced an underlying aggressiveness and a lack of empathy for others. No surprise there: a background like his makes for a whole raft of behavioural problems and mental health issues.

But circumstances had forced Stephen's mother to relinquish him. She wasn't alone: in 1968 about 10,000 children were adopted in Australia.[26] Back then there was no social acceptance of children born outside marriage. Something desirable, a stable family structure, was underpinned by something harsh, a social stigma on illegitimacy. It's probably a good thing, but disgrace is a greatly weakened social force these days – if it still exists at all.

In those days many children were adopted out and it didn't always work, no matter how devoted the adoptive parents. The kids thought that if their

---

26 In 2018-19 the number was 310. Australian Institute of Health and Welfare.

mum had given them up, there must have been something wrong with them. Or, even worse, something wrong with their mum. And that's if they knew they were adopted. Those who didn't and found out later faced other problems adjusting. I sometimes wonder how much good tracing the birth mothers really does. Often both sides think only of the lost years, and go through more sorrow and anguish.

As for the mad, I encounter plenty. Take the bloke charged with importing prohibited goods. He'd ordered a PSP4 Phaser Shock Wave device, a plasma gun, a BLS3 Blaster wand, a Stun 4 Security Plus stun gun, a Z force-ultra stun gun, and a ZBLS Blaster Wand kit 120,000 volt stun gun. He had a crook back, he explained, and wanted to build a medical device. He was planning to zap himself with 120,000 volts to ease the pain! Or so he said.

I was representing a schizophrenic one day, a young man who suffered from paranoid delusions. He had a grudge against a farmer he believed was trying to kill him. Voices told him to sabotage the potato harvest by pinching the farmer's tractor. So in the middle of the night he hitch-hiked 80 kilometres to the farm and stole a $70,000 tractor. Then he drove it 200 kilometres to the other side of Ballarat and dumped it. On the way back to Melbourne he found himself in a railway carriage at Deer Park. The voices had gone quiet and he phoned his mental health worker and said, 'I think I've fucked up.' He was breaching a suspended sentence.

In the course of the drive, the client had managed to stuff the tractor's gearbox to the tune of $8000. At court, when the cops asked for restitution, I told them to forget it. My man was an undischarged bankrupt, which was pretty quick work as he was only twenty-two. As is the norm, the schizophrenia was mainly self-inflicted through drugs, though I can't speak for the bankruptcy.

Schizophrenia is a mental illness, but some clients are just weirdos. You assume most people want to get out of trouble, but some have an agenda you don't know – and which sometimes they don't even know themselves.

Jules, for instance, seems a bit Bohemian. He's accompanied by his mother, who definitely looks way-out. She's a tai chi instructor with peculiar hair and lots of jingling things around her neck and wrists. I tell Jules, 'Burglary is a serious charge.'

'Wow!' he exclaims, 'am I going to go to jail?'

'I don't think so,' I say, and he looks disappointed. It wasn't what he wanted to hear.

'But it's possible?' he asks hopefully.

'Anything's possible.'

'Cool!'

His mother seems equally delighted. When I arrange a new hearing date, she's thrilled. She tells me it's a good moon date, something to do with harmonious energy. Whew! I'm glad I've done something right! Before they leave she offers to sell me an accelerated personal growth program. They're having a breathing weekend for only $490. Sounds pricey so I give it a miss; I'll just keep breathing free of charge.

Another denizen of the counter-culture is at court for dangerous driving. She's an entrepreneur and gives me her business card. It lists her specialities: 'Clinical hypnosis, Counselling, Sekhem energy healing, Crystals, Psychic and intuitive healer, Flower remedies, Essential oils, Kinergetics.' The card is pink and has a drawing of a butterfly on it – or is it a flower? I'm feeling a bit run-down so twenty bucks' worth of Sekhem energy is tempting, but apparently that's not the way she sells it.

This lady, though, is no flower child; once we start discussing her case, her expression turns sour. She exudes a sense of resentment that the traffic rules apply to her. She takes it for granted that I share her own high opinion of herself, and if I don't, I'm in trouble. She's someone with an acute sense of injustice; probably been to university and done a major in Grievance Studies, she's got that sort of look about her.

She fits into the category we call querulous litigants. Their traditional habitat is the Family Court but they can pop up anywhere. You see them coming, the ones with armfuls of folders and notes, all underlined and highlighted in four colours. You can't pin them down on factual matters and certainly not on what they actually hope to achieve. They wallow in a generalised sense of victimhood and their present case is the defining moment in their lives. They expect to be vindicated, but whatever the outcome, it won't be what they want.

And what about the bad? Some are pretty clear-cut. A bloke with a Slavic name is charged with possessing child pornography, military explosives, detonators, fuses and a sawn-off .22 with a hundred rounds of ammo. 'Might be something to do with him being a mercenary in Africa,' suggests his lady friend. Luckily for him, it was before our present panic over bombs and terrorism.

Then there's Cameron. He's on parole when he reoffends. He turns up to court with a rough-looking mate and a rougher-looking girl he fails to introduce. 'Who's this?' I ask.

'Wouldn't know,' he says, shrugging. 'Only just met her.'

Cameron seems drug-affected; he's just shared some Xanax with his new acquaintance. He's facing charges of theft and criminal damage. He ripped a toilet fixture out of a public toilet and tried to make off with it. When the police asked him his reason, he said, 'They're new, those things. I've been in jail that long I'd never seen one like that before and thought I'd like to have it.'

Magnus, another young man, is charged with attempted theft by smashing open a railway ticket machine with an iron bar. The damage runs to thousands of dollars. He's pleading not guilty because he denies intending to steal. He explains: 'I wasn't going to pinch anything. I just felt like smashing something up.'

These people are basically social problems, but their conduct causes them to become legal problems too. The essence of growing up is learning to take responsibility, and these people simply aren't grown up yet. The last parts of the brain to mature are the parts that govern things like judgment and risk assessment and self-control, but this type haven't got that far. They're sexually mature at thirteen but not mentally mature till twenty-six – if ever. The Romans knew how long it took for males to grow up: you couldn't be a senator till you were approaching thirty. Yet in Australia you can legally get a job at fifteen, leave home and have sex at sixteen and join the army or get married at eighteen. Call it progress, but it doesn't change biology.

Some of these people's lives are so devoid of purpose that getting into trouble then getting out of it becomes an achievement. One major activity is copulating with each other's girlfriends, which also provides them with something to fight over. They rot their minds with television and video games, addle themselves with drugs, leave school early and then seem baffled when their lives don't come up to expectations.

What do you do with them? One idea is to call in the experts. Once the psychologists are on the job, there's no end to what can be discovered. With a bit of luck they'll prove to be suffering from some hitherto undiagnosed condition. Today I read a psychological report which diagnoses an offender as suffering from 'generalised psycho-pathology of moderate intensity'. Cripes, it sounds just like me – or most of my barrister friends, anyway.

According to the psychologist, a lengthy course of psychotherapy would be beneficial. Beneficial to whom? Certainly the psychologist if he can bulk-bill Medibank – but to the client? It makes you wonder. The client himself isn't interested in treatment, but he's very interested in his diagnosis. When he hears it, he agrees absolutely. 'Yeah, it's ruined my life.'

Psychologists deploy a whole battery of tests to justify their conclusions. A famous one is MMPI, which stands for Minnesota Multiphasic Personality Inventory. A questionnaire of 567 questions, it's designed to evaluate a person, and contains built-in checks, they say, to catch out those who under-report or exaggerate. It may have its uses, but I start to wonder when I notice incompatible scores on the 'Ego Strength Scale' and the 'Over-Controlled Hostility Scale'.

Excuse my cynicism, but there's another test called the HTP kinetic family drawing test. It sounds scientific and costs a couple of hundred bucks. But it turns out HTP stands for House, Tree, Person. When you've bought your test papers and cut open the sealed envelope, you find the test consists not of a questionnaire, but of three blank pages on which the subject has to draw – yes – a house, a tree and a person. The drawings are then interpreted by an expert who knows what conclusion their client wishes them to come to.

If the drawings are a good likeness, then the subject is exhibiting a sound grip on reality and fine attention to detail. If they are poor, they are 'primitive'. Jagged lines indicate anxiety, but straight lines indicate rigidity. If no hands are visible it suggests the subject is heavily into masturbation. Truly! What if the subject is rotten at drawing hands? What if they gave Picasso one of these tests?

People who throw tantrums or tell outrageous lies are diagnosed as ill. Sudden rages aimed at coercing or intimidating others are 'mood swings'. We're asked to perceive them as something like epileptic fits, rather than deliberate self-serving behaviour. Any anti-social behaviour which follows a recognisable pattern is given a label and provides an excuse for its continuation.

And if you haven't got psychological problems, maybe you've forgotten them. Talk to the right therapist for a dozen sessions and you've got a Recovered Memory! Dig deep enough and someone, somewhere, at some time or other will turn out to have touched you inappropriately in a way detrimental to your well-being.

I'm glad to say, courts don't swallow this stuff wholesale, but it does have an influence that starts to displace common sense.

Some of these people are very cunning. A colleague tells me of one young woman who's caught shoplifting. She informs the police she's got mental health problems and has been diagnosed as 'irrational'. They take her to the hospital where she asks to be admitted to the psych ward. The doctors refuse, so the police bail and release her. She goes straight into a nearby bottle shop and creates a scene by running amok and smashing a few bottles. The cops take her back to the psych ward and this time she's admitted. Irrational, you wonder? Evidence of reasoned thinking is more like it! She knew exactly what she wanted and how to get it.

And how well does 'the system' cope with cases like this? A schizophrenic marries another schizophrenic. They produce a son they can't look after, surely no surprise. The son is fobbed off onto the grandparents till he's thirteen, by which time he's grown into a big, rebellious, anti-social boy. He spends twelve hours a day playing violent computer games. He's completely divorced from reality.

The old folk can't control him and want him out. They apply for an intervention order, but the Department of Health and Human Services get to hear about it. Not wanting to be saddled with the kid, they intervene and negotiate a 'settlement'. They have him sign a 'contract' to limit his X-box to an hour a day and twist the grandparents' arms to have him stay on with them. The oldies still can't cope but the deal's been done. Their lives are a misery again but the Department have closed their file. Problem solved.

Sad, bad or mad? As I said, they're hard to tell apart. The categories seem to merge into one. Somehow you always come full circle and end up back at the sad.

A young woman already has one child she can't look after and is pregnant again to the same violent, drug-addled moron. When she's not out committing crimes, she spends her time smoking dope with her mother and grandmother. When her babies are old enough they'll be able to join in: four generations sharing a bong. Such togetherness! How can the law solve something like this?

Like begets like: a melancholy thought.

34

Places of Judgment

Court buildings

A courtroom isn't your average workplace. A relaxed and pleasant environment? Hardly. Privacy? Forget it. Natural light? None. Personal safety? Well, you're not going to be dragged into a machine and physically maimed, but for a barrister there's a definite risk of limping away with a bruised ego.

Courts represent the coercive power of the state. They aren't as laid-back as a coffee shop, nor should they be. Court houses symbolise justice; they are the visible state. They ought to be formal, dignified, imposing. Some are.

Every state has some splendid court buildings, New South Wales especially. Goulburn has a dome and colonnade; Bathurst is like the Vatican on a smaller scale; Deniliquin conjures up a Roman temple. Perth and Adelaide have magnificent Supreme Courts;

Queensland and Tassie have distinctive court houses that match their climates.

Historic buildings like these are unsuitable by modern standards. Some were built without electricity in mind, much less broadband. The waiting areas are small and congested, the offices are cramped, security is poor, toilet facilities are prehistoric and the buildings are cold in winter and hot in summer. Need I go on?

By the time I came to the bar, many of Victoria's historic country court houses had been closed down. A few still function, like the one at Mansfield, 190 kilometres from Melbourne, which continues to sit twice a month. Built in 1880, it was the very first court in which Bob Menzies, our longest-serving prime minister, appeared as a barrister. His fee was six guineas but he spent five quid of it on travelling expenses.

I sometimes get a gig at Mansfield and my solicitor mate Coxy also appears there. As a keen gardener, he tells me how on one occasion he noticed the rose bushes out the front looking neglected. On his next visit, being public-spirited, he took secateurs and gardening gloves with him. After appearing in court, he changed into work clothes and started pruning the roses. A passing local stopped, commended the job he was doing and asked how many hours he still had to go. He'd mistaken Cox for some old codger performing unpaid work on a Community Corrections Order!

The old bluestone court house in Kyneton[27] is still going, too. Ned Kelly appeared there in 1870 for robbery (and got off). They used to have an open fire until a few years ago, when a barrister stood too close and set his pants alight.

Until recently, many of Melbourne's suburban courts were of the cream brick, flat-roofed, public urinal style of architecture. The facilities were lousy. There were hardly any interview rooms and you conferred with clients and witnesses on the front steps. If you wanted more privacy you moved further along the nature strip.

---

27 Readers with an interest in history are referred to my own Historic Court Houses of Victoria, Palisade Press, 2001

My least favourite court was at Sunshine. It was a woeful, cramped building on the far side of the railway tracks, remote from the main shopping area. The court staff were unfriendly and didn't open the doors till 9.30. By then there'd be two dozen punters jostling to get inside to be first at the counter. I rarely got a good result there. It must have had bad *feng shui*.

The few shops nearby included an adult bookshop a few doors along and a bottle shop directly opposite. If I got to court early I used to kill time in the grog shop, checking out the Croatian liqueurs. Some of the other customers were also waiting for the court to open, and I took pains not to watch what they were up to. Citizens who were soon to swear to a magistrate that they were total abstainers would exit with brown paper bags in hand. They'd carry their clinking purchases across the road and deposit them in the boots of cars they shouldn't have been driving.

Sunshine now has a new court house up near the highway. It's laid out like an airport terminal but with fewer toilets, no legible signs and a drink machine instead of a duty free shop. First you go through security, of course. Then you walk down a sort of concourse with a glass wall on your right and the doors to the courts on your left, numbered like boarding lounges. The comparison isn't completely far-fetched because some of my clients do actually go on a trip after passing through their doors.

Box Hill Court (now demolished) adjoined the police station and was another unattractive venue. One morning my car wouldn't start so I rode my push-bike to court. To avoid being spotted by my client, I went round the side of the cop shop and started to padlock the bike to a railing. A policeman came out and said, 'You can't leave that there.'

'Why not?' I asked.

'It might get stolen.'

The prosecutors' office was in a separate annexe at the back. For a time it had a sign on the door reading: 'No Admittance to Solicitors'. Luckily, I was a barrister. Sometimes, when the prosecutors were especially keen to sort out a case, they'd take me the back way and usher me through to the cells without signing in at the watch-house counter.

I'd follow the overgrown path to a sort of out-house. The cells didn't have bars, they had wire mesh, like cages at the zoo but harder to see through. There was a painted line you had to keep behind and a busted metal chair you could drag to the line and sit on.

Because of the wire you couldn't really make eye contact with your client. There was no privacy whatever; the other prisoners lurked in the shadows listening to everything you said and sometimes contradicting it. Occasionally they'd prompt my client from the sidelines and he'd say, 'My mate here reckons you're wrong.' I'd think to myself: if your mate knows so much, how come he's in there and I'm out here?

I was giving advice once to a bloke who'd spent several days locked up there. A fellow prisoner had convinced him he'd beat most of his charges and would get a bond on the rest. I broke the news that he was looking at a couple of months more in the slammer.

The bush lawyer kept interjecting till finally I said, 'Mate, can you please shut up. We don't need your advice. I'm meant to be the lawyer here.'

He grunted, 'Yeah, meant to be.' A point to him, but he did stop talking.

Preston cells were the worst. They were more dungeon than cage. We lawyers would stand in a sort of alcove in the police station and the cops would open an inspection hatch on the door. In winter it was freezing. The cells were so cold, vapour billowed out as from a deep freeze.

Things are much improved these days, with proper interview cubicles in police stations and court houses. You speak to your clients in private through the reinforced glass. If they lose their tempers or put on an act, they can shout and bash their heads against the glass in perfect comfort. Occasionally you'll be interrupted by a custody officer taking orders for morning tea. The prisoners are always at their well-mannered best for this: 'Milo with four sugars, please.' The officers are always polite, too – at least while I'm there.

In the past, the most shabbily housed of all jurisdictions was the Children's Court. The old building in Batman Avenue was made of breeze blocks and fibro. Conditions were dire, though I'm told the corridor was handy for the clerks to play indoor footy after hours with a screwed-up newspaper. The place was demolished, thank goodness, and with Federation Square no trace of it remains.

The court transferred to a rented building overlooking the casino – very convenient for parents with a gambling problem. It was miles better than Batman Avenue, but it wasn't purpose-built as a court and some of its design features were far from suitable. The courtroom doors, for instance, opened inwards, a very bad idea.

I was appearing there once in a child welfare case. My client, the child's mother, was serving a jail sentence and had been brought to court in custody to take part in the proceedings. At the end of the day, after the magistrate had adjourned, my client's boyfriend went to kiss her goodbye. The courtroom was empty except for the loving couple, two police and myself.

Officially, physical contact with prisoners is forbidden, but in the Children's Court where family members are separated, security sometimes allowed a bit of leeway. Not this day, worse luck. One of the police was super-officious and roughly pulled the mother away. She took umbrage and resisted. The second policeman was drawn in and a regular brawl ensued.

The two police wrestled the woman to the ground, but in the confined space they couldn't subdue her. For several minutes she goaded them: 'You fucking dogs, you think you're so tough.' Police reinforcements couldn't get in from outside because the three struggling bodies prevented the door from opening.

I didn't distinguish myself in the fracas. I stayed put at the bar table, mumbling, 'Hey there', 'Steady on' and other facile remarks. The boyfriend screamed abuse and threats to sue the police. He couldn't join the fray himself as he was recuperating from three broken vertebrae sustained in a drunken stupor, when he'd been hit by a train.

Finally, extra police managed to force their way in and drag my client down to the holding cells. I hurried downstairs to speak to her. A senior sergeant met me and asked what the hell had happened. I told him the incident had been avoidable and didn't reflect well on anyone. I went into the cell, where my client was nursing a blood nose, split lip and sore wrists. Nothing came of the barney, though. Both sides called it quits. Nobody was charged and nobody was sued.

Now there's a new purpose-built Children's Court in Little Lonsdale Street, diagonally opposite where the old VD clinic used to be. I don't think the layout is ideal here either, but the courtroom doors open outwards and it's light years better than the previous building.

Half a block away, opposite the Flagstaff Gardens, is the newish Commonwealth Courts building. Before it was completed, the various federal courts were spread among a number of leased city buildings. Part of the Family Court was housed in an office building in King Street, quite a walk from the legal precinct.

I was never keen on family law – as if I haven't got enough domestic turmoil without buying into other people's! – but I did a little of it in my early years. One day I had two undefended divorces in King Street, one in a court on the sixth floor and one on the eighth. I hadn't met either client and I was alternating between the two floors in the hopes of making contact with them. The lifts were slow so I was using the stairs.

After a couple of ups and downs in the stairwell, I lost count of what floor I was on. Thinking it was the sixth, I tried the door handle, only to find it locked. I looked to check what level I was on but there was no floor number marked. That was strange because a minute earlier the floors *had* been numbered – or so I thought.

I feared the stairwell door had clicked shut and that now I'd have to run down to the ground floor, exit onto the back lane and re-enter the building. I let fly at the door with some colourful language and rattled the handle forcefully. As I applied maximum torque, the handle gave way and fell to the floor with a clang.

Within seconds I heard doors opening on the landings on floors above and below. Voices rang out – 'Stop! Security!' – and hurried footsteps started to converge on the floor I was on. I sprinted one level up, dashed into the lobby (the door was unlocked) and flung myself into an armchair. A sign indicated I was on the eighth floor. What had happened was that I'd been on the seventh which, unknown to me, was locked and unmarked because it was where the judges had their chambers.

I was just in time to grab a newspaper and pretend to be reading. Two security guards burst into the lobby, looked around then disappeared. Soon they were back, brandishing the door handle. One approached and demanded, 'Did you do this?'

I lowered the *Age* nonchalantly. 'Beg pardon?' I wasn't going to ruin my career by admitting to criminal damage and contempt of court. I brazened it out.

They shook the handle at me. 'Did you damage this?'

'No way.'

'We know it was you.'

'Well, if you know, why are you asking?' (Yeah, I was quick with that one!)

By this time I'd strolled to the lift doors. 'Excuse me, please,' I said as the doors opened and I stepped in. I felt guilty telling those blokes a fib; they were only doing their job. Still, it wasn't the first lie to be told in the Family Court, nor the worst.

At lunchtime, when it was time to leave I made sure I was in the middle of a gaggle of fellow barristers. As I exited, the guards said, 'Sir, we know it was you, please just tell us it was,' but I didn't admit anything. Soon after, I told my clerk I'd lost interest in matrimonial law. That was the end of my career in the Family Court.

Of course, security in all courts is now tighter than ever. It was upgraded in one suburban court as a direct result of one of my clients. The prisoners' dock at the time was an enclosed, waist-high wooden stall. It lacked the usual shoulder-high perspex partitions and offered an athletic prisoner a chance to jump the dock and do a runner.

I'd never seen it attempted, and I hadn't picked Colin as an escape risk either. He'd breached a suspended sentence but seemed resigned to serving the three months he owed. Apparently, as the mago was pronouncing sentence, Colin's wife in the body of the court became a bit emotional, got to her feet and left the courtroom. I didn't see this myself, as she was behind me.

But I did see the next part. Quick as a flash, Colin vaulted the dock and dashed the width of the courtroom, heading for the door. A staff member tried to block his path and Colin lost half his shirt in the scrimmage. Even so, he made it out the courtroom door, through the foyer, out the main entrance and – a miracle – across the busy main road without being hit by a passing car. On his way through the foyer, he shed the rest of his shirt so he was bare-chested as he disappeared into the multi-level car park of Shopping Land.

The court orderlies took off in hot pursuit because they were going to get into terrible trouble if Colin got away. They cordoned off the carpark and recaptured him within the hour. Colin claimed to have surrendered voluntarily, saying he'd never really intended to escape. His feelings had just got the better of him and he'd wanted to comfort his wife and give her a farewell kiss.

It sounded touching but the story didn't quite match the facts. He'd shot past his wife in the foyer without offering her a word, much less a kiss. The wife told me afterwards she'd been the only one to say anything.

'What did you say?' I asked.

'Go, baby!' she grinned.

Colin faced court the next day, charged with escaping from legal custody. I represented him again, even though I was potentially a prosecution witness. Our version fell flat as the magistrate noticed there was an intervention order in force, so for Colin to have given his wife a hug would have constituted an additional offence. The mago gave Colin an extra month for the escapade and the dock was enclosed in perspex within the week.[28]

What with metal detectors, X-ray machines and long queues, getting in and out of court houses these days can be time-consuming. It makes it hard on clients wanting to nip outside for a smoke. On a busy day in the city the whole process, including waiting for the lifts, can take a good ten minutes. Of course, I do exhort my clients to give up smoking, but only once their case is over. I don't expect them to quit when they're all stressed out. It's easier on me, too, if they soothe their nerves with nicotine one last time.

One female client of mine was waiting for her case to be called and asked if there was time to pop out for a cigarette. I said, 'There is, but didn't you tell me you were pregnant?'

'Yes, with twins.'

---

28 I can't resist recording the excuse another escaping client once gave: 'Just giving the police some exercise.'

'In that case,' I said, 'better have two.'

35

The Rough and Tumble

Coping with the bench

Every year barristers have to do ten hours of Continuing Professional Development. One of the seminars on offer last year was 'How to Handle Difficult Tribunals'. It was a one-hour session and I was puzzled how they could cover such an extensive topic in so short a time.

Courts and tribunals are presided over by judges, magistrates and other judicial officers. These people are in control and they can make things easy for you – or difficult. All are individuals and many have their idiosyncrasies. Some decide quickly, others are slow and meticulous. Some are amiable, others irritable. Some tell you what they're thinking, others are inscrutable. Some are plain speaking: 'Tell your client to bring his toothbrush next time.'

Others are prolix: 'I don't wish to inhibit your client's vocational aspirations.' (The kid was half-way through a dog-grooming course!) And some are just plain unpredictable.

The barrister's job is to persuade a court to decide the way their side wants. It pays to keep the judge or magistrate on-side. Sometimes it's wiser to back down a tad than to press a point. When a magistrate shouts at me: 'Sit down! Your submissions are nonsensical!' I take the hint.

Decades ago things were much worse. Being a magistrate then was a licence to be a bully. I remember one jailing five defendants in a row because it was his golf day and he wanted to get away early. Another was famous for having told a police prosecutor he was a 'cretin' and for interrupting a barrister by saying, 'That's the most pusillanimous submission I've ever heard'! The barrister didn't even know what pusillanimous meant. (It means gutless, in case you don't know either.)

About twenty years ago, audio recording was introduced. When that happened all court proceedings were taped, so these old-time magistrates had to moderate their manner and curb their more extreme remarks. In theory, you can now get a recording of everything said in open court. In practice it's different: a couple of times I've applied for one at $55 a throw, only to be told it's 'unavailable', can't be found or didn't come out. The first time I got a useful copy I was horrified at the fidelity of the recording. It picked up all the coughs and asides at the bar table, including me whispering to my opponent, 'Shit, I don't even want to be here. Let's get this over with.'

I hope the magistrate didn't hear the remark, but part of the problem in court is knowing what the magistrate *has* heard or – more to the point – heard and actually taken in. Often in a case it's more important to emphasise the obvious than to elucidate the obscure. Sometimes, then, you repeat a question or comment in slightly different words to get the point across. In doing so you risk annoying the mago.

'His last conviction was in 1999, Your Honour. That's twenty years ago.'

The mago, testily: 'Twenty years? You don't say! I've been able to do sums since grade three.'

And once they're peeved, magistrates will seize on any slip. A short-tempered one asks a colleague, 'How old is your client?'

The barrister fumbles with his papers and plays for time as he does some quick mental arithmetic: 'He's ... er ... he was born on the twenty-first day of ... er, February...'

'I'm not going to send him a birthday card,' snaps the mago. 'I just want to know how old he is.'

The cardinal rule, then, is not to antagonise the court. Yet at the same time you have to advance your client's case. You need to judge when to press on and when to desist. Sometimes the decision is made for you. I was expounding a legal argument once before an irascible magistrate. She said, 'You've wasted fifteen minutes on that. Move on to your next point.' I thought: Strewth, I haven't got a next point – and ground to a halt.

At other times you plough ahead no matter what. One mago some years ago was so indecisive he was at the mercy of the last thing he heard. Fifty-fifty Fritz, we called him. With Fritz it was essential to stay on your feet and have the last word. The last person standing would win the point.

With most tribunals, though, you need to judge when to ease off. You need an 'off' switch and know when to use it. I remember making a series of submissions to a judge and striking a brick wall at each step. It was obvious he disagreed with everything I was saying. Perhaps I was over-persistent. I said, 'I know I'm annoying Your Honour to press this point.'

He grunted, 'Well, you've finally said something that *is* right.'

On one occasion I did a case about a lease of a shop, a crooked Chinese versus a crooked Lebanese. It wasn't my usual field and there'd been a fair bit of paperwork to it. Partway through the hearing the magistrate exploded, 'These pleadings are unintelligible! What does Clause 13 mean?' I waffled on a bit and he interrupted me, saying, 'When I was at the bar I practised in this field and I've never seen pleadings like them. Who drew them?'

'I did, Your Honour.'

He said, 'Well, I've read Clause 13 four times and I'm none the wiser.'

'None the wiser, perhaps, but hopefully better informed!' That's what I should have answered. It's the classic retort and was on the tip of my tongue, but I wasn't game to say it.[29] The mago was already cranky with me and by the third day he threatened to order all the costs against me personally for wasting time. It was said of him that he was often wrong but never in doubt.

Another time I was running a case for a bloke with a long history of violence. He was docile with me, but the sight of a blue uniform tended to inflame him. He had issues with anyone in authority. His outbursts were quite alarming and on a previous appearance in court he'd leapt to his feet and made a wild lunge at the bench.

---

[29] Coined by Victorian barrister Walter Coldham before the Chief Justice of the High Court in 1905.

Before the case began, the magistrate called the prosecutor and me into his chambers and told us he was aware my bloke might pose a security risk. He said he'd given orders to double security, though he'd told them to keep a low profile. He'd also directed they weren't to carry firearms. 'If there's any trouble,' he said, 'I don't want the wrong person shot.' A prudent decision certainly, but I wondered afterwards who he thought was the right person to be shot.

On occasion, judges and magistrates are sarcastic. I generally don't mind, provided it's directed at the client, not at me. Indeed, it sometimes expresses bluntly what I can only tell them politely. A client of mine charged with refusing to blow into a breathalyser claimed a sudden asthma attack had rendered him physically unable to blow. The mago said, 'Yeah, nothing brings on an asthma attack like the sight of a flashing blue light.'

Even pleasant magos can be unpredictable. Years ago there was a lovely one we called Gentleman John. One afternoon he was on auto-pilot. He gazed absent-mindedly at the ceiling while a colleague made a plea in mitigation for a fellow barrister who'd been caught speeding. Trying to do his best for his pal, my colleague delivered some high octane rhetoric. At the end, Gentleman John gave a start and said, 'Could you repeat that, please?'

'Which part, Your Worship?'

'All of it. My mind wandered.'

So my colleague tried again, but it had been a one-off. His inspiration had waned and he managed only a pale imitation of his original peroration. Gentleman John wasn't impressed and suspended the barrister's licence for six months.

There are magistrates and judges whom you try to avoid, but sometimes you just can't help a bad draw. I once represented a kid who'd made a few crank calls to the fire brigade. I dealt with it light-heartedly, but unknown to me, the mago was the chairman of the Metropolitan Fire Brigade Tribunal and didn't share my levity.

Just as druggies go doctor-shopping for an obliging medico, so we go mago-shopping – or try to. For us it isn't easy because the rosters of judges and magistrates are only made public on the day of the case or the night before. Some days if you have a case in two separate courtrooms and play your cards right, you can get one transferred so both are dealt with by the more favourable magistrate. Otherwise, all you can do is to think up a reason to ask for an adjournment. Recently, at one court, a tough reserve magistrate turned up unexpectedly and there was a rush to the lifeboats. The courtroom emptied as five cases in a row were adjourned. But you risk facing the same mago again next time – or one who's even worse.

By worse, I mean tougher. In general, that will be the one who's been a magistrate the longest, for they all get tougher as time passes. When they've heard the same excuse a hundred times they tend to tire of it.

It also pays to have local knowledge. One day I appeared at a country court for an accused who'd embezzled a lot of money. Some local solicitors were at court and since I didn't know the mago I asked them what he was like. They said he was a model of fairness and common sense. That was disappointing because they weren't qualities I wanted in a magistrate that day; I preferred credulity.

Still, I waxed lyrical that the proceeds of the thefts hadn't even been usefully spent. 'Dissipated on joyless luxuries,' I described it, 'a fancy car with mag wheels and a cabin cruiser.'

A couple of the solicitors congratulated me later. They said, 'We loved your plea, especially the bit about the joyless luxuries.' It turned out the mago had bought himself a new car and boat the week before!

I might add that for pleas of guilty there exists a whole lexicon of clichés: 'wrong choices', 'turning his life around', 'pulling his socks up', 'taking strides', 'a cry for help'. They're hard to avoid no matter how much you try. The grammatical passive voice also comes in handy: 'an injury was sustained', 'loss was incurred', 'the vehicle was damaged'. Anything to camouflage the unvarnished truth.

Humour certainly has its place in court and a harmless jest can serve to lower the tension. Indeed, in the highly-charged atmosphere of the courtroom any droll remark can seem wildly comical. Often it's less so in retrospect, when what seemed the height of wit proves less funny in the re-telling.

Humour, though, is the prerogative of the bench. Mostly the advocate is wise to play it straight, though with due appreciation of any sally from the bench, no matter how feeble.

A Chinese bloke who was a disqualified driver was caught driving to his local KFC. The mago remarked dryly, 'Only last week I had another Asian gentleman driving while disqualified. Also on his way to Kentucky Fried. This seems to be a prevalent offence.'

The same mago dealt with a another of my clients who got into a scrape in a pub. I tendered a report which said he regularly consumed twenty beers a day. The mago quipped, 'I suggest he cut it down to nineteen.'

Interruptions from the bench can be a problem. They throw your train of thought and prevent you expounding any coherent argument. One magistrate, now retired, was notorious for it. He barely let you get started.

'My client is nineteen years old...'

'Well, he should have known better...'

'He's beginning to mend his ways, Your Honour.'

'Yeah, I've heard all that before.'

And so on.

I was once on my feet before this magistrate when a prosecutor quietly passed me a note. It read, 'Congratulations. You just managed three whole sentences in a row.'

My mate Coxy was a model of how to handle this particular mago. He was appearing for a bloke on his fifth drink driving charge and he just kept plugging away without contradicting the mago one jot. Whatever the mago said, Coxy would agree, then continue: 'That's a very good point, Your Honour ... except on the other hand...'

'This offence, there are very heavy penalties now,' grunted the mago.

'Yes, Your Honour, the Act was amended ... when was it now? ... (Coxy makes up a date at random) ... in December 2018, I believe.'

Cox just keeps talking till the mago mumbles, 'Nnnn – yeah I suppose when you look at it that way ... Well, he's got to do some community work.'

'Exactly my first impression,' says Cox, 'but then, Your Honour, I don't want to create a problem for the Office of Corrections. Unfortunately my client may have difficulty performing the community work.'

'Nnnn – yeah. Why's that?'

'A work injury, Your Honour. He was a metal polisher.'

'What sort of metal did he polish?'

'Er ... various kinds of metal, Your Honour. Yes ... er, any type of metal that needs polishing. Burnishing, I believe they call it.'

'So what's his problem?'

'His elbows, Your Honour, they're completely shot, what with all that polishing.'

'All that drinking wouldn't have helped!'

'Very true, Your Honour. Good point.'

'All right, it'll have to be a fine then.'

'A fine, yes Your Honour. But the problem with a fine is he's got very limited means.'

The upshot was that Coxy, having talked the mago out of imposing jail or community work, worked it down to a minimal fine.

'When can he pay it?' asked the magistrate.

'Well, it'll have to be the same way he pays his legal costs, Your Honour. On the drip feed.'

The mago was going to make it $100 a month but Cox bargained him down to $80. Brilliant!

Personally, I never managed to handle the magistrate so adroitly.

The mago: 'This behaviour is outrageous!'

'It is, Your Honour.'

'It's deplorable! And this report! It's just a joke.'

'It says he's making progress, sir. Page 4.'

'That's just a euphemism.'

I look down. 'Possibly.'

'So he forgets to take his medication but remembers to smoke marijuana!'

I didn't have a good answer to that one, not on the spot, anyway. Sometimes it's hard to make a clever retort no matter how alert you're feeling. Being quick-witted is slightly different from being sharp-witted. I'm sharp enough but not always quick enough. When I get asked a hard question I do always manage to think of a smart reply, but sometimes it takes me a week to come up with it.

I occasionally wonder why judges and magistrates get so cantankerous. After all, they're are on a very good wicket. Quite apart from the generous pay and super, they have a fun job, sitting in comfort and sending people to jail. They have short hours, and the best job security you could ever get. They can't be sacked except by Act of Parliament – and for that to happen they need to be pretty-well totally deranged.

I applied twice to become a magistrate. I filled in an enormous questionnaire but never even scored an interview. I shouldn't have been surprised; at Nunawading High School I polled second in the election for prefects but the headmaster vetoed me on the grounds I was unfit to exercise authority. It might sound like sour grapes to quote this, but one wag described a barrister being appointed a judge as the only example in nature of a butterfly turning into a slug.

I remember one fairly bumptious barrister who was appointed a magistrate. The promotion went to his head and at a social function he announced that in his new role his aim would be to improve the standard of the junior bar. A voice sang out: 'You already have!'

I used to keep a dossier on the judges and magos from when they were appointed and written up in the Bar News: what school they went to, whether they had a family, what their interests were. If I knew they were into horse-racing, for example, I'd pepper my submissions in court with turfing metaphors.

It didn't always work. I appeared before one magistrate I knew to be a Catholic. My client, who'd been knocking off stuff from his employer, had formerly been a student at a Catholic school, and I alluded to the fact. 'Attended a very good school, Your Honour, Marcellin College.'

'Yes,' she shot back, 'this court gets a lot of thieves from that school.'

This mago was a very plain-speaking lady. I was before her one day for a client who had an excuse for everything – all of them preposterous. He carried a machete because he used to work on a road gang; he had Woolworths 'Reduced' price stickers in his wallet because he'd previously worked as a supermarket cleaner and used to help the baker reduce the prices on yesterday's stock. The mago heard me out then turned to the accused. She said, 'Your barrister's just told me what you've told him. That's his job. He has to tell me.' Then she paused for effect, fixed him with a look like a cobra and added, 'But *I* don't have to *believe* it. And I don't.'

The same point was once made more subtly by another mago. My client was an old lag with a long string of convictions. He was putting in his own two-bob's worth about how he'd finally reformed. 'I've turned the corner, Your

Honour,' he insisted. 'I truly have! I give you my word I'll never break the law again as long as I live.' The mago nodded sagely at the promise and went relatively easy on the bloke. As the chap left the courtroom he sang out, 'Thanks, Your Honour.'

The mago, deadpan, replied, 'Bye-bye. See you next time.'

36

Compassion Fatigue

Getting sick of it all

After more than forty years in the law and thirty-plus as a barrister, I have a confession to make. Occasionally – just occasionally – my tolerance and good humour run low. It happens to many lawyers from time to time, some of whose reserves drop to near empty.

A while ago a magistrate I'd known since law school retired and I wrote him a note wishing him well for his retirement. His reply was succinct. He said it was a relief to leave the court with its 'endless parade of human violence, stupidity and deceit'.

Compassion fatigue, then, is an occupational hazard. It isn't a chronic condition, though; it comes in bouts. When I suffer an attack, I feel like getting up and addressing a court like this:

Your Honour,

My client is a worthless parasite. He is lazy, dishonest, cowardly and violent. He acknowledges no authority but his own whims. He is oblivious to anything worth knowing, and proud of his ignorance.

He had some bad luck in childhood and has been trading on it ever since. The chip on his shoulder is the size of Uluru. He's had mental health issues – self-inflicted of course – which he regards as a complete excuse for his persistent law-breaking.

He complains of physical ill-health which modern medicine is at a loss to explain, but which previous generations would have diagnosed as malingering.

I recommend he be sent for a lengthy period to a secure, drug-free environment.

I don't say it, though. It's my job to advocate for him and that's what I do. A magistrate once told one of my clients, 'I'm filled with admiration for Mr Challinger. I don't know how he thought up so many good things to say about you.' I didn't know myself.

On the whole I like my clients, and most of them seem to like me. Respect is an essential element in a friendly feeling and I can summon up some respect for an honest thief, or for clients who show a scintilla of genuine remorse. I wish my clients the best, both for their own sakes and the community's. The future's unpredictable, though, and you can never tell how they'll end up. Some do well, some do time.

But clients want to get their own way and some of them think the first step is to manipulate their advocate. Some are cunning and well-practised at it, indeed, absolute experts. They take every advantage and exploit any flicker of sympathy from others. Self-pity infiltrates their every utterance. They tell you ludicrous lies and when you warn them the court is unlikely to swallow them, they whine, 'But you believe me, don't you?' I tell them it's not my function to believe or disbelieve, and some get the message. Others don't; they plead and wheedle and whine till my patience wears thin.

Often I have to give them bad news. 'Your chances of bail aren't too good,' I say. In fact I'm breaking it to them gently: their case is hopeless. But they still arc up and act aggrieved and accusing. 'Whose side are you on anyway?' they demand. I wonder whether they react the same way when a doctor gives them a bad result from a pathology test.

A colleague had a client, aged thirteen, in the Children's Court. He asked the boy a question about his case and the kid snarled back, 'No comment.'

My colleague admits he just about exploded. He shouted, 'Who the fuck do you think I am? I'm your bloody lawyer!' But this was a child so inured to the system, so jealous of his rights, so distrustful and devious, that he wouldn't help even his own barrister.

There are clients who argue, quibble and split hairs. They contradict themselves without noticing. They tell you to argue legal points that are untenable. They nudge you in the middle of a case, 'Object to that! Don't you know your job!' They put you on the spot by making stuff up as they go along. They expect you to sacrifice your good standing with the court by being party to some subterfuge they've just thought up.

With these clients you need to set boundaries, maintain formality, and focus on what you're there for – and on what can or cannot be achieved. The more you let these clients off the leash, the more confusion they generate. With some you reach the stage where you're too tired to argue. You don't have the time or energy to overcome their invincible stupidity.

Occasionally a client threatens suicide. With some, I gently laugh it off. I say, 'Don't kill yourself, mate, you'll live to regret it.' But often it's a fellow in custody, busting to get out on bail. If he doesn't get bail, he tells me, he'll kill himself.

Now, to start with, it's not my decision whether or not he gets bail. My duty's to present his case as well as I can, which is what I do, with or without a death threat. Secondly, I don't believe he means what he says. Of course, I understand it's an expression of distress and an appeal for sympathy, but it's also, I think, a ploy to exert some moral blackmail. I've reached the stage where I simply don't want to put up with this nonsense. I'm the man's lawyer, not his best friend. Counsellors get paid for listening to that stuff; I'm there for a different purpose.

So I disregard the threats clients make, and if they persist I give them legal advice. On one occasion when a client threatened suicide I told him, 'It's up to you. Attempted suicide isn't a crime any more. If you go ahead and botch it, you won't be charged. If you succeed you'll be beyond the reach of the court.'

He went right off! I wondered for a moment if I'd misjudged him and that he really was a suicide risk. (I hadn't. He wasn't.) These days I put on my saddest face and pander to them for five minutes. When time's up I get back to the job in hand.

Many clients look to me to solve their self-made problems. As I mentioned earlier, some who lose their driving licences demand, 'How am I supposed to get to work?' They can't accept it's their own problem, not mine.

When I suggest the bus, they flare up: 'I'm not taking the fucking bus!' The loss and inconvenience is of their own making, yet to organise their life without a car – as do millions of their fellow citizens – is intolerable. These are self-centred, irresponsible people.

What about consideration for others? A state-supported female flounces into court with her litter of many-fathered bastard offspring. 'I'm a single mum,' she declares defiantly, as if to say, 'Wanna make something of it!'

Well, I don't want to, not in the least. Good on her if she's a good mum, but I wonder if she is. Her kids run about noisily in the court foyer, annoying other people and trampling their spilt Twisties into the carpet. First she ignores them, then, in turn, yells at them, pleads with them, laughs at their antics till finally she does her block and creates a scene. The children learn that discipline depends on their mother's degree of exasperation and nothing else. They already know they can behave anywhere exactly as they please and that other people sharing a public space merit no consideration.

What about self-respect? A client was in the cells without shoes. I asked the Salvation Army welfare officer if he could help out. I thought he'd go up to the Salvos' op shop and grab a pair. Instead he went to a full-price shoe shop and bought the kid a brand new pair. The kid removed the shoelaces and threw them away. He wanted to look slovenly and impoverished.

It's at such times that I mourn the loss of ordinary, old-fashioned virtues like hard work, thrift, politeness, common sense, punctuality, sobriety, fortitude. Fortitude, by the way, entails controlling your own emotions so as not to embarrass or inconvenience other people – and to retain some self-respect. These days it's seen as psychologically damaging.

Also psychologically damaging, apparently, are those minor misfortunes which at one time were simply coped with as ordinary vicissitudes of life. These days they're blown out of all proportion and become traumatic events. Clients who copped a dirty look from an unfriendly neighbour tell me they were 'devastated'. Some even manage to contract Post Traumatic Stress Disorder in the expectation of getting compensation. Yes, these days it pays to be pathetic.

Some families, of course, are prisoners of their own history. They're not capable of change. They've grown up in homes with a complete absence of authority. They're locked into multigenerational patterns of bad behaviour: of drink, of drugs, of lousy driving, of hatred of the police. They pass their lives with violent video games and a diet of high-cholesterol junk food. What else is there to do but go through life breaking the law?

Their problems are compounded by homelessness. Once upon a time everybody had a home, but the situation seems to get worse year by year. Even in this area, though, things are not always as they seem. I recall a young couple living in their car; a tragic situation, I thought. They couldn't go home to their parents, they told me, neither his nor hers.

But at court I got to meet the parents. Both sets said the kids were welcome back home. The parents simply insisted their children get up by 9 o'clock because they didn't want them lying in bed all day. But that was too tyrannical for the young people! Their motto was: 'You can't tell us what to do.' Everything was about their rights. They revelled in being homeless transients, relying on their social worker to wangle them an occasional night of emergency housing in a motel. For them, any restraint was intolerable.

It's the hypocrites who get you down. Dole bludgers, for example, who reckon their Centrelink benefits are too low and help themselves to more. I had a client who was drawing the dole while working at Ingham's chicken plant, processing chicken guts. Her excuse was that it was such a rotten job, and paid so poorly, she deserved more. I accept she was poorly paid, but what about her workmates on the chicken line? They were being paid the same and their taxes were subsidising her double-dipping. She didn't care about that.

People don't like cheats; apparently we're hard-wired that way. Cheating is one area where people overcome their aversion to dobbing others in. Social security fraud is essentially theft from the poorest members of the community because it depletes the total fund available for the needy. The detection of social security cheats, I'm told, relies half on data matching and the other half on people informing on them.

I once represented a dole cheat who'd been systematically stealing from the public purse, not just with false declarations but with multiple false identities. I asked him what we could offer in mitigation. He told me, 'I'm a born-again Christian. I've found the Lord.'

Well, it was something. 'When were you re-born?' I asked.

'In 2016.'

I couldn't believe his effrontery. 'But that's before you started submitting false declarations month after month and thieving public money!'

My indignation must have shown. He looked mildly crestfallen and shrugged, 'Well, no-one's perfect.'

37

Serious Stuff

Society and the law

A sense of justice seems to be innate in human beings. People want to be treated fairly – or at least, not unfairly. As any parent knows, even tiny tots are sensitive to the appearance of one child being favoured over another. This aversion to injustice raises unreasonable expectations. People expect the law to provide a remedy for every ill.

People also confound law with justice. They're not the same thing: law amounts to the rules themselves, justice is what you get when the rules are applied fairly. To expect the law to be infallible is sheer folly. At best it can be a blunt instrument, and some who come into contact with it are likely to go away bruised.

Of course, to some people 'justice' means simply getting their own way. In their disappointment at not getting the result they want they make silly remarks; they tell me the law is 'all bullshit'. Comments like that annoy me. If their car breaks down they don't proclaim the internal combustion engine to be 'all bullshit'.

Often those who complain the loudest are the very kind the law most protects. Without the law, death squads and rogue cops or vigilantes would shoot some of my clients. I don't exaggerate. Extra-judicial killings are happening right now in Brazil and the Philippines with presidential encouragement.

Without the law, property rights would not exist, contracts and promises would be meaningless, life and limb itself would be at risk. The law isn't oppression; it's a mechanism that protects people and their property and gives them some chance of a fair go.

Courts exist to apply the law, to give considered judgments rather than make snap decisions on a gust of emotion. Of course, courts sometimes make mistakes. In every system which handles a large number of cases, mistakes happen. The machinery to correct mistakes is a right of appeal. It's not infallible either, but it's the best we can do.

As I get older I come to appreciate more the importance of our institutions. The legal system is only one of them, but it underpins the others. Much as we grumble about the state of the country, our police aren't lawless thugs, the currency doesn't turn worthless overnight, the press can publish awkward facts, the army keeps out of politics, our votes are counted honestly, government statistics aren't lies, and we can get on Centrelink without paying a bribe. We take all this sort of thing for granted, but many countries don't enjoy anything remotely similar. A century ago Argentina was as rich and free as Australia. It isn't now. A major reason is that our institutions worked and theirs didn't.

Institutions depend on trust, by which we mean confidence that other people will act fairly. Surveys indicate that trust is diminishing. People increasingly view institutions as corrupt, strangers as suspect and facts as negotiable. Organisations, such as banks, which were once the epitome of prudence and propriety, turn out to be thieves and racketeers.

The undermining of trust flows over into a general attitude of suspicion and self-interest. If banks can make millions by laundering money for terrorists and pedophiles, what's so wrong with pinching a car or two? If multinationals can juggle their figures and pay no tax, what's wrong with fiddling your own tax return? The problem is compounded by politicians rorting the system, breaking promises and flouting the constitutional rules and conventions that hold our system of government together.

Even small things matter. A fellow complained to me the other day how police receive free meals at McDonald's. In fact, I understand they get their Big Macs half-price, not free, but he was right to take exception. The police are well paid. Why should they get a discount? Currying favour with the police may seem trivial, but favouritism feeds resentment. Even in small things we should strive for fairness and trust.

As an example of old-time standards, let me cite Sir Owen Dixon,

Australia's most revered jurist. As Chief Justice of the High Court till 1964, he had a Commonwealth car and driver at his disposal. On returning to court after lunch, he'd sometimes give a lift to friends or acquaintances, but he wouldn't detour from the direct route. If his friends weren't going back to court they had to get out at some point and walk the rest of their way. Dixon said that the people of Australia had provided him with the use of a car in his capacity as Chief Justice and not otherwise. How different standards are today!

So far as the law goes, and society in general for that matter, I'm in favour of what works. Often we don't know what works till we try it. One benefit of our federal system is that with six states and two federal territories we have eight laboratories in which to try out ideas. Victoria was the first to make seatbelts compulsory in cars and the rest of the country followed, then the world. The territories led the way with laws on voluntary euthanasia, till Victoria assumed the lead. South Australia introduced deposits for drink containers years ago and reduced litter by half. Now even Queensland has followed suit, with Victoria belatedly promising action in two years time.

Some things work for some people but not for others. Alcoholics Anonymous succeeds by changing alcoholics' routine and replacing one habit with another. Instead of going to the pub and getting a skinful, members go to meetings and talk about addiction. It's not for everyone, but for some it's the answer.

So let's just give things a try. Supervised drug injecting rooms, medical cannabis, weekend detention, Koori Courts, alternative dispute resolution, restorative justice, parenting courses for prisoners, conjugal visits, drug courts, unpaid community work for young offenders. I'm even in favour of the 'Multiple and Complex Needs Initiative', whatever that may be!

People's behaviour can be changed. It has changed with regard to smoking cigarettes, recycling plastic bottles, racial abuse – even sitting in the sun without a shirt on. Attitudes to drink driving and family violence have been completely reversed. And it hasn't all been done by compulsion. Education and reason and appealing to people's better nature have contributed. Except for sociopaths, everyone has a conscience.

Some ideas sound outlandish but might actually merit consideration. *Gulliver's Travels* was published in 1726, not as a children's book but as a satire on government and human nature. In it the inhabitants of Lilliput thought it ridiculous to punish people for breaking the law. To their way of thinking, it made more sense to reward citizens for obeying. Instead of force and punishment they favoured persuasion and reward. It bears thinking about.

Our driving habits are in obvious need of change. Drivers in other countries don't regard someone else changing lanes as a personal affront, but in Australia road rage is ubiquitous. This is strange as in most things Australians are an easy-going people. Education and encouragement might be the way to more civilised driving. And once the pendulum starts to swing it may just lead to a collective change of heart; the tendency to follow suit and conform is a strong one.

On the subject of driving, consider this. In Mexico everyone used to pay a bribe to get a driving licence, so half the states simply abolished driving tests. In Mexico City there is now no compulsory training or testing of any kind.[30] Paradoxically, accidents and the death rate have fallen. No-one knows why. Perhaps, knowing the average driving skills of the population have fallen, road users take more care. I'm not advocating we copy Mexico in this, but something unexpected is happening and it might be helpful to work out what it is. It may have application in other ways.

Another interesting idea comes from Estonia. In a recent experiment, instead of being pulled over and fined, speeding drivers were made to take 'time out', cooling their heels by the side of the

30 Grabiszewski and Horenstein, 'Driving tests do not Increase Road Safety; Evidence from Mexico', Instituto Tecnologico Autonomo de Mexico, reported in The Economist, 22–28 October 2011.

road for an hour or so, depending on their speed. The idea was to discover whether lost time might be a greater deterrent to speeding than lost money.

It seems it actually might: drivers saw the delay and their interaction with the police as more off-putting than receiving a fine, which they tended to pay like any other bill and then forget about. Estonians also saw the scheme as more egalitarian in the sense that while some people have lots of money, everyone has only 24 hours in each day. It also answered the complaint that fines for traffic offences are just revenue-raising.

Consider now the causes of crime. In my experience poverty doesn't 'cause' crime. Not one of my clients has been caught stealing bread; none will starve. In terms of my parents' generation none of us is poor. Before World War II most men owned only two pairs of trousers: a work pair and their Sunday best. Many didn't have bicycles, much less cars. A meal in a restaurant was a treat. Even into the 1970s an interstate trip was a thrill and overseas travel beyond the reach of most people. In material terms even the poorest in our community enjoy comfort, safety, freedom and mobility absolutely undreamt of, even by the rich of previous generations.

But relative poverty is what counts. Well-being depends on comparison with others. The most equal societies, such as Scandinavia's, are the best-off by almost all social indicators: unemployment rates, gender equality, maternal health, education, mental health, crime. It's something outside the control of the law. It's a social and political choice. At present in Australia, alas, unfairness and inequality continue to increase.

As well as letting inequality rise, we've also contrived to loosen the social glue that holds us together. The community has fractured into competing tribes, all bristling to take offence at something said, or opinions held, by others. Exaggerated notions of political correctness can make ordinary, unselfconscious conversation difficult, and sometimes impossible.

Lollipop ladies are forbidden to touch the children they shepherd across the road; help a kid tie her shoelaces and it's an assault. These days no male stranger dares to help a child for fear of being denounced as a pedophile. Nobody ventures to intervene with vandals. When a girl started scribbling in texta on the wall of a brand-new train, I remonstrated with her, but not one person in the crowded carriage supported me.

This lack of social censure has produced a whole tribe of kids who are pampered yet resentful. They've been trained to know that nothing's their fault and there's always someone else to blame. Tell them off at your peril.

I think two factors are underrated in their contribution to crime among young people. One is vanity. By this I mean the desire for acclaim we all have, especially males. Those with few accomplishments have no way of drawing attention to themselves other than getting into trouble. Their entire lives become a form of performance, with each escapade publicised on social media as an incentive for others to outdo. Some of these kids would be willing to die for their misdeeds if the audience was big enough. Often they're urged on, I might add, by imbecilic females, some of whom enjoy the fact that young men will come to blows over them.

The other factor is boredom. The desire for excitement is deepseated in human beings, especially the young and, again, especially males. These days, though, the capacity to endure boredom seems much reduced. Young people have to be constantly entertained. They can't do without their iPods, mobile phones, DVDs and incessant 'music'. Many young people would prefer disaster to boredom.

Insofar as there is a cure, the cure for boredom is work. Quite apart from the money earned, it has many advantages. It occupies young people, it channels their time and provides an outlet for their energy. It confers the satisfaction of doing something useful. It earns respect from others and thereby creates self-respect. It helps cure a sense of entitlement.

One's contemporaries are more important in adolescence than at any other time of life. In evolutionary terms it makes sense: there's nothing to be gained in cultivating old folk who are going to die off soon. So a less obvious benefit of work is that it takes young people out of the exclusive company of their peers and into the general community. The audience they now play to is not one of foolish, immature kids but of grown-up men and women, who are a harder group to impress.

But if you can't cure crime, how do you deal with those who break the law? Punishment is the first thing commentators think of. Are sentences too light? they ask. Well, are five-year-olds too young to start school? Are twenty-year-olds mature enough to get married? The answer is: it depends. Some are and some aren't.

Sentencing is a matter of weighing different factors and exercising judgment. Reasonable people may differ on particular cases but it's surprising how much unanimity there is when a panel of people hear the same facts. Normal people reach a consensus. Admittedly, lawyers and police prosecutors know the general tariff that applies to different offences, but at court we're generally on the same page regarding the appropriate sentence.

You can be pretty sure of one thing: that what you read in the media won't be the full story. And know-all advocates of mandatory sentencing quickly change their tune when they're personally affected. Years ago, I happened to be in a court when a *Herald-Sun* journalist was being sentenced for drink driving. Unlike the editorial-writers, he wasn't in favour of heavy penalties; he wanted a light penalty. Nor did he want to lose his licence, even though its cancellation was mandatory. How curious.

Those who are so cavalier about advocating jail often don't think things through. Obviously there are crimes for which there's no alternative but jail; some criminals absolutely belong behind bars. But young men who go to jail are going to come out in due course. To imprison someone amounts to sending him at public expense on a residential training course for criminals. You lock him up with a gang of thugs and degenerates so he learns aggression, limited conscience and the law of the jungle. He then rejoins the rest of us a more accomplished criminal. We only need to look overseas to see if more jail is such a good idea. In the US they jail their citizens at six times the rate we do – and look what a gentle, safe and just society they've created!

Many of the huge jail population in America are there as a result of mandatory sentencing laws. 'Three strike' rules and suchlike may seem attractive, but they're a recipe for injustice. Every case is different, and facts and circumstances can present in ways entirely unforeseen. Every law that mandates a fixed sentence produces injustice when the crime doesn't merit it.

Three years ago Victoria amended the law relating to bail, removing much of the court's former discretion. Recently, I represented a young Aboriginal man with an intellectual disability. One afternoon he'd lost his cool and deliberately flung his girlfriend's phone, value $40, to the ground and smashed it. (She then did the same to his phone, but wasn't charged.)

The man was charged with criminal damage and breaching an intervention order. Because he was subject to a corrections order at the time, the *Bail Act* precluded bail unless he could show exceptional circumstances. You'd have thought the length of his time on remand was exceptional in itself, but he stayed in jail for thirty-nine days before facing court. He pleaded guilty and was sentenced to the time he'd already spent in custody. Effectively then, he served a day's jail for each dollar of value of the phone – which on any reckoning is wildly disproportionate. And keeping him in detention for those thirty-nine days had cost the community about $9000. Hardly value for money.

At last count it costs $88,000 per year to keep a criminal in jail. That's $241 a day. For the same money you could afford to put them up at the Hyatt – though obviously the locks on the doors wouldn't be as strong. By contrast, it costs about $7000 a year for an offender to remain in the community under supervision.

Jail is meant to both deter and rehabilitate, but it doesn't do terribly well on either measure. Four in ten prisoners reoffend badly enough to go back to jail. There, prisoners are warehoused in conditions of boredom, futility and physical violence, with some jails awash with drugs. The prisoners' only companions are other criminals, so new alliances and allegiances are formed which continue on the outside.

Lip-service is paid to rehabilitation, but little more. The physical environment of concrete walls, steel bars and razor wire is dehumanising, the routine monotonous and the discipline arbitrary. Prisoners' sex lives are unnatural, psychiatric treatment is perfunctory and the available work is stereotyped and limited to things like screwing nuts and bolts together. There's little scope for self-improvement and no chance to develop a sense of individual responsibility.

But here's something strange. There's a fear of the unknown in all of us, and most clients facing jail for the first time are desperately anxious not to go inside. It creates the paradox that jail isn't an efficient deterrent, but fear of jail is. The deterrent though, once lost, is lost for all time.

It can be lost pretty quickly too. I had a client who spent twenty-two days on remand. It was his first time in custody and when he appeared in court I told the mago he'd had plenty of time to reflect; I implied the experience had been a salutary lesson. The magistrate spoke to him directly and asked him what jail had been like. To the surprise of us all, he said, 'Yeah, it was pretty good, actually.'

'Good?' she asked.

'Yeah, all the bro's were there, like, lots of my friends. I could work out in the gym and the food wasn't bad.'

Of course, some offenders deserve jail; for some there is no alternative. When a serial rapist is locked up, the streets are safer. But jail needs to be the punishment of last resort. Crime is a young man's game; the statistics indicate that if you can keep a young man out of jail until he's about twenty-five, he'll come to his senses of his own accord. If you send him to jail, he's as likely as not to go back in. The readier you are to send someone to jail the greater the risk of creating an intractable social problem for the next twenty years.

I wish I could end this book with a simple solution to society's ills and a cure for the law's many imperfections. I can't. I don't purport to have the answers but at least I can see some of the questions. Let me end, then, by giving one of my clients the last word.

As I mentioned, almost everyone who goes to jail comes out eventually. Some are my former clients and from time to time I run into them in the street. A bloke said hello to me in the supermarket the other day, but I couldn't place him. He reminded me I'd been his barrister so I asked him how he was. He said, 'Not that good. I've been in jail. Don't you remember?'

'Of course I remember,' I lied. 'How was it?'

'Most of it wasn't too bad,' he said. 'The worst thing was the prison officers.'

'How so?' I asked.

'They treated us like criminals.'